FIXING FRAGILE STATES

FIXING FRAGILE STATES

A New Paradigm for Development

SETH D. KAPLAN

PRAEGER SECURITY INTERNATIONAL
Westport, Connecticut • London

Library of Congress Cataloging-in-Publication Data

Kaplan, Seth D.
  Fixing fragile states : a new paradigm for development / Seth D. Kaplan.
    p.   cm.
  Includes bibliographical references and index.
  ISBN 978–0–275–99828–8 (alk. paper)
  1. Developing countries—Politics and government.   2. Political stability—Developing
countries.   I. Title.
  JF60.K36   2008
  320.9172'4—dc22   2008008791

British Library Cataloguing in Publication Data is available.

Library of Congress Catalog Card Number: 2008008791
ISBN-13: 978–0–275–99828–8

First published in 2008

Praeger Security International, 88 Post Road West, Westport, CT 06881
An imprint of Greenwood Publishing Group, Inc.
www.praeger.com

Printed in the United States of America

The paper used in this book complies with the
Permanent Paper Standard issued by the National
Information Standards Organization (Z39.48–1984).

10 9 8 7 6 5 4 3 2 1

This book is dedicated to my
parents, without whom none of this would
be possible, and to the children of fragile
states.

"People don't rebel because they are poor but because they are excluded from the system. To give people a stake in the economy, to prove to them that government is in the business of including them in formal society, is to put the terrorists out of business."

—Hernando de Soto

"Of all the ills that kill the poor, none is as lethal as bad government."

—*The Economist*

"The events of September 11, 2001, taught us that weak states, like Afghanistan, can pose as great a danger to our national interests as strong states. Poverty does not make poor people into terrorists and murderers. Yet poverty, weak institutions, and corruption can make weak states vulnerable to terrorist networks and drug cartels within their borders."

—*The National Security Strategy of the United States, 2002*

"The best protection for our security is a world of well-governed states."

—*European 2003 Security Strategy*

"Weak states are cracks in the foundation of our international system. Left untended, they can threaten the entire edifice of political and economic stability.... Those states can destabilize their neighbors and whole regions, creating humanitarian crises as severe as any natural disaster.... We have both a humanitarian obligation and a national security mandate to pay attention."

—Senator Joseph R. Biden, Jr.

Contents

Illustrations

Preface

Within a period of just a few months in late 1988 and early 1989, I made two journeys that kindled a passion that through two decades of exploration and reflection has culminated in this book. First, I went to Lagos, Nigeria, to work for an enterprising young bank; there, I lived with a family and soaked up a fascinatingly diverse but deeply divided young country. Over many months, I learned the fine arts of navigating the anarchic roads in rundown taxis, living through long power outages, and inducing government officials to follow the law. My coworkers and friends taught me how to survive the daily challenges of life—including how to conduct business, how to travel, and how to make ends meet—in this most unpredictable of environments. Then, I flew across continents, traversing what seemed like whole worlds, to arrive in a completely different civilization: Japan. In my four years there, I became fluent in the language and culture and tried my best to acculturate to the Japanese worldview. I again spent many months living with a family, and worked inside one of the country's best manufacturing companies. I learned the nuances of behavior in the world's most cohesive nation-state, agonized over the smallest of details in a society obsessed with quality, and was charmed by how precisely every system seemed to work.

The contrast between these two experiences fermented in my mind, stirring a fervent interest in how societies work and why only some foment societal and state progress. As a businessman who had to regularly contemplate what socio-economic conditions encouraged investment, what actions influenced government bureaucrats to behave a certain way, and what factors within countries augured well for their futures, my daily profession stimulated the thoughts that would in time become hypotheses and, later, conclusions about these issues. My intoxication with the allures of developing countries—the excitements of the markets, the electricity of the streets, the warmth of the people, the variety of the experiences—led me to wander farther and farther afield in an attempt to soak up as many places as was humanly possible. My empathy for the people I met led me to try to absorb their worldviews, to feel for their hopes and struggles, and to seek out what forces either assisted them or held them back from reaching their dreams. The more societies I saw, the more states I experienced, the more data I had to feed into my evolving theories.

Fundamentally, this book is about the process of development, about why some countries have been able to prosper while others seem to be forever held back by dysfunctional political and economic climates, trapped in dismal poverty. In attempting to fashion an all-encompassing paradigm of what forces drive—and, for that matter, what forces make possible—development, economic growth, and societal progress, I have sought answers beyond the formulas that have dominated the field of development since its inception and which continue to be the mainstay of specialists in the field. Although nobody can deny the importance of competitive elections, free market reforms, and social development spending, I believe that certain fundamental sociopolitical, historical, and geographic forces are more influential in the very first stages of development in influencing a country's chances for success, and unless that state's institutions are designed to harness these fundamental forces, it is unlikely that forward progress will result, no matter how well intentioned leaders are or how much aid is forthcoming.

This book is a journey across seven countries and regions—almost all of which I visited in preparing this manuscript—selected for what, individually and collectively, they can teach us about struggling states and development. Each case study focuses on a different facet of the complex array of sociopolitical conditions to be found in the underdeveloped parts of the world. While many issues and proposed solutions overlap significantly from case study to case study, each of these seven parts of the world—the Andes, West Africa, the Horn of Africa, the Democratic Republic of the Congo, the Levant, the Caucasus, and South Asia— has different problems resulting from its unique historical evolution. Some of the ideas I propose here will be fairly seen as unconventional, but they are not, I trust, impractical. Indeed, I asked veteran policymakers, seasoned practitioners, eminent scholars, and local experts to review drafts of each chapter and to point out anything that seemed unreasonable or unworkable. But while I have thus done my best to ensure this book's analyses and recommendations are realistic, I have no qualms about offering ideas that lie outside the mainstream of current thinking in development circles. After all, people in fragile states have lived through decades of war, misgovernment, and destitution that current development formulas did little or nothing to ameliorate; isn't it time that alternatives were considered?

Acknowledgments

Twenty years is not a long time, yet in that period one comes in contact with a lot of people. Some of them are formally introduced. Others brush by you on the street, sit next to you inside of a bus, or stroll with you around a village. Many have spent countless hours patiently explaining their life, their culture, and their values, giving me a deep appreciation for the uniqueness of their people's traditions, society, and land. Whether it was a small Pashtun town outside Peshawar, a college campus in Accra, an Aymara farm in the Andes, a wedding in Hargeisa, an official government dinner in Nanjing, a company outing in Tokyo, or a coffee house in Damascus, innumerable people have over and over again helped me find my way, invited me into their homes, and showed me hospitality and care beyond my wildest expectations. In the process, they have taught me the distinct beauty and melody of their own ethos. I am deeply grateful to them and can only apologize where I have fallen short as a student. There is always more for the heart to learn.

Although the book's contents—including any errors of commission or omission—are solely my responsibility, a number of people were especially helpful in assisting me understand various cultures and in giving me critical feedback on portions of the book. There are too many to name them all here, but I would like to specifically thank the following people:

- In Azerbaijan and Armenia: Anar Ahmadov, Leila Alieva, David Eizenberg, Farid Guliyev, Avaz Hasanov, Tabib Huseynov, Ulvi Ismayil, Shavarsh Kocharyan, Ilgar Mammadov, Seda Muradyan, Nasib Nassibli, David Shahnazaryan, and Aynur Yusifova.

- In Bolivia: Antonio Aranibar Arze, Miguel Buitrago, Miguel Centellas, Jules Lampell, Fernando Mayorga Ugarte, Jose Mirtenbaum, Godofredo Sandoval, Zulema Torrez Laguna, Carlos Villegas Quiroga, and Moira Zuazo.
- In Nigeria: Ebitimi Banigo, Tosa Ogbomo, Callistus N. Udalor, and Derego Williams.
- In Pakistan: Cyril Almeida, Hameed Haroon, Pervez Hoodbhoy, M. Ilyas Khan, Ahmed Bilal Mehboob, Mariam Mufti, Arifa Noor, Rasul Bakhsh Rais, Aasiya Riaz, Hasan Askari Rizvi, Muhammad Waseem, and S. Akbar Zaidi.
- In Somaliland: Adan Yousuf Abokor, Abdillahi Duale, Bobe Yusuf Duale, Yusuf Abdi Gabobe, Mohamed Saeed Mohamed Gees, Mohamed Abdillahi Harbi, Mohamed Hashi, Mohamed Rashid Sh. Hassan, Mohamed Ibrahim, Edna Adan Ismail, Mohamed Ahmed Mahamoud (Silaanyo), Ulf Terlinden, Lulu Farah Todd, and Amina Yusuf.
- In Syria: Samir Altaqi, Talal Atrash, Ziad Haidar, Ibrahim Hamidi, George Jabbour, Karem Moudarres, Raed Nakshbandi, Yassin Hajj Salih, Samir Seifan, and Jihad Yazigi.
- In North America: Fran Biderman, Marcus Brauchli, Edouard Bustin, Tom Callaghy, Stephen Cohen, Chester Crocker, Stacia George, Jeffrey Herbst, Joshua M. Landis, Princeton Lyman, Robert Pringle, Harris Reinhardt, Rochelle Sharpe, Peter Takirambudde, and I. William Zartman.
- In Europe: Daniel Bach, Christopher S. Clapham, and Denis Tull.
- In Japan: the Babas, Fujimaki Yoshihiro, Katai Shinbu, Kousaka You, Mitani Fumio, Mochizuki Yukinaga, Morimoto Toshio, Nishio Susumu, Ohkubo Kazutoshi, the Shimas, the Shimoies, Suzuki Takanori, Tada Masanobu, Takeshima Hiroshi, Toyooka Kurumi, and Watanabe Yuji.
- In China: Gao Ming, Harold Lerner, Li Ling, and Wu Kung-ting.
- Elsewhere: Kwesi Kwaa Prah and Rebecca Zeffert.

Beyond these, I need to give special heartfelt thanks to my splendid editor, Dr. Nigel Quinney, without whom this book would probably never have been realized. And Jeff Urbancic did a terrific job designing the cover. Kim Rusch drew all the maps. My editors at Praeger, Hilary Claggett and Heather Staines, were extremely lenient with my many special requests and queries on issues few authors normally bother them with. Phil Costopoulos of the National Endowment for Democracy, Trudy Kuehner of the Foreign Policy Research Institute, and Alexander Lennon of the Center for Strategic and International Studies helped shape some of the chapters through their comments on submissions to journals they edit.

Several of these chapters are outgrowths of articles that have already appeared in print:

- Chapter 5 is based on an article published in the *Washington Quarterly* 29(4) (Fall 2006): 81–97.

- Chapter 6 is based on an article that appeared in *Orbis* 51(2) (Spring 2007): 299–311.
- Chapter 8 is based on an article that appeared in the *Journal of Democracy* 19(3) (July 2008).
- Chapter 9 is based on an article that appeared in *Orbis* 50(3) (Summer 2006): 501–517.

1

Introduction: Why Fragile States Matter

Fragile states are a menace unlike any other, endangering international security, while ruining the lives of hundreds of millions across the globe. Although everyone agrees that they should be dealt with, no one seems able to formulate a strategy to do so. Even worse, few seem even to understand the underlying causes of their dysfunction.

Certainly, fragile states have received a surge of attention in the years since 9/11. Government bodies, think tanks, academics, intergovernmental organizations, nongovernmental organizations, and even corporations have convened commissions, conducted inquiries, and launched programs that focus on these dangerous places. Yet, while these studies have produced a number of significant proposals on how to respond to the breakdown of such countries, nobody seems able to explain how to fix them—and why decades spent pumping money, peacekeepers, and advice into fragile states have been unable to reform them. Must we just learn to live with them?

Fixing Fragile States emphatically rejects this gloomy conclusion, but it also rejects both the diagnosis and the treatment that the West has long prescribed for these benighted countries. If we are to transform failed and failing states in Africa, Latin America, the Middle East, and elsewhere, we need to adopt innovative policies that challenge conventional wisdom. In particular, we need to embrace a new way of thinking about development.

This book presents a new way of conceptualizing—and solving—the riddle of development. It blends political science, economic, sociological, and business theory together with firsthand experience in the art of helping developing countries prosper to explain why some states succeed and some states break down. And it shows in seven case studies how its new paradigm can be applied to alleviate the problems of fragile states.

By focusing on group identities, state capacities, and business conditions, *Fixing Fragile States* examines the underlying foundations of institutional potency. This analysis of local sociocultural environments shows the impracticality of many current efforts to reform weak countries, thus unraveling the enigma of why so many efforts have gone awry. Instead of arguing about how to prop up existing governing bodies, which is how the international community typically deals with these places, this book shows that these very bodies often clash with local realities, making it highly unlikely that they will ever work as prescribed.

In essence, this book argues that inappropriate institutions cause fragile states and that only by redesigning those institutions can dysfunctional places craft the commercial environments necessary to attract investment—without which no development can occur or be sustained—and jumpstart a self-sustaining cycle of growth. The new development paradigm proposed in the following chapters would create the positive incentives that drive successful economies, empowering diverse peoples, leveraging limited governance capacities, and catalyzing multinational corporate investment to advance regions that have struggled up to now.

THE CONSEQUENCES OF STATE BREAKDOWN

Fragile states are widely recognized as a danger both to international security and to the security of their neighbors, as well as to the well-being of their own people. Their lawless environments spread instability across borders; provide havens for terrorists, drug dealers, and weapons smugglers; threaten access to natural resources; and consign millions to poverty. They are the source of much of the violence and many of the humanitarian crises around the world. Even when harshly repressive rulers manage to impose some degree of domestic control, their societies fail to provide positive incentives for productive behavior and thus become breeding grounds for criminals and extremists who disrupt the international order.

Fragile states have marched from the fringe to the very center of Western security concerns. Whereas once U.S. defense analysts worried only about competing powers such as the Soviet Union and China, now even the weakest of countries is considered a potential threat. "The events of September 11, 2001 taught us that weak states, like Afghanistan, can pose as great a danger to our national interests as strong states," the 2002 U.S. National Security Strategy declared. Poverty may not turn people into terrorists, but "poverty, weak institutions and corruption can make weak states vulnerable to terrorist networks and drug cartels."[1] In a similar vein, the United States Agency for International Development has declared, "Fragile states . . . are now recognized as a source of our nation's most pressing security threats. There is perhaps no more urgent matter facing [us] than fragile states, yet no set of problems is more difficult and intractable. Twenty-first

Table 1.1. Links between State Instability and International Terrorism

Terrorist network requirement	Level of dependence on instability	How unstable states act as enabler
Basing: leadership haven and training of recruits	High	Ungoverned territory provides a secure area for leadership cadres. Recruits can be trained and integrated within organisation
Conflict experience	High	Normalisation of violence and places terrorist activities in context of conventional conflict
Weapons/equipment testing	Some	Ungoverned territory provides small arms and explosives training, weapons R&D
Finance/resources	Some	Lack of checks and balances mean that monies can be obtained through corruption and misused
Operations	Some	Base for mounting attacks on local targets (embassies, infrastructure)

Source: U.K. Prime Minister's Strategy Unit, *Investing in Prevention: An International Strategy to Manage Risks of Instability and Improve Crisis Response* (London, UK: Prime Minister's Strategy Unit, February 2005), Table 1.2, 12.

century realities demonstrate that ignoring these states can pose great risks and increase the likelihood of terrorism taking root."[2] Other Western governments have similarly reoriented their foreign policy and aid toward fragile states since 9/11. Table 1.1, from a British government strategic policy document, summarizes the links between instability and international terrorism.

The list of weak countries threatening international stability and Western interests grows with time. Terrorists originating in Afghanistan, Pakistan, and Somalia have attacked American and European homelands, embassies, and militaries. Western troops and United Nations' peacekeepers have intervened in dysfunctional states such as Sudan, Sierra Leone, Haiti, and Bosnia-Herzegovina. Meanwhile, ethnic fighting in Nigeria, civil unrest in Ecuador, and concerns over the stability of Iraq have all contributed to rising oil prices, threatening to derail growth worldwide. Fragmented countries such as Colombia and Afghanistan continue to be the source of much of the world's illicit drugs.

The growing presence of Western troops and defense assets in fragile states and regions in recent years reflects this new reality. Although the wars in Iraq and Afghanistan are the most prominent instances of this form of intervention, they are far from being the only ones. Interventions in the Balkans in the 1990s helped stabilize the historical tinderbox of Europe. Troops have been deployed to East Timor, Haiti, Liberia, the Philippines, and Sierra Leone to fill vacuums created by weak local governments. Western soldiers and advisers can be found from Colombia to the African Sahel to Central Asia, upgrading local capacities to deal with threats posed by terrorists and drug lords.

The dangers are expected to persist—indeed, most people think they will grow more acute—impeding the work of diplomats, humanitarian workers, and corporate executives. According to a World Bank report, the number of fragile countries that could provide a breeding ground for terrorism jumped from seventeen in 2003 to twenty-six in 2006.[3] "It is very likely that the rise in instability observed over the last decade will be an enduring characteristic of the strategic landscape rather than a temporary phenomenon," explains *Investing in Prevention*, a report issued by the United Kingdom's Prime Minister's Strategy Unit in early 2005. It concludes that fragile countries "have a significant impact on the achievement of a wider range of domestic and international objectives, including: security, humanitarian assistance, promotion of human rights, poverty reduction, terrorism, trade and prosperity, asylum, energy security and organized crime."[4]

Meanwhile, the debilitating combination of weak governance, ill-conceived policies, and feeble institutions force the peoples trapped in these places to endure the world's most miserable lives. Depending on how broadly fragile states are defined (see next section), up to 2 billion people suffer the consequences of these countries' meltdowns. Generally poor, undereducated, and undernourished, these communities are denied any opportunity to benefit from the explosive growth of international trade and investment. Three out of four of those living in the most dysfunctional places (some thirty countries) are affected by ongoing armed conflict. The 500 million people in these states "share bleak socioeconomic indicators—from GDP per capita levels typically half that of low-income countries; child mortality rates twice as high as other low income-countries; mortality rates plummeting by up to thirty years as HIV afflicts over 42 million; and over 200 million lacking access to improved water and sanitation."[5] Fragile states are the main barrier impeding international efforts to meet the United Nations' Millennium Development Goals—which include eradicating hunger, reducing child mortality, and achieving universal primary education—by 2015. They are fifteen times more prone to civil war than developed countries, and they are the source of most of the world's refugees.[6]

Sadly, amid the surge of interest among multinational companies in the developing world, and the concomitant rise in trade, investment, and outsourcing, fragile states are unable to garner anything but the paltriest fruits from globalization. Although leading natural resource companies such as Exxon, Shell, and BHP Billiton source significant amounts of minerals in fragile states, and major multinationals such as Coca Cola, Nestlé, and Unilever seek markets for their products in these places, their business conditions discourage any venture that could be done elsewhere. As a result, fragile states typically export no more than a handful of commodities, often produced in protected enclaves that limit opportunities for embezzlement and violence. Few outside firms are tempted to invest in any add-on business activity that would increase the value of goods produced locally, while spreading the benefits of higher productivity. The flawed commercial environment hinders corporations from making their greatest contributions to local economies: few managers are trained, hardly any local companies learn how to supply internationally competitive products, and governments are not challenged to improve their standards of performance.

The seemingly irredeemable nature of fragile states suggests a new global bipolarity forming between, on the one side, those countries gaining from globalization and, on the other side, those that are losing. Countries that enjoy a reasonable degree of stability and the rule of law, such as China, India, Turkey, Botswana, and Chile, are able to develop greater interdependence with the international market economic system, which brings greater investment and prosperity. But where a state is too dysfunctional to establish these conditions, instability feeds on itself, emasculating efforts to improve institutions, thwarting attempts to cultivate a business climate that attracts investment, and permanently disconnecting territories from the benefits of trade.

DEFINING AND ANALYZING FRAGILITY

Scholars and practitioners use terms such as "fragile states," "failed states," and "weak states" to describe countries unable to administer their territories effectively. While there is no set definition for these expressions, and therefore no consensus on which places qualify, most experts agree that any country where the government is unable to deliver even the most basic public services—such as territorial control and security—to a significant portion of the population is *failing*. A completely *failed* state—such as Somalia, Haiti, Liberia, and the Democratic Republic of the Congo (DRC)—is one where the state has withered away in the face of violence, warlordism, or criminal activity.

Fragile, or *weak*, states, however, encompass a much wider group of territories where the national government operates, but has institutions so dysfunctional that they perform many of their tasks badly—or not at all. Although many developing countries have flimsy institutional foundations, are plagued by corruption, are handicapped by ineffectual governing bodies, and suffer from the weak rule of law, most scholars and practitioners agree that fragile states are only those where these problems have grown to such systemic levels that they threaten stability. The state is so incapacitated that it cannot provide many essential services: public schools and hospitals barely operate in many places, police and judges are beholden to the rich and the powerful, and the black market trumps legitimate moneymaking activities. Depending on the degree of dysfunction, fragile states can be either close to collapse, as in Nepal, or functioning at a bare minimum level, as in Nigeria, or working haphazardly, as in Ecuador and Bolivia.

In a number of cases, the governing regime operates reasonably well but is unable to impose its rule throughout its territory. In the Philippines, Colombia, and

Pakistan, secessionists, drug gangs, and militants limit the national government's writ. Rebellious armies have carved out unrecognized mini-states in Azerbaijan, Georgia, and Sri Lanka. In other cases, such as Syria and Uzbekistan, the state may seem anything but weak, but highly repressive policies may actually hide a combustibility that can erupt into flames if the authorities lose control, such as in Iraq after the U.S. invasion.

There are as many lists of fragile states as there are definitions. Britain's Department for International Development (DFID) has designated forty-six states "fragile" using the World Bank's Country Policy and Institutional Assessment (CPIA) scorecard to measure governance performance.[7] As mentioned above, the World Bank itself has identified twenty-six countries as "fragile states" (formerly the Bank called them "Low-Income Countries Under Stress" [LICUS]).[8] *Foreign Policy* magazine has listed sixty states as "weak or failing" in an annual ranking of vulnerable places using twelve social, economic, political, and military indicators.[9] The Center for Global Development (CGD), a think tank based in Washington, DC, that focuses on development issues, has listed forty-nine "poorly performing states" that do not qualify for the U.S. government's Millennium Challenge Account aid program because of their poor governance.[10] The Commission on Weak States and U.S. National Security has estimated that there are between fifty and sixty weak states.[11]

Since 9/11, Western governments, militaries, think tanks, aid agencies, intergovernmental organizations (IGOs), and scholars have all increased their research into various aspects of failed and fragile states because of their now proven capacity to damage Western interests and disrupt international peace. The reports published by governments and leading think tanks have been less interested in analyzing weak states than in exploring how to improve Western governments' capacities to handle crises erupting in such places. The articles and books issued by aid agencies and academics tend to have a different focus and pay more attention to the question of how to fix the troubled countries; their answers, however, often offer only generic, one-size-fits-all solutions that concentrate on rebuilding existing state structures. The recurrent theme is to hold elections, reform economies, and increase aid to nongovernmental organizations (NGOs), all within a relatively short time. Although there is a growing body of work on how to better respond to and deliver aid in such places, there are very few new ideas that challenge the conventional wisdom on institution building and that offer alternative prescriptions for fostering development in fragile states.

Almost all analyses ignore any structural issues that might hold back development. Instead, they tend to focus only on either the incapacity or the unfortunate attitude of the actors governing weak states, as if the states' problems would be solved if these players could be replaced. DFID's *Why We Need to Work More Effectively in Fragile States* argues that "states are fragile because of weak capacity or lack of political will—or both."[12] The Organization for Economic Co-operation and Development's Fragile States Group expresses a similar concept in *Principles for Good International Engagement in Fragile States* (2005): "States are fragile when governments and state structures lack capacity—or in some cases, political will—to deliver public safety and security, good governance and poverty reduction to their citizens."[13]

The fact that international efforts to repair fragile states have yielded few positive results has not escaped attention. As the co-head of a CGD initiative on fragile states noted, "even as the number of fragile states is rising, and despite an increasing amount of attention paid to the topic, our knowledge of the factors that make states fragile, as well as policies and programs that could reverse the trend, is very much in early stages."[14] The World Bank's own Independent Evaluation Group, which reports on the organization's activities to its board of directors, concluded that "past international engagement with [fragile states] has failed to yield significant improvements, and donors and others continue to struggle with how best to assist [them]."[15]

Just a few books specifically focus on failed and fragile states. Robert I. Rotberg, head of the John F. Kennedy's School of Government's program on interstate conflict, conflict prevention, and conflict resolution, has published *When States Fail* (2004) and *State Failure and State Weakness in a Time of Terror* (2003). Although delving deeply into the causes, consequences, and differences between cases of state failure, both of these also assume that prevention and reconstruction of fragile states require "getting nation building right," which "is possible if there is sufficient political will and targeted external assistance."[16] Francis Fukuyama's *State Building* (2004) emphasizes the importance of strengthening "stateness" through upgrading government administrative capacities. CGD's *Short of the Goal* (2006), edited by Nancy Birdsall, Milan Vaishnav, and Robert Ayres, effectively critiques U.S. policy in weak states, but while calling for "situation-specific analysis," it does not significantly depart from the focus on personalities and state capacities. Only *Making States Work* (2005), edited by Simon Chesterman, Michael Ignatieff, and Ramesh Thakur, focuses on issues related to state legitimacy, the role of identities, and the need to gear development "to the way the society is structured and functions economically."[17]

Beyond the narrow field of fragile states, there are, of course, many books on what drives state performance, including works in the fields of political science, economics, history, and sociology. There is a long record of such research, going back to the earliest products in these fields by such renowned writers as Aristotle, Adam Smith, and Max Weber. Among recent volumes, a few stand out as touching on subjects important to the ideas discussed here. Robert Putnam's *Making Democracy Work* (1993) was a landmark study that showed the importance of civic community in developing successful state institutions by comparing diverging regional performance in north and south Italy. Douglass North pioneered the study of institutions to explain the quality of governance and economic performance.[18] Others have tried to explain differences in state performance in terms of culture, level of democratization, nationalism, legal structures, historical circumstances, the quality of administrative organs, geography, systems of formulating property rights, and the intensity of vested interests.[19]

The author of this book is indebted to the work of these and many other scholars. Their analyses have helped me to refine ideas that I first formulated while working in fragile states as an employee of, consultant to, and, finally, CEO of local companies. Fifteen years spent experiencing firsthand why some countries make substantial progress while others struggle mightily to deliver basic services fed a curiosity to see many other states and regions and to explore the literature on development. It also underscored the fact that while much excellent work has been done toward diagnosing the problems of fragile states, the prescription for remedying those problems has so far remained elusive.

A NEW APPROACH

The cure for fragile states is development. But, as discussed in the next chapter, development is often misunderstood. Although usually equated with economic growth, it is really a process of transforming the system of how the members of a society work together. Although education and health care can better prepare individuals to participate in development, a country's ability to advance is crucially tied to its citizens' ability to cooperate—both among themselves and in partnership with the state—in increasingly sophisticated ways. A community's capacity to foster progress is therefore highly dependent on its social cohesion and its set of shared institutions—especially its set of shared informal institutions in the early stages of development when strong, formal governing institutions are typically absent.

The illegitimacy and poor governance that debilitate fragile countries can be traced to many factors—colonialism, for instance—that have combined to detach states from their environments, governments from their societies, and elites from their citizens. Whereas a successful state uses local identities, local capacities, and local institutions to promote its development, a dysfunctional country's state structures undermine all of these indigenous assets. As a consequence, a dysfunctional state cannot leverage its people's histories and customs to construct effective formal institutions with wide legitimacy; nor can it draw on the social capital (defined here as "the norms and networks that enable people to act collectively")[20] embedded in cohesive groups to facilitate economic, political, and social intercourse; and nor is it able to employ the traditional governing capacities of its citizens to run the affairs of state.

The new development paradigm proposed in this book takes a far more nuanced approach to state building than the policies currently promoted by the international community. Instead of emphasizing the will and capacity of leaders and administrators (both of which, if absent, cannot of course help things), it instead places the local sociocultural and socioeconomic environment—encompassing identities, governance capacities, and investment climates—center stage and provides a set of analytical tools that can help explain why some countries have thrived, why others have not, and what must be done to help the latter succeed.

In doing so, it simultaneously explains why rich countries such as the United States, Japan, and Germany evolved as they did and why the few development success stories of recent decades—Korea, China, India, Turkey, Botswana, and Chile among them—are managing the modernization process far better than their neighbors.

Instead of focusing on economic restructuring as the World Bank does, social policies as NGOs do, and administrative reforms as aid agencies increasingly do (all of which are helpful in their own—narrow—ways), this book argues that only redesigning governing bodies to better fit local conditions—that is, connecting the state with its surrounding society—will be able to win legitimacy, develop competency, and encourage investment, the rule of law, and the other ingredients necessary to foster a self-sustaining, internally driven process that will lead to development. Such an approach would involve not only reshaping existing formal institutions to enable them to better utilize informal institutions and local identities and capacities but also, where necessary, using the resources of regional, corporate, and Western actors to foster an environment in which local actors have a better chance of developing on their own. Where a state contains multiple cohesive identity groups, for example, structures will function most effectively when they reflect these underlying group loyalties and their traditions of governance, not generic forms imposed by outsiders. Iraqi Shiites, for example, will never support a government that ignores the role of Islam in their lives. Iraqi Kurds, in contrast, being a minority that has often suffered from state repression, insist on a federal, highly decentralized governing structure because they do not trust their neighbors to manage their affairs. Countries such as Guatemala, Ecuador, and Bolivia (Chapter 9) are unlikely to stabilize until their large indigenous populations feel themselves to be active participants in national policy formation.

Strong states also need powerful economic engines, which in turn depend upon the existence of an environment that rewards investment, whether by multinational corporations or by local entrepreneurs. Investors' money is the fuel that drives the wealth-creation process that is the prerequisite for any development. Many of the small states that proliferate in West Africa (Chapter 5), Central America, and elsewhere in the developing world have markets so tiny and administrative capacities so weak that they will always be unlikely, by themselves, to generate enough investment and competition to jumpstart growth.

Where state institutions cannot form the basis for a process of self-regenerating development, it is foolish for the international community to continue propping them up. Somalia (Chapter 8), for example, is never going to overcome its dysfunction until outsiders stop encouraging a centralized, Western-style administration. If states are to be successful, they must be made more relevant to their populations by interconnecting them with local, informal, internally driven political and economic processes, and not divorced and autonomous from the societies they are supposed to serve, which is the situation now. Fostering accountability loops that make politicians responsive to small population groups (Chapter 6), using tax systems to make governments dependent on their citizens, basing more laws on local customs, adopting traditional symbols, and constructing governing structures around identities all help to empower local societies.

It should be noted that the benefits of fixing these states would extend far beyond their borders. To begin with, such an outcome would go far toward stabilizing larger regions plagued by the strife they cause. Military budgets could be reduced, resources could be concentrated on social and infrastructure investment, and aid could start yielding genuine dividends and even start being drawn down. Adding hundreds of millions of new workers and consumers to the international economic system offers immense opportunities to increase growth and jobs elsewhere. Much as the people of China, India, and Eastern Europe have helped unleash a new wave of economic dynamism over the past two decades that contributes to rising incomes everywhere, the 2 billion people trapped in fragile states could someday make their own contribution to the world economy.

Social and economic development would also reduce the incentives that drive many people to choose careers of crime and terrorism. As a report issued in 2003 by RAND has noted, "Social and economic development . . . provides economic alternatives to potential (terrorist) recruits, and it creates a new middle class that has a vested interest in maintaining peace. This conclusion is not to suggest that poverty causes individuals to join terrorist groups. Rather, it is based on our assessment that members of the communities included in this study considered terrorist activity as a viable response to perceived political, economic, and social injustices, thereby sustaining a pool of willing recruits."[21]

THE SCOPE AND STRUCTURE OF THIS BOOK

This book's scope of study differs from others that focus on fragile or failed states in two important ways. First, it considers as fragile all countries in which (1) the state in some form—for example, its borders, its governing structures, its legal system, its method of choosing leaders and making important decisions—is not recognized as legitimate by a significant proportion of the population because of a mismatch between the state and traditional group identities; and (2) the state suffers from governing bodies so meekly and corruptly administered as to be unable to foster any legitimacy on their own.

Second, this book does *not* examine states whose current fragility is caused not by their fundamental design, but by the personality or policies of their leaders. North Korea, an extremely cohesive state, might actually thrive if it introduced the type of reforms that have allowed Vietnam and China to prosper since abandoning Communist economic ideology (though it might then be swallowed up by South Korea). Cambodia's decline into class warfare during the 1970s was more the result of circumstances and characters than of a fundamental conflict between identities

Table 1.2. Fragile States within Various Regions of the World

Africa	Latin America
Angola	Bolivia
Côte d'Ivoire	Ecuador
DRC	Guatemala
Ethiopia	Guyana
Mozambique	Nicaragua
Nigeria	Peru
Somalia	
Sudan	**Middle East**
Uganda	Iraq
	Lebanon
Balkans	Syria
Bosnia and Herzegovina	
Serbia	**South Asia**
	Nepal
Caucasus and Central Asia	Pakistan
Afghanistan	Sri Lanka
Azerbaijan	
Georgia	
Kyrgyzstan	

Note: This list is meant to be illustrative, not comprehensive.

and institutions. Places such as the Democratic Republic of Congo (Chapter 6), in contrast, are unlikely to develop even if a set of highly skilled politicians emerged in Kinshasa.

In short, a fragile state is defined here to mean any state highly unlikely in its current form—even if blessed in the future by better leaders and policies—to be able to cultivate the kind of state bodies that can manage an effective process of development. Put another way, a fragile state is any country highly unlikely to become prosperous and stable without first undergoing some form of institutional reengineering. See Table 1.2 for a list of some of the more prominent fragile states as defined in this book.

With this definition as its starting point, this book sets out to discover what ails fragile states and what can be done to improve their situations. It is intended for everyone who has a stake in the fate of these desperate places: policymakers who must deal with the security and economic consequences of the breakdown of fragile states; NGOs, supranational bodies, international financial analysts, and scholars who strive to devise effective ways of fostering economic growth in dysfunctional territories; businesspeople who are searching for new markets for their products, cheaper places to manufacture their designs, or more reliable sources of minerals; everyone, indeed, who makes decisions related to these places, who sympathizes with their long-suffering citizens, or who works with or travels to some of the territories discussed here.

The book is divided into three parts: Diagnosis, Prescriptions, and Application:

- *Diagnosis.* Chapters 2 and 3 explain how development works and why fragile states are seriously disadvantaged in their current form from promoting it. Chapter 2 begins by discussing the development process and what drives it, before reviewing the histories of successful state development and identifying those traits that are common to both developed countries and successful developing countries but are absent from stagnant territories. It ends by examining the role of identity and social cohesion in fashioning the robust governing systems necessary for stability and growth. Building on these foundations, Chapter 3 untangles the historical roots of state fragility and diagnoses the enduring structural cause of fragility—the reinforcing nexus of fragmented identities and weak formal institutions. It then examines the environments these produce, including the low levels of trust and high transaction costs that yield such widespread opportunism and corruption.
- *Prescriptions.* Chapter 4 prescribes ten bold but practicable remedies designed to help fragile states replicate the processes that have generated development elsewhere. All ten are intended to improve the effectiveness of the systems that govern societies and states, and through such changes to transform the informal institutional environment that affects all social, political, and economic activity. Four recommendations discuss how to better leverage local capacities, while three discuss how to better leverage outside capacities. The remaining three are intended to improve the effectiveness of efforts to enact these recommendations—or, for that matter, any program designed to fix fragile states. Rather than calling for wads of new cash—a mantra often heard within the development community—most of the remedies prescribed in Chapter 4 call for a change in the way that we think about the development process.
- *Application.* Chapters 5–11 dissect seven instances of dysfunction: West Africa, the Democratic Republic of Congo, Syria, Somaliland, Bolivia, Pakistan, and Azerbaijan. These cases have been chosen to highlight both the different sociopolitical contexts existing in various regions and the similarities between the problems faced by fragile states throughout the world. Each of the seven chapters start by examining the local history, geography, identity groups, governance structures, administrative record, and investment environment, and names the core issues holding back stability and growth. Recommendations tailored to each situation focus on reengineering institutions and reshaping policies in ways that will change the institutional dynamics of these countries and enable them to better leverage local identities and capacities to foster development. (The case studies have been written to be free-standing, so readers interested in particular cases can turn to one or more of Chapters 5–11 without having first read

Chapters 2–4. Reading all the chapters sequentially, however, will create a much richer understanding of how the development process works both in theory and in practice.)

*   *   *

Fragile states face seemingly insurmountable problems. As this book makes clear, however, they are far from hopeless places. History and circumstances have conspired to impede their development, but they are not doomed to eternal misery by any sinister design or tragic flaw. If local, regional, and international actors embrace the new paradigm of development, fragile states can look forward to a much brighter future for their inhabitants and can begin to play a constructive role in the world at large. We all stand to benefit from this transformation.

Part I _____

Diagnosis

2

Fostering Development: The Missing Ingredients

Development—the key to fixing fragile states—is much discussed today by everyone from presidents and prime ministers to intelligence agents and military officers, academics and aid specialists, and even financiers and business executives. Yet, there is little understanding of what conditions foster it and why some countries are able to accomplish it while others struggle mightily, seemingly eternally dysfunctional. Moreover, despite the increasing awareness of its importance to the West's own security and well-being and the annual investment of tens of billions of dollars in aid in an attempt to promote development, many of the policies designed to help the most desperate places actually undermine it.

The purpose of this chapter is to explain how development takes place. Essentially, it identifies two key ingredients—social cohesion and a society's shared, productive institutions—that have been missing from other analyses of how countries work. It begins by explaining what development is and how the development process works, and explores the relationship and the differences between formal institutions, informal institutions, and governance. Next, the chapter charts the history of successful state building by nation-states and "state-nations," paying particular attention to the roles played by these two missing ingredients and how they combine to foster effective governance systems. The chapter concludes by examining the role of identity in the formation and functioning of institutions.

THE DEVELOPMENT PROCESS

A Lack of Understanding

Although usually regarded as an economic process, development is in fact ignited or stifled by noneconomic factors. Two factors above all others decide how a country's political, economic, and societal life evolves: a population's capacity to cooperate (which depends, for the most part, on the level of social cohesion) and its ability to take advantage of a set of shared, productive institutions (especially informal institutions at the crucial early stages of development when formal institutions are usually feeble and ineffectual). These two ingredients shape how a government interacts with its citizens; how officials, politicians, and businesspeople behave; and how effective foreign efforts to upgrade governance will be. In short, they determine to what degree a society is able to nurture a locally driven, productive system of governance—a prerequisite for any attempt to develop. Together with the set of policies adopted by the government, they make up the three major determinants of a country's capacity to advance (see Figure 2.1).

Far too many programs designed to help fragile states simply ignore these immeasurable yet all-important drivers of societal and individual action, as if local histories and sociocultural conditions simply did not matter. As the Institute of Development Studies (IDS), a major British research institute, has noted, "for decades the development community has intervened in poor countries with little understanding of the political and institutional landscape, and with scant regard for the impact of their actions on local political relationships and incentives."[1] The international community, in fact, has generally assumed that any governance models other than those used by Western countries are undesirable. But current state structures in fragile states—almost always imported from abroad and inappropriate to their environments—often have little relevance to local populations. As the ex-president of Liberia, Amos Sawyer, has repeatedly stressed, "institutional arrangements of governance have been inherently flawed and have been a structural source of breakdown and a significant contributor to violent conflicts; to reconstitute order, there is a need for a new constitutional paradigm and a new institutional design that depart significantly from those that have failed."[2]

People from developed countries have great difficulty understanding fragile, undeveloped states for several reasons. First, the gospel of multiculturalism and the ideological commitment to democracy and respect for diversity that has so pervaded academia, the media, and other places where much development research and policymaking takes place precludes the type of sociopolitical approach that states riven by group identity divisions require. Americans, among others, see "the world through the assumptions, definitions, and goals of liberal thought"; indeed, it is "their very mechanism of comprehension."[3] For example, a recent Rand Corporation publication, *The Beginner's Guide to Nation-Building*,[4] "has almost nothing about what is clearly the Achilles' heel of recent nation-building adventures: culture. No single chapter is devoted to it—nothing on the role of

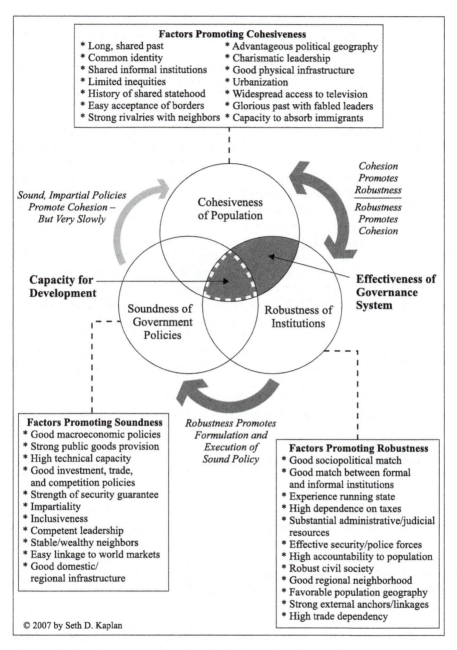

Factors Promoting Cohesiveness
* Long, shared past
* Common identity
* Shared informal institutions
* Limited inequities
* History of shared statehood
* Easy acceptance of borders
* Strong rivalries with neighbors
* Advantageous political geography
* Charismatic leadership
* Good physical infrastructure
* Urbanization
* Widespread access to television
* Glorious past with fabled leaders
* Capacity to absorb immigrants

Sound, Impartial Policies Promote Cohesion – But Very Slowly

Cohesiveness of Population

Cohesion Promotes Robustness

Robustness Promotes Cohesion

Capacity for Development

Effectiveness of Governance System

Soundness of Government Policies

Robustness of Institutions

Factors Promoting Soundness
* Good macroeconomic policies
* Strong public goods provision
* High technical capacity
* Good investment, trade, and competition policies
* Strength of security guarantee
* Impartiality
* Inclusiveness
* Competent leadership
* Stable/wealthy neighbors
* Easy linkage to world markets
* Good domestic/ regional infrastructure

Robustness Promotes Formulation and Execution of Sound Policy

Factors Promoting Robustness
* Good sociopolitical match
* Good match between formal and informal institutions
* Experience running state
* High dependence on taxes
* Substantial administrative/judicial resources
* Effective security/police forces
* High accountability to population
* Robust civil society
* Good regional neighborhood
* Favorable population geography
* Strong external anchors/linkages
* High trade dependency

© 2007 by Seth D. Kaplan

Figure 2.1. The Development Framework: Understanding Societal Systems

culture in countries being rebuilt and, just as importantly, nothing on the culture of the nation-builders themselves," as an *International Herald Tribune* op-ed noted.[5]

Second, development is about far more than economics, but because economists so dominate the discipline and because their quantitative tools of analysis play well to the needs of policymakers and academics, the development agenda has been unnecessarily limited in scope, precluding the broader approach that it requires. This narrow outlook has been particularly influential in Western countries, where the policy not just of Western governments but of most inter-governmental organizations is made. Many of the remedies proposed—such as the World Bank's ubiquitous structural adjustment programs—are "fundamentally driven by economic analysis and have difficulty in factoring in their impact on political stability and development."[6]

A third reason why people from developed countries have problems understanding state fragility is that they have forgotten, or have never been taught, how their own countries had to struggle to build robust state structures. Moreover, the problems facing fragile states—for the most part postcolonial countries struggling to deal with the imposition of unnatural borders and governing bodies—are different from anything their own countries ever had to deal with.

Among the most difficult issues for Westerners to understand is the role that traditional identities and institutions must play if effective governing bodies are ever to be built. Without a greater appreciation for the tribal, ethnic, religious, and clan institutions and loyalties that drive behavior—and which are far too often dismissed both by Westerners and local elites as being primitive impediments to development—and without a greater understanding of how these interact with weak formal state structures to destabilize fragile states, the international community will be unable to design institutions that can actually promote development.

How the Development Process Works

Development describes a complex process that transforms both the way people think and behave and the system of how they work together. Although economics drives development, politics plays a far greater role in the key take-off stages, with social, business, and government modernization inextricably linked as the process advances. Development requires not just the right economic and human resource policies (as usually stressed by the international community), but also a system of informal institutions that encourages entrepreneurs and financiers to take the necessary risks. Incentives matter, but at a more fundamental level than policymakers usually recognize.

Historically, only one process has led to development: market-driven economic modernization spearheaded by the business sector. This process usually occurs slowly, with change seeping through a society gradually, often fueled by the demands of expanding companies and new taxpayers. Competition plays an important—and underappreciated—role here. When people try to meet customer needs and raise productivity, they change their outlooks on how to manage time, assess information, and judge quality. Growth feeds rising incomes and expectations, which in turn leads to increasing demands on private firms and public service providers. As companies undertake projects of growing complexity and scale, and the division of labor between firms becomes ever more intricate and refined,[7] they demand greater security in property rights and reductions in transaction costs. Where a government must depend on taxes from local businesses and citizens, it, in turn, becomes more accountable and responsive to a population's needs. The cycle feeds upon itself: progress generating confidence, profits yielding more investment, rising expectations forcing reform upon one sector after another. As Adam Smith wrote in *The Wealth of Nations*, "commerce and manufacturers gradually introduced order and good government and, with them, the liberty and security of individuals among the inhabitants of the country who had before lived . . . in a state of servile dependency upon their superiors."[8] East Asian nations have vividly shown over the past few decades that creating internationally competitive economies is the best way to modernize because the process efficiently reorganizes society, importing and diffusing modern values and skills far more rapidly than any domestic-focused program could. The more compact the entity or region, the faster the transformation; in larger populations, such as in China and India, the cycles of development naturally take longer to spread.

However, for this process of societal development to start and gather momentum, people and companies must have enough confidence in the surrounding institutional environment to make the investments necessary to nourish it. Individuals must see in their future earnings the benefits of more education and training. Entrepreneurs must believe that their property and contract rights will be respected without undue hassle, allowing risk taking to yield adequate returns. Illicit behavior must be sufficiently penalized so as to funnel activity into projects that yield benefits for all. Although business owners and workers in rich countries take such conditions for granted, most poor states struggle to create even their most basic elements.

Development is therefore fundamentally about a society's capacity to nurture productive risk-taking, which depends on its ability to offer a secure and low cost environment for the possession of private assets and the carrying out of private transactions. These naturally depend on that society's institutions as they "together with the technology employed determine [the] transaction costs" necessary to "protect property rights and to enforce agreements," as Nobel Prize winner Douglass North explains in his landmark work on the subject.[9] Communities in the early stages of development, lacking the robust formal institutions that drive developed states, have little choice but to rely upon their informal institutions to impart these. One of the chief differences between successful states and struggling states is their ability or inability to create a system of informal institutions that can foster productive behavior at the very early stages of development. Fragile states repeatedly prove unable to do so, often producing toxic behavioral incentives instead—even when well-meaning leaders try to introduce the well-meaning policies promoted by the international community.

INSTITUTIONS AND GOVERNANCE: A BRIEF INTRODUCTION

Institutions are the framework within which human interactions take place—the rules of the game in a society—structuring "social interaction by constraining and enabling actors' behavior,"[10] affecting all "political, economic and social interactions" within countries. Consisting of "both informal constraints (sanctions, taboos, customs, traditions, and codes of conduct) and formal rules (constitutions, laws, property rights),"[11] they mold all activity through their incentives and disincentives, deciding where individuals funnel their energies in the process.

The ability of any country to foster private investment—the engine that should drive economic expansion and development—depends on the robustness and predictability of its formal and informal institutions (see Figure 2.1). Similarly, the ability of any poor country to jumpstart the virtuous cycles that underpin the development process depends on its capacity to construct "good" institutions, such as competent regulatory agencies, widely accepted property rights, and constructive social norms. If these provide the right positive incentives, they will channel people's behavior in productive ways, motivating them to take the risks that create wealth and jobs, advancing their country in the process. These can only be built, however, when state institutions are widely accepted and cultivated by citizens.

Governance describes how a country is run, referring to the "nature of relations between state and society" and the "nature of rules that regulate the public realm—the space where state and economic and societal actors interact to make decisions."[12] While there are widely accepted concepts of good governance—requiring that a state is "capable, accountable, and responsive," using the Department for International Development (DFID) terminology,[13] and that it therefore acts efficiently, transparently, accountably, decently, fairly, and with the participation of stakeholders[14]—the state governance systems that might satisfy these criteria are highly contextual and vary across the world. A country's historical background, previous regimes, sociocultural setting, economic system, international environment, and geography can all influence the character of its formal institutions. Japan, the United States, and Sweden, for example, all are marked by highly effective governance systems, even if their state structures and laws differ in some important ways.

Good governance—which has recently come to so dominate the development policy debate that many consider it to be "perhaps the single most important factor in eradicating poverty and promoting development," as ex-United Nations Secretary-General Kofi Annan has said[15]—is intimately linked to good institutions, and could not come about without them. However, and in contradiction to how the international community is diagnosing the ailments of poor countries,[16] there are many examples of states rapidly developing with what would be judged as highly unsatisfactory governance, such as China and South Korea. In fact, most of today's rich countries grew rapidly in the nineteenth century, during which period, notes Ha-Joon Chang, the Assistant Director of Development Studies at the University of Cambridge, their judiciaries, levels of political participation, financial intermediaries (such as banks), and property rights were "*less* advanced compared to today's developing countries at similar stages of development." As "the developed countries in their earlier times grew much faster than the developing countries over the last two decades.... [Thus,] contrary to what is assumed in the 'good governance' discourse, many [of these high standards] follow, rather than lead, economic development."[17] In a similar vein, IDS notes that "the astonishing economic growth of countries in East Asia" was achieved "despite a lack of formal institutions generally thought essential to good governance. Research in China shows how informal relations effectively substituted for more formal property rights in the early stages of market-led growth."[18] What all of these successful states *have* had in common is a widely accepted system of institutions that have encouraged risk taking and moneymaking. Good governance, although highly important in itself, is clearly not the cause of these countries ability to develop. Something more fundamental is at work here.

Although formal institutions are the main drivers of behavior in developed countries, *informal institutions* "are relatively more important in poor countries" because people there "are often ill-served by the limited formal institutions available," as a recent Organization for Economic Co-operation and Development (OECD) working paper on institutions and development concluded.[19] Yet, most programs and policies devised by the international community to assist developing countries focus almost exclusively on formal bodies of government, ignoring, in effect, the most significant factors influencing how most people in those countries act. The research community is no different: "informal rules have remained at the margins of ... comparative politics. Indeed, much current literature assumes that actors' incentives and expectations are shaped primarily, if not exclusively, by formal rules. Such a narrow focus can be problematic, for it risks missing much of what drives political behavior and can hinder efforts to explain important political phenomena."[20]

This situation is all the more disappointing because there are abundant examples of the powerful hold of informal institutions on behavior. In post–World War II Italy, for example, norms of corruption were "more powerful than the laws of the state: the latter could be violated with impunity, while anyone who challenged the conventions of the illicit market would meet with certain punishment."[21] In Mexico, for decades an unwritten code "gave the sitting president the right to choose his successor, specified the candidate pool, and prohibited potential candidates from openly seeking the job.... In Central Asia, clan-based norms have 'become the rules of the game,' while the constitutional structures created after the collapse of the Soviet Union are 'increasingly ... inconsequential.' And in much of the developing and postcommunist world, patterns of clientelism, corruption, and patrimonialism coexist with (and often subvert) new democratic, market, and state institutions."[22] Indeed, informal institutions can have such a powerful grip on societies that even if there are dramatic changes in formal rules, such as those caused by a revolution, by colonialism, or by a change in law as a result of a political or judicial decision, their high degree of "path-dependency"—whereby an outcome depends on the series of preceding patterns of conduct—means that behaviors stay the same. "Although a wholesale change in the formal rules may take place, at the same time there will be many informal constraints that have great survival tenacity because they still resolve basic exchange problems among the participants, be they social, political, or economic."[23]

One of the reasons fragile states have such difficulty constructing good governance systems is that their foreign-imposed formal institutions are weak and conflict and compete with—and lose to—the informal institutions that drive much behavior. "Informal institutions structure incentives in ways that are incompatible with the formal rules: to follow one rule, actors must violate another."[24] As North explains, "putting in place the formal institutions that have undergirded the spectacular growth of the developed world does not produce the desired results. That is because the formal rules must be complemented by informal norms of behavior (and enforcement characteristics) to get the desired results."[25]

STATE BUILDING: A BRIEF HISTORY

History shows that only two types of countries—nation-states and "state-nations"—have been able to create robust systems of governance able to jumpstart this process of development, in both cases because the great majority of their populations—or at least of their elites—share a common national identity and accept the state's most fundamental rules of the game (see Figure 2.1). In each case, the success of the state has rested "in its ability to provide stable and enabling institutions . . . For institutions to be successful, they must be both legitimate in the eyes of the citizens and effective and efficient in their ability to undertake the development agenda and governance functions."[26]

The Developed Nation-States

For almost two centuries, the nation-state has been the main driver of political and economic modernization. What has made that possible is the nation-state's cohesion, usually based on its shape—one "imagined community" of people in one territory.[27] In the nation-state, the affinitive power of identity and group allegiance channels itself into country development, yielding states that are more stable, faster growing, less corrupt, better governed, and more development oriented. By starting with the deep-rooted cultural heritage shared by an identity group with a long history, modern governing forms could be constructed upon time-tested manners of working together informally, ensuring that productive activity would be relatively low cost to transact and well rewarded whereas unproductive opportunism would be penalized by the social community. Similarly, the trust and social capital[28] built up between members of a cohesive group with long experience working together could be leveraged to stimulate the economic activity necessary to drive development forward. Later, these states' cohesion encouraged the creation of more democratic and more liberal forms of government because their common identities made it easier for populations to accept changes in government, unfavorable court decisions, and disparities in wealth.[29]

All kinds of relatively cohesive societies, ranging from England to Germany to Japan, have successfully transformed themselves into modern states because they could leverage their past throughout the development process. These countries were able to form states and build nations in tandem, strengthening group identity in the process and building robust and legitimate formal institutions based on shared customs. Core groups came together in nations, rallying around a common tongue, a common culture, and shared political and economic organizations. The evolution of these countries, rarely enlightened or even deliberate, often involved brutal wars, savage power politics, ethnic cleansing, forced assimilation, and considerable greed and egotism (as well as the construction of schools and highways). "The state used its institutions and resources to promote national identity in order to consolidate and legitimize itself by manipulating . . . powerful new symbols [of the nation]."[30] In the end, the best-managed groups became stronger militarily and economically. They expanded over broader areas, absorbed neighbors and formed sociopolitically coherent, economically logical, effectively governed states. Citizens came to view outside countries as their true competitors rather than other groups within the state, pulling together to advance their homeland's power and standing, and further delimiting their identity in relation to others.

This natural evolution—"natural" in the sense that states were created by the common historical experience of their inhabitants, through a long process of trial and error—leads to formal governing bodies that enjoy widespread legitimacy among citizens, which is a good predictor of better governance, more robust institutions, and higher growth.[31] Formed "through a local political process of state/society bargaining,"[32] institutions are the "products of lengthy processes of institutional development involving political struggles, ideological battles, and legal reforms,"[33] yielding "a balance between state effectiveness and accountability."[34] Even where authoritarianism was the norm for much of the process, state dependence on taxation produced a "governance dividend" whereby "a fiscal social contract" played a major role in "constructing new relations of accountability, based not on patronage but on mutual rights and obligations."[35] In Western Europe, for example, "the need for rulers to collect tax to fight interstate wars forced them into negotiations with taxpayers, resulting in the creation of representative institutions, administrative machinery to collect revenue and implement public programmes, and formal mechanisms of accountability. The effectiveness of the state was enhanced, while at the same time state power was constrained by the growth of organised interest groups and institutions."[36]

This progression is a part of human history around the globe, but only in Western and Central Europe, Northeast Asia, North America, Oceania, and a few places in the developing world has it produced unified, effectively governed nation-states.[37] That is because the process is protracted, typically involving many detours and taking far longer than is usually appreciated. England and France, for instance, took three to five centuries to evolve into modern nation-states.

In regions dominated by these countries, borders are more stable, state structures are stronger, institutions are more robust, and growth is faster than elsewhere because populations are more cohesive.[38] Europe, after a torturous process lasting centuries, is now mainly made up of states that are based on a single dominant national identity group. The economic dynamos of Northeast Asia all have long histories as cohesive states. In North America and Oceania strong new nations formed, with the help of the institutions bequeathed by the British, fed by immigrants who actively embraced their new identity as Australians, Canadians, New Zealanders, or Americans. (In the case of the United States, it took a war—the Civil War—to create a unified nation.) Although some rich countries still have groups seeking autonomy or even independence—for instance, the Basques and the Quebecois—there are far fewer of them, and their differences with their countrymen are far narrower, than in the developing world.

Outside the Western world, the countries that have developed most successfully are the economic dynamos of Northeast Asia. It is no coincidence that the Japanese, Chinese, and Koreans each have thousands of years of common social, economic, and political evolution and that their strong identities are underpinned by some of the world's most sophisticated institutions. They were the most cohesive states in the premodern world, and each has been able to call upon deep reserves of group affinity to make modernization a national mission. Similarly, Taiwan, Hong Kong, and Singapore have prospered because of their citizens' common Chinese past (the latter two have also benefited from British institutions, as discussed below).

The Developing Nation-States

A handful of successful developing nation-states in other regions have a lot in common with these countries, although their location in bad neighborhoods far from other successful countries has hampered their development. These developing nation-states are far more cohesive and unified than other countries in their regions because they are based on a common identity, and thus contain fewer identity-driven rivalries and conflicts than their neighbors. Some, such as Kuwait and Korea, organized themselves around a common cultural heritage and a recognizable political unit, while others, such as Botswana and Costa Rica, had colonial borders that fortuitously left them relatively homogeneous. All of them were able to develop by leveraging community-wide informal institutions, governance capacities, and rich reserves of social capital. In some cases, the cohesive groups successfully adopted the modern state system of governance even though they had no or limited experience managing state institutions in the pre-colonial era.

Turkey, one of the very few non-Western and non-Northeast Asian countries that entered the modern era with "a relatively homogeneous population and a pre-existing high culture on which to base a modernizing nationalism,"[39] is the only large country in the Middle East that is successfully developing, partly because it is one of the region's few nation-states. Almost uniquely in the region (Iran is the other example), it has a "sense of group solidarity [that] rests on the solid base of country; it is sustained by a common sense of nationhood and upheld by centuries of sovereign independent statehood."[40] Mustafa Kemal began molding a modern, European-style identity in 1923 upon the ashes of the Ottoman Empire. He created a state that eschewed imperial ambitions, downplayed the role of religion, and zeroed in on economic, political, and social modernization as the way to ensure Turks' continued independence and strength.

Botswana, one of the few African countries with a "favorable geography"[41] (its population density and shape make it relatively easy to consolidate power) and one of "only four states [that] came remotely close to being ethnically homogeneous at independence,"[42] has regularly conducted competitive elections since independence in 1965 and has created a fairly efficient civil service with "remarkable levels of operational autonomy."[43] Despite building its economy on a nature resource (diamonds), it has avoided the "resource curse" that has befallen the great majority of similarly endowed developing countries—precisely because its cohesiveness has yielded a far different attitude among leaders towards assets held by the state. Botswana has, in fact, enjoyed one of the fastest growth rates in the world since independence. The country creatively based modern institutions on traditional patterns of governance, reinforcing long-established loyalties. Tribal heads, for example, have two distinct roles: they are symbolic leaders at the local level and they sit in the national House of Chiefs.

Chile's history as the most stable country in Latin America "must ultimately be ascribed to the peculiarity of [the country]. . . . Its agrarian economy was dominated by a close-knit oligarchy . . . ethnic divisions were not as deep as in most other countries of Latin America: the lower classes comprised large numbers of whites and mestizos, the small black population declined fairly rapidly after independence, and few separate Indian communities survived. . . Chile, therefore, was a very integrated country by comparison with her fellow Spanish American republics."[44] This relatively homogenous state built inclusive, legitimate institutions with a special "strength of constitutional legality"[45] early on, enabling it to become the only country in the region that translated its exploitation of natural resources (copper and nitrates, chiefly) to produce productivity dividends for the whole economy.[46]

A few other countries also fit this pattern. Costa Rica, for example, "founded a constitutional system which was able after 1889 to evolve into a wider democracy with free elections and genuine political freedoms . . . largely due to its geographical isolation and its small, homogeneous population."[47] Its "small indigenous population and limited natural resources" fostered a "homogenous, egalitarian smallholder society" that "had the virtuous effect of contributing to social integration and stability over generations."[48] Vietnam and Thailand, both among the fastest developing countries in Asia over the past two decades, are natural nation-states that bring together people with a common history, language, and culture dating back a millennium. Mongolia's close-knit population partly explains the ease and speed with which it has abandoned Communism and become one of freest countries in Asia.

Mali's ability to achieve "a record of democratization . . . that is among the among the very best in Africa" in recent decades, despite it being one of the poorest countries in the world, stems from its "coherent geography," a social cohesion rooted in a common precolonial past, and its ability to adapt its governing structures to the area's very rich and widely shared precolonial societal norms.[49] Senegal, despite an unfavorable geography that has encouraged a long-standing secessionist movement in its south, has been able to foster a national identity among its other inhabitants through their shared Islamic heritage and customs. It has one of the best records of democratic government on the continent.

Elsewhere, there are territories that—given the right leaders and policies and the readiness to fit formal institutions to local circumstances—could use their peoples' common identity and past to develop around a nation-state model. Burkina Faso, for example, may have enough in common with Mali that it could follow in Mali's footsteps.[50] Somaliland, the secessionist state in the north of Somalia, has already made substantial progress as a political entity by leveraging its past to build a cohesive state rooted on traditional forms of self-government (chapter 8). Uruguay, like Chile, enjoys "natural [geographical] advantages and . . . [a] relatively small, homogenous population of predominantly European origin," that has given it extensive "social harmony" throughout its history.[51] States such as Iran and Cambodia are similarly endowed.

The Colonial Exceptions: State-Nations

Among the states that emerged from colonialism with multiple strong identity groups, few have developed cohesive national identities or robust national governing systems from the institutional structures bequeathed by Europeans. The small number of heterogeneous countries that have succeeded all share a history where the colonizing power—in every case, the British Empire—invested substantially over many generations in establishing and legitimizing new state institutions and a new national identity so robust such that after independence local elites adopted these as their own, helping to unify populations with disparate backgrounds. In time, these states have managed to integrate their citizens' diverse traditions with the transplanted colonial governing bodies to form a cohesive political entity focused on national development. These state-nations offer important lessons about the challenges of constructing new institutions and identities in divided polities;

they also help explain why other postcolonial countries have had such enormous difficulties constructing new legitimate governing bodies from scratch.[52] Table 2.1 offers a comparative summary of some of the defining characteristics of state-nations, nation-states, and fragile states.

India is one of the few places that benefited from colonialism because the British Empire invested significantly more money and manpower over a far longer length of time in "the Jewel in the Crown" than in its other possessions. Colonialism conditioned Indians to see the whole of South Asia as one country—a vision without precedent before the British arrived. As Sunil Khilnani, the director of the South Asia Studies Program at Johns Hopkins University, explains in *The Idea of India*, "before the nineteenth century, no residents of the subcontinent would have identified themselves as Indian. . . . What made possible the self-invention of a national community was the fact of alien conquest and subjection."[53]

The country was one of the few colonies to gain independence with both the administrative and military capacity and necessary transportation and communication infrastructure to govern its territory. "The state . . . that could in practice enforce a constitutionally defined identity . . . had to rely largely on its inheritance of military and bureaucratic capacities from the Raj . . . these colonial legacies were the sole instruments to impose a political identity over the whole territory . . . The army and civil service gave the Indian state a professional class recruited from an all-Indian base, able to operate and move easily across the country—an elite of 'functionary Indians.' "[54] The fabled Indian Civil Service and other arms of the colonial government employed and trained hundreds of thousands of Indians in modern forms of bureaucratic administration whereas most colonizers prepared very few, if any, locals to take the reins of government.

Generations of Indians grew up under the Raj, with the elite attending British schools in India and England before independence, fashioning a new national, multiethnic identity and, eventually, cooperating in the fight for independence. The men who fought for Indian independence—Mohandas K. Gandhi, Jawaharlal Nehru, Muhammad Ali Jinnah, Vallabhbhai Patel, Bhim Rao Ambedkar—were all trained as lawyers, passed the bar in England, and imbibed British ideas of effective governance. As Khilnani notes, "British domination helped to create the opportunities for Indians to acquire a modern self, a political identity guaranteed by the state."[55]

South Africa's experience (in the struggle to end apartheid) was in some ways similar to India's: a long time in which to grow accustomed to a new, colonially imposed national identity and to new formal institutions; indigenous leaders acculturated to British norms of government through education (Nelson Mandela, for example, was trained as a lawyer, and Thabo Mbeki studied for many years in England); an elite committed to taking over, not undermining, the state's institutions; and the inheritance of a robust administrative, security, and judiciary apparatus. Despite an ethnic and linguistic mix comparable to some of the most dysfunctional states on the continent, the country is by far the most politically and economically advanced in sub-Saharan Africa, containing a far more modern

Table 2.1. Comparing Characteristics across States

Nation-States
1. Formed around cohesive group with shared history
2. Common national identity
3. National governing bodies viewed as legitimate; highly stable political order
4. Common set of informal institutions
5. Robust governing system
6. State closely integrated with and highly reflective of society
7. State security, administrative, and judicial organs competent or better
8. Borders accepted as legitimate
9. High levels of trust and social capital
10. Low costs to hold property and to transact business
11. High incentives to invest given right policies
12. Typically able to avoid natural resource curse
13. Usually found in region of robust states

State-Nations
1. Formed around colonial identity and long-established, robust colonial formal institutions
2. Common national identity stronger than all or almost all subnational and supranational identities
3. National governing bodies viewed as legitimate by the great majority of population; political order becomes increasingly stable as time passes
4. Subnational groups may have common set of informal institutions, but whole population may not
5. If sufficiently rooted, the governing system will be stable in the short term and possibly robust in the longer term
6. State becomes more integrated with and reflective of citizens' diverse traditions over time
7. State security, administrative, and judicial organs able to enforce security, overcome political fragmentation, and rule impartially
8. Borders accepted as legitimate by the great majority of population
9. High levels of trust and social capital within subnational groups; moderate levels of trust across groups
10. Low costs to hold property and conduct business transactions within cohesive subnational groups, especially in homogenous areas; moderate costs across groups
11. Generally good incentives to invest given right policies
12. May be able to avoid natural resource curse
13. Location within a region of robust states assists process of state consolidation during early years of independence

Fragile States
1. Formed around diverse population with little shared history and poorly established, weak formal institutions
2. Weak national identity overwhelmed by conflicting subnational or supranational identities
3. National governing bodies viewed as illegitimate by a significant number of population; political order highly unstable and difficult to reform
4. No common set of informal institutions
5. Dysfunctional governing system
6. State sits on top of and is disconnected from society
7. State security, administrative, and judicial organs so weak or discriminatory that they exacerbate political fragmentation
8. Borders not accepted as legitimate by a significant number of people
9. Low levels of trust and social capital
10. High costs to hold property and conduct business transactions in most cases
11. Little incentive to invest even if good policies are adopted
12. Typically unable to avoid natural resource curse
13. Usually found in region of fragile states
14. In some cases, state's undersized market, dearth of human resources, unfavorable geography, or population distribution makes it especially unstable
© 2007 by Seth D. Kaplan

and extensive infrastructure, a more sophisticated financial and legal system, and a stronger administration than any other state. Hong Kong, Singapore, and Malaysia are other examples of this phenomenon, though the former two territories have also been able to draw upon the strong Chinese identities of the great majority of their populations.

Few other ex-colonies, British or otherwise, have benefited from the impact and legacy of colonialism. For the vast majority of states, colonialism was a disaster at the time and its legacy continues to hobble their efforts to develop. In Africa, Europeans sought from the beginning "conquest on the cheap," as they were "unwilling, given the high cost of administration and the low probability of reward, to develop extensive administrative networks." Vast areas were never effectively taken over. "The colonial state was notably slow in expanding the spatial reach of the security forces, arguably the essence of any state." Infrastructure was neglected where it did not lead directly to a financial return. Trains, for example, were built to ports, but rarely to connect inland territories.[56] In many colonies, such as the Congo (see Chapter 6), few people were educated above primary school level and the higher echelons of the national civil service were closed to locals. In most of the Middle East, Europeans drew up new borders at the end of World War I, spent just two decades administering the new states (and did so with little enthusiasm), and then promptly withdrew after World War II, leaving barely any mark on the region except for badly drawn borders. Colonial rule in Latin America, although lasting for centuries and leaving an indelible mark on the region's societies, created a new set of identity divisions and institutional weaknesses by systematically discriminating against a significant portion of the population, a discrimination that vitiated the ability of national governing bodies to unite populations.[57] There was also little experience in creating national identities in most places, as, with the exception of Brazil, most of the newly independent countries had no history as separate entities. Central Asia and the Caucasus suffer today from a Soviet policy designed to "divide, conquer, and tie up in trouble" nationalities by forcing rivals to share homelands (see Chapter 11 on the Azerbaijan-Armenia conflict).[58]

The experience of all these states shows the difficulty of implanting new formal institutions and new concepts of identity into foreign lands. Only a sustained and coherent program lasting generations, led by one outside power, and featuring significant foreign involvement in the management of governing bodies and security forces and large investments in the education of local elites can hope to pay dividends. The failure of recent attempts by the international community to build new institutions in failed states such as East Timor, Haiti, and the Democratic Republic of the Congo (DRC), despite the outlay of billions of dollars in some cases, can easily be explained by the brevity of such efforts. In East Timor, a small country of about 1 million people, the UN effort—lasting only thirty-two months—became known as Quickfixville and largely provided for just "the minimum to keep the government functioning," as the UN's top man on the ground explained it. The spectacle became "a saga of short-termism, ill-directed aid and conflicting priorities," not atypical for any such project undertaken by the highly unfocused and undisciplined international community.[59] Resolving the problems created by divided populations and weak—or in some cases almost nonexistent—formal governing bodies that most postcolonial states were born with requires far more creative approaches.

IDENTITY AND INSTITUTIONS

The important role played by social cohesion in constructing the legitimate, robust national governing systems necessary for development (as portrayed in Figure 2.1) can be traced back to the role of identity in how people view the world and in how institutions are formed. Nation-states, by definition based on a cohesive population with a long, common past and identity, have, through a process of trial and error and over the course of many centuries, created a set of shared institutions; these institutions have formed the basis for governing bodies that are regarded as legitimate because they reflect the underlying sociocultural fabric of the state. State-nations, while made up of diverse peoples that may have significantly different pasts and local customs, have, over the course of generations, grown accustomed to a new common identity and to a new formal governing system that is also viewed as legitimate. By contrast, the diverse populations in fragile states have very limited common historical experience and thus possess neither a strong unifying identity nor widely accepted institutions (whether formal or informal), both of which are essential to the formation of a robust and legitimate national governing system. In fragile states, formal institutions are often empty shells "suspended in 'mid-air' over society and . . . not an integral mechanism of the day-to-day productive activities of society."[60] Disconnected from the local population, they are seen as "an external entity that should be shunned. Unless, of course, a citizen has access to state resources, in which case the state is an entity to be exploited."[61]

Identity lies at the heart of how people see themselves and the world around them. Molded from birth by family, skin, blood, place, community, language, religion, and culture, identity reflects and affects the ties that bind people to groups. Cohesive groups—of whatever kind—are "integrated not by one but by a combination of several kinds of objective relationships (economic, political, linguistic, cultural, religious, geographical, historical) and their subjective reflection in collective consciousness."[62] These "people who share the same collective identity think of themselves as having a common interest and common fate."[63]

The dominant force driving identity is different in different places. In some regions of the world, religion is the defining aspect, in others ethnic group, in still others language. In much of the Middle East, for instance, "a region of old and deep-rooted identities," "not nationality, not citizenship, not descent, but religion, or more precisely membership of a religious community, is the ultimate determinant of identity."[64] In India, "a sense of region and nation emerged together, through parallel self-definitions."[65] In pre-colonial Africa, "identities, allegiances, and loyalties revolved around lineage, the clan, the chief and cultural practices related to these institutions."[66] In Latin America, identities have been "historically so fragmented and mixed" because subgroups combine deeply varied ethnic and cultural "*mestizaje* of Iberian, Indian, and African traditions."[67] In Central Asia, "smaller solidarity groups based on locality, kinship, or a combination of the two remain at the core of political action."[68]

Identities have an important role to play in the construction of effective governing systems (whether constructed around a state or not). Cohesive groups with a long history have naturally developed a set of common "norms, beliefs, practices and traditions with which" they "engage [the] environment."[69] The shared social customs, extended period of working together, and ability to discipline their own members generate over time significant amounts of intragroup trust and intragroup social capital that nonmembers naturally cannot generally benefit from, though the levels depend on each unique group background. These informal institutions not only play important roles in regulating the security, political relationships, and economic ties of group members, but also, in conjunction with this built-up social capital, significantly reduce the cost of transactions and of holding property, thus greatly increasing the capacity of companies and individuals to conduct business within the group, enlarging their scope to produce wealth, even where they hold no formal role in state management. "Dispersed ethnic groups" such as diaspora Jews, Chinese, Lebanese, Indians, and Armenians, for example, "have exercised a disproportionate influence on the growth patterns of nations, cities, and regions"[70] partly because they could leverage a "strong sense of ethnic identity," a "sense of mutual dependence that helps the group adjust to changes . . . without losing its essential unity," a strong sense of "mutual trust that allows the tribe to function collectively," as well as a "passion for . . . knowledge."[71] Unsurprisingly, states that can take advantage of these group synergies on a national level have great advantages over those that cannot.

But just as a strong identity can unite a population and strengthen the state, so a weak national identity or a multiplicity of competing identities can divide citizens and undermine the state. Even a country with robust state institutions and a long history of good governance, such as the United States, cannot completely eliminate the negative effects of diversity. Recent research by Robert Putnam, one of the world's most influential political scientists, suggests that diversity and trust are inversely related. "In the presence of diversity, we hunker down," notes Putnam. "We act like turtles . . . And it's not just that we don't trust people who are not like us. In diverse communities, we don't trust people who look like us."[72] Research by other social scientists confirms that "racial divisions and ethnic divisions reduce incentives for people to be generous to others through social welfare," undermining "support for government spending on 'public goods' of all types, whether health care, roads or welfare programs for the disadvantageous."[73] For instance, in sub-Saharan Africa, per capita spending on HIV prevention and treatment correlates closely with ethnic division, the least divided societies spending five times more than the most divided societies.[74]

In fragile states, where the state's formal institutions are weak and society is fractured, making overall conditions quite unstable, the effects of diverse identities are far worse. Although each individual's identity is "constructed on the basis of various traits and experiences" and often encompasses membership in multiple identity groups, whose "relative importance and compatibility differs in various times and circumstances,"[75] fluid, unstable environments encourage polities to split along the most profound cleavages: ethnicity, religion, tribe, clan, and so forth. In Yugoslavia and Iraq, although diverse populations lived peaceably side-by-side for decades, the instability and uncertainty of rapid change led religious and ethnic subnational (or supranational) identities to reemerge as the dominant factors determining an individual's identity; both countries swiftly fragmented along allegiances a millennium in the making and descended into ferocious civil conflict. "Nations don't behave this way," said Timur Göksel, the former spokesman for the United Nations Interim Force in Lebanon. "It's groups of people who share the same land."[76]

A multiplicity of competing identity groups, when combined with weak formal state structures, does not always result in bloodshed, but it does always cripple efforts to promote development. As we will see in the next chapter, this toxic combination—the absence of social cohesion and the lack of a set of shared, productive institutions—prevents states from fashioning a robust nationwide governing system, yielding instead a host of chronic problems, ranging from state illegitimacy to political instability to economic impotency.

3

Fragile States, Fractured Societies

The divided natures of fragile states have left them with no unifying identities, no unifying institutions, and no unifying governance systems with which to bind their peoples together. Usually based on arbitrarily drawn borders that ignore local sociopolitical, geographical, and economic conditions, the designs of these states force their peoples to discard hundreds of years of institutional memory, devalue the stored-up social capital of their communities, and make the incorporation of informal norms into formal governing bodies highly problematic. Even where populations have shared the same political space for centuries, deep ethnic, religious, clan, social, geographical, and cultural divisions estrange their various identity groups. Predictably, given these circumstances, such states are riven by severe factionalism, undermined by their illegitimacy, and enfeebled by weak formal institutions.

This chapter shows that the root causes of fragile states' many troubles can be traced back to the absence of social cohesion and a set of shared, productive institutions—the two ingredients discussed in Chapter 2. Without these, fragile states are unable to create an effective governance system on their own. This chapter also makes clear that only by rethinking and refashioning these states' formal institutions can their problems be ameliorated. It starts with a brief explanation of the historical roots of state fragility and a discussion of how current aid policies often prolong past dysfunction. It then diagnoses the structural issues at the root of state fragility and explains why fragile states are unable in their current form to harness the driving forces that enable other countries to develop. It concludes with an explanation of some of the problems these structural flaws have produced.

THE HISTORICAL ROOTS OF FRAGILITY

Many of the difficulties confronting fragile states stem from how those states are structured. Mostly based on borders arbitrarily drawn by Westerners, their very births forced together disparate—and often incompatible—identity groups. This left precolonial communities (or in some cases a mixture of precolonial communities and settlers) not only unable to continue their evolution into more mature entities[1]—to evolve as nation-states have done—but also without the strong, inclusive institutional framework necessary to govern newly established countries—the kind of framework that state-nations have been bequeathed by their colonial masters.[2] Institutions, norms, and systems of governance that had developed over centuries of adaptation to local conditions were discarded by the colonizers and a very Westernized "concept of the state was grafted onto a wide variety of pre-existing forms of government and social organization. In some cases, the state was even superimposed where order had traditionally been maintained without central institutions of any kind,"[3] such as in Somalia. Similar maladies plague the few fragile states that were not the product of colonialism—such as Ethiopia—because their histories also yielded countries with comparable societal divisions.

The pattern established when the colonial powers arrived and built their administrations on top of, and disconnected from, local societies was essentially continued in most countries at independence: governments are largely divorced from and autonomous of the societies that they are supposed to serve.[4] "The state . . . [is] in most of Africa [and to various degrees elsewhere—SK] an essentially artificial one, 'suspended above' a society which would never have produced it and did not demand it. This 'mis-match' between state and society is the essence of the problem."[5] In such environments, there is an enormous gap between a small cadre that manipulates or controls the state—and therefore favors its perpetuation—and the general population, who are highly ambivalent at best toward their own government. "The State is the estate of the new nobility."[6]

The postcolonial order, whereby Westerners have sought to help their past wards by providing aid and other forms of assistance, has in many ways only prolonged their agony by preventing any reorganization of the state so as to make it better suited to local conditions and more connected to its surrounding society. (Western policy toward fragile states may, in fact, be regarded as a new form of colonialism insofar as it tends to extend those states' dependence on the West.)[7] The "weakness of the [policies of] international financial institutions is particularly problematic where the state has failed to strike deep roots."[8] As a USAID Democracy Fellow concluded in a report for the agency, the "political disconnection [that existed at independence between state and society] was exacerbated by the economic disconnection that arose from the growing availability of external financial support. As the state became increasingly dependent on these foreign resources for its survival, it also grew increasingly autonomous of its own society and local resources, and so lost interest in that resource base as anything other than a source of plunder."[9] A DFID research program similarly pointed to "the complicity of rich, highly developed countries in the governance problems of poor countries, and to the need for external actors to take much more care about the impact of their actions on internal incentives and relationships in poor countries."[10] Abundant natural resources, such as oil, when controlled by a narrow ruling elite, can yield a similar result or exacerbate a society's dysfunctionality.

DIAGNOSING THE STRUCTURAL CAUSES OF FRAGILITY

Fragmented Identities, Weak Institutions, Illegitimate States

Fragile states are plagued by two structural problems—political identity fragmentation and weak national institutions—that together preclude the formation of any robust governing system, severely undermining the legitimacy of the state and leading to political orders that are highly unstable and hard to reform.

State legitimacy lies at the base of any stable political order; it is an essential ingredient influencing any country's capacity to foster economic, political, or social progress and is a powerful predictor of economic growth and the quality of governance.[11] The most secure such order "will derive from the conviction on the part of the member that it is right and proper for him to accept and obey the authorities and to abide by the requirements of the regime. It reflects the fact that in some vague or explicit way he sees these objects as conforming to his own moral principles, his own sense of what is right and proper in the political sphere."[12] Such regimes work effectively because of "the obedience of officials and subjects to a legally established impersonal order."[13] This legitimacy can be derived either from the citizenry seeing the state as the result of a socioculturally appropriate historical evolution that has yielded a just order (as is the case in nation-states, and, to a lesser degree, in state-nations), or from the citizens accepting the state because it has been established by or is governed by a revered leader (such as in the case of Turkey and Atatürk). A governance system that has become deeply rooted in and widely accepted by a society is by far the strongest and longest-lasting form of legitimacy—and the best basis on which to promote development.

The role of identity is crucial to the creation of legitimacy, because a legitimate political order is usually built around a cohesive group—and uses institutions that are a reflection of that group's historical evolution. As Michael Hudson explained in his classic study of the "legitimacy shortage" in Arab politics, "a legitimate political order ... has to be [based on] some consensus about national identity, some agreement about the boundaries of the political community, and some collective understanding of national priorities. If the population within given political boundaries is so deeply divided within itself on ethnic or class [or, for that matter, religious or clan—SK] lines, or if the demands of a larger supranational community are compelling to some [significant] portion of it, then it is extremely difficult to develop a legitimate order."[14] "Without authoritative political structures endowed with 'rightness' and efficacity, political life is certain to be violent and unpredictable."[15]

Political fragmentation and weak governing bodies feed upon each other, further undermining state legitimacy. As William Easterly, a well-respected development economist, explains, "Ethnic diversity has a more adverse effect on economic policy and growth when institutions are poor. To put it another way, poor institutions have an even more adverse effect on growth and policy when ethnic diversity is high. Conversely, in countries with sufficiently good institutions, ethnic diversity does not lower growth or worsen economic policies."[16] Their very divisions, for example, prevent the formation of "one of the most important requirements for making states work . . . the creation of apolitical bureaucratic structures (civil service, judiciary, police, army) supported by an ideology that legitimates the role of neutral state authority in maintaining social order through prescribed procedures and the rule of law."[17] The tribalism inherent in their political cultures engulf their already weak governing bodies, tribalizing them in the process, and preventing any apolitical bureaucratic structure emerging that could gain some allegiance from their populations. Similarly, the weakness of the state makes each identity group fall back upon its traditional loyalties because these are the only form of protection and support available. As Easterly explains in a more recent paper, "good institutions are most necessary and beneficial where there are ethnolinguistic divisions. Formal institutions substitute for the 'social glue' that is in shorter supply when there are ethnolinguistic divisions."[18]

Table 3.1, adapted from Hudson's work, summarizes the fragile state dilemma clearly. Political systems with low fragmentation and low government capabilities (square III)—features of some cohesive but not yet developed countries such as Mali, Armenia, and Mongolia—are relatively stable but inert. These have potentially bright futures if they can foster good investment climates and improve state capabilities because they should be able to create unified regimes backed by all their people. States with high identity fragmentation but also high government coercion capabilities available to quell internal conflict (square II), such as Syria,

Table 3.1. Alternative Political Orders

| | | Political Culture Fragmentation | |
		Low	*High*
Government Capabilities	*Low*	**III Inert**	**I Unstable**
	High	**IV Dynamic**	**II Controlled**

Source: Based on Michael Hudson, *Arab Politics: The Search for Legitimacy* (New Haven, CT: Yale University Press, 1977), 391.

Iraq under Saddam, and the former Soviet Union, are controlled. These countries may appear secure but are inherently weak, unable to adapt to change unless they either foster greater cohesion among their people or find a structural design or modus operandi that compensates for their divided natures. Systems marked by low political fragmentation and high state capabilities (square IV), as in the case of almost all developed countries and to a sufficient degree in the state-nations, are genuinely dynamic. Only this group is institutionally capable of attaining strong legitimacy and fully tackling the challenges of development. As this grid makes apparent, states that combine low-capability governments (especially low coercive powers) with highly fragmented political cultures (square I), such as the Democratic Republic of the Congo (DRC), Nigeria, and many other African states, give rise to the worst of all circumstances, and are inherently unstable orders. Fragile states are concentrated in squares I and II.

Much of the history of the better-led postcolonial states that start with both these disadvantages, such as Syria under Hafiz al-Asad (Chapter 7) and Ghana under Jerry Rawlings, can, in fact, be interpreted as attempts to move from square I to square II (as movement to square III is far more difficult). These countries seek to increase their legitimacy by fostering at least some semblance of national unity and by slowly increasing their ability to provide real services, including the maintenance of law and order, the construction of reasonably effective administrative organs, and the extension of education, health, and employment opportunities to a growing proportion of the population. As states develop, they will move from one of the upper squares to one of the lower squares, and from the right to the left. All Latin American countries, for instance, suffered from some form of instability during the first hundred years or so of their independence, but while progress has since been haphazard, most have become more stable and more development-oriented over time. The more cohesive entities, such as Chile, have been able to harness their unity and steadily enhance their capabilities and therefore have been able to create robust, dynamic, democratic, and increasingly prosperous regimes in recent years. Most African, Middle Eastern, and Central Asian countries are at a much earlier point in this trajectory.

Low Levels of Trust, High Transaction Costs

This political fragmentation directly impinges on the ability of these countries to foster the positive institutional environment necessary to encourage productive economic, political, and social behavior because it undermines the usefulness of traditional informal institutional systems and squanders built-up social capital while disabling attempts to construct robust formal governing bodies. The net result is societies with low levels of interpersonal trust and extraordinarily high transaction costs.

As discussed in Chapter 2, cohesive groups with long common histories naturally develop their own sophisticated political, economic, and societal system of self-governance (which is incorporated into the formal governing bodies of the nation-state as it matures). This system includes various mechanisms to police members' behavior, to lower the cost of various transactions between members, and to encourage the security of property. Even without the governing bodies of the modern state, such groups can create complex societies with advanced institutions, such as the nations of East Asia did centuries ago. These processes do not necessarily require a formal state role, as in the case of many precolonial communities in Africa and the Middle East that functioned without a state (such as the Igbo people) or relatively independent of the Ottoman state (such as the semi-autonomous confessional communities). People, after all, "tend to obey the rules not because they are worried about cops but because they have obligations to other people."[19] In many of these cohesive groups, "virtuous" circles develop that result in "social equilibria with high levels of cooperation, trust, reciprocity, civic engagement, and collective well-being,"[20] and a variety of formal and informal procedures to penalize the nonproductive activities that might undermine the general welfare.

Most, but not all, cohesive societies create such virtuous patterns; few, if any, fragile states do so. States made up of many identity groups with no common history of cooperation and no robust governing institutions to stimulate and regulate such cooperation tend to gravitate toward "a suffocating miasma of vicious circles" whereby, as Putnam notes, "defection, distrust, shirking, exploitation, isolation, disorder, and stagnation intensify one another."[21] Once such dysfunctional, unproductive institutions come to predominate in a society, they will persist because, as North explains, the high degree of path-dependency of a given institutional framework provides "disincentives to productive activity . . . [by creating] organizations and interest groups with a stake in the existing constraints,"[22] which "is an important factor in explaining persistent low growth rates in developing countries."[23] Easterly contends that "high ethnic diversity is closely associated with low schooling, underdeveloped financial systems, distorted foreign exchange markets, and insufficient infrastructure . . . interest group polarization leads to rent-seeking behavior and reduces the consensus for public goods, creating long-run growth tragedies."[24]

Trust—which Putnam describes as "an essential component of social capital"[25]—is a prerequisite for any economic and political development because it "lubricates cooperation. The greater levels of trust within a community, the greater the likelihood of cooperation. And cooperation itself breeds trust. . . . In communities where people can be confident that trusting will be requited, not exploited, exchange is more likely to ensue."[26] Democratic systems cannot function without trust; where there is little trust, there is, for instance, little incentive to obey the results of elections. Prosperous economies likewise depend upon a certain level of trust. "Virtually every commercial transaction has within itself an element of trust, certainly any transaction conducted over a period of time. It can be plausibly argued that much of the economic backwardness in the world can be explained by the lack of mutual confidence."[27] Putnam concludes that "for political stability, for government effectiveness, and even for economic progress social capital may be even more important than physical or human capital."[28]

State structures in divided countries delegitimize informal institutions without replacing them with effective formal bodies while destroying built-up social capital by forcing people with no common history to work together. (Indeed, to quote from an article published in 2000 by the World Bank, in many underdeveloped countries, "a society's social capital inheres mainly in primary social groups disconnected from one another."[29]) This combination significantly raises the cost of exchange while lowering the price of assets, severely crippling economies, and sharply reducing the capacity of societies to foster development. As North explains, "the greater the uncertainty of the buyer, the lower the value of the asset... the costs per exchange in [Third World countries] are much greater [than in advanced industrial economies]—sometimes no exchange occurs because costs are so high."[30] Conducting legitimate business activities—or for that matter conducting any form of productive social, political, or economic exchange—carries far greater risk in fragile states than in cohesive environments, dramatically influencing societal dynamics and the incentives that guide behavior. According to Paul Collier, "ethnically fractionalized societies were liable to have worse economic performance than more homogenous societies... [because they] can reduce income, namely, by reducing trust, and so raising transactions costs."[31]

Opportunism, Corruption, and Neopatrimonialism

Political fragmentation warps incentives, encouraging short-term opportunism at the expense of long-term investments that could advance development. Society becomes obsessed by the conflict between identity groups, not with generating wealth or increasing national prestige. Meanwhile, formal governing bodies and regulations, disconnected from their surrounding environments, and not having become an integral part of the informal institutional frameworks that guide people's behavior, command only superficial allegiance and compliance. Real life goes on outside them. State laws go unheeded because no one acknowledges them as legitimate. Corrupt governments, biased courts, and weak property rights are a natural product of such conditions.

In these fragile states, individuals are more likely to feel allegiance to a tribe, religious leader, or clan with which they and their forefathers have been closely connected than to a state with which they have few ties. "It is difficult to overestimate the enduring importance of patronage networks in societies that are still largely organized within ethnic communities and along kinship lines."[32] Groups compete to use the formal institutions for their own selfish objectives. If one group gains control of the state apparatus, it inserts its members in important positions and drains the country's wealth. Instead of formulating policy that might encourage growth, the ruling clique acts to control wealth-producing assets, restrict markets, disenfranchise portions of the electorate, and even dupe foreigners into providing more aid. Groups out of power see the state as illegitimate and seek to bypass it. Where cooperation does extend across clan lines, it is usually only a temporary alliance of opportunity, as cliques of various backgrounds compete to take advantage of the general lawlessness in society to siphon off money from everything from state construction projects to gold mines to warfare. In such cases, identity divisions may be manipulated for short-term personal or political gain, widening the gulf between groups.

In Côte d'Ivoire, for instance, the state was mired in a civil war for most of the 2000s due to the disenfranchisement of northerners. Ethnic tensions prompted southerners to amend the national constitution, marginalizing millions of people and denying them the right to identity cards, without which one cannot legally vote nor work. "We needed a war because we needed our identity cards," explained one rebel fighter. "We took weapons, not for oil, diamonds or power, but to say that there are people in Côte d'Ivoire that are living as second class citizens in their own country," said another.[33] Many Latin American countries, such as Bolivia, Ecuador, and Guatemala, have discriminated against their indigenous populations for centuries in everything from the provision of public services to the eligibility to vote to the recognition of languages (Chapter 9). States such as Nigeria, Sudan, and Bolivia have even failed to provide the most basic infrastructure and public services—for generations in some cases—to peoples living near many of their oil and mineral deposits.

Entrepreneurs in this environment must offer large payoffs to a corrupt regime or act illegally outside state structures and the formal legal framework. The businesspeople who flourish are not those with the best education or the best ideas but those connected by blood or marriage to the ruling clique or skilled at manipulating and bribing officials in charge of handing out licenses and contracts. Corruption and illegality thrive even where they were not a problem in local cultures originally. Paperwork and procedures expand to create new opportunities for bureaucratic wealth production, starving the legal private sector and fueling the growth of a shadowy black market. In Niger, for example, it takes eleven steps and costs four times the average annual income to register a business.[34] Investors stay away; roads, airports, telephone lines, and other infrastructure do not get built, or if built are not maintained; businesspeople and those with advanced degrees flee to other, better places to live and work; and the country makes no progress toward eliminating poverty, developing sound institutions, or modernizing. Table 3.2 shows how deficient fragile states' governments are when compared with their more cohesive neighbors.

Such environments naturally affect the actions of officials. "Politicians are beset by insecurity and fear of the unknown. If their behavior appears at times quixotic or even paranoid, the irrationality lies less within themselves than in their situation . . . [these] politicians must operate in a political environment in which the legitimacy of rulers, regimes, and the institutions of the states themselves is sporadic and, at best, scarce."[35] These supposedly bad leaders may enact bad

Table 3.2. Comparing State Performance within Various Regions of the World

Cohesive Countries Perform Far Better Than Fractured States
The more cohesive states listed above the line in each region consistently outperform their more divided neighbors on a number of indicators of government effectiveness

Country	World Bank Aggregate Governance Indicator, 2006*	Telephone Mainlines Per 1,000 People, 2004**	Corruption Perception Index Score, 2006	Political Freedom Rating, 2006
	+ 2.5 = best governed; - 2.5 = worst governed		*10 = most clean; 0 = most corrupt*	*1 = most free; 7 = least free*
Africa				
Botswana	+ 0.7	77	5.6	2.0
Mauritius	+ 0.7	287	5.1	1.5
South Africa	+ 0.5	N/A	4.6	2.0
Seychelles	+ 0.1	253	3.6	3.0
Uganda	− 0.6	3	2.7	4.5
Ethiopia	− 0.9	2	2.4	5.0
Angola	− 1.1	6	2.2	5.5
Nigeria	− 1.2	8	2.2	4.0
Sudan	− 1.5	29	2.0	7.0
DRC	− 1.7	0	2.0	5.5
Somalia	− 2.3	0	N/A	7.0
Balkans				
Croatia	+ 0.3	425	3.4	2.0
Bosnia	− 0.4	N/A	2.9	3.0
Serbia	− 0.4	330	N/A	2.5
Caucasus				
Armenia	− 0.3	192	2.9	4.5
Azerbaijan	− 0.9	118	2.4	5.5
Latin America				
Chile	+ 1.2	206	7.3	1.0
Uruguay	+ 0.6	291	6.4	1.0
Costa Rica	+ 0.6	316	4.1	1.0
Peru	− 0.4	74	3.3	2.5
Guyana	− 0.4	137	2.5	2.5
Guatemala	− 0.6	92	2.6	3.5
Nicaragua	− 0.6	40	2.6	3.0
Bolivia	− 0.7	69	2.7	3.0
Ecuador	− 0.9	124	2.3	3.0
Middle East				
UAE	+ 0.6	275	6.2	5.5
Israel	+ 0.5	441	5.9	1.5
Kuwait	+ 0.4	202	4.8	4.0
Turkey	+ 0.0	267	3.8	3.0
Lebanon	− 0.7	178	3.6	4.5
Syria	− 1.0	143	2.9	6.5
Iraq	− 1.8	N/A	1.9	6.0
South Asia				
Bhutan	+ 0.3	33	6.0	5.5
India	− 0.1	41	3.3	2.5
Pakistan	− 1.0	30	2.2	5.5
Nepal	− 1.1	15	2.5	4.5

*The World Bank figure averages six governance indicators: voice and accountability; political stability; government effectiveness; regulatory quality; rule of law; and control of corruption.
**2004 or most recent year available.

Sources: http://info.worldbank.org/governance/wgi2007/sc_country.asp; http://hdr.undp.org/hdr2006/statistics/indicators/; http://www.transparency.org/policy_research/surveys_indices/cpi/2006; http://www.freedomhouse.org/template.cfm?page = 365&year = 2007.

policies or act in a despotic fashion because such behavior is their only viable survival strategy. "These leaders are more likely to resort to patronage, nepotism, corruption, and other patterns of political behavior that are occasionally subsumed under the category of *neopatrimonialism*."[36] Hudson concludes, "in short, the insecurity of the ruling elite, based not necessarily on selfishness but on what impartial observers might call a realistic appraisal of the situation, causes it to act autocratically . . . [outsiders] may be wrong in ascribing the behavior to innate human evil; placed in the same situation, they invariably [would] do the same thing."[37]

RETHINKING THE DEVELOPMENT PARADIGM

Given enough time, fragile states suffering from severe identity fragmentation and weak formal institutions *might* be able to integrate their citizens into new nations—gaining clearly demarcated boundaries and cohesive national identities—and to build governing systems that are both robust and that have gained the allegiance of their peoples. This evolution, however, would take a long time, stretching into centuries in many cases.

The deadly combination of weak social cohesion and feeble state institutions (in some cases complicated by difficult political geographies and a lack of a necessary critical mass of human resources and market size) creates problems that are not amenable to the types of solutions—such as more aid, competitive elections, and economic reform—typically advocated by the international community. States such as the DRC, Sudan, Bolivia, and Iraq cannot easily democratize because political campaigns and voting often exacerbate, rather than ameliorate, domestic tensions. For some identity groups, self-determination actually means secession; for many, it means a chance to capture control of the state—and a determination to not relinquish it thereafter. The leaders of fragile states are reluctant, anyway, to compete in competitive elections because they—and their group or clique— have far more to lose than in legitimate, cohesive states. Equally, these countries cannot create strong institutions because few, if any, people profess any loyalty to the state or have any incentive—given the state's sociopolitical dynamics and informal institutional environment—to respect its laws. Bad governance in such countries cannot be fixed merely by enacting macroeconomic or administrative reforms because far more fundamental issues are causing their dysfunction. Such states, in any case, generally have a dearth of competent and honest officials willing to uphold an impersonal order—a prerequisite to introducing effective reforms.

Most divided countries will never develop if they continue evolving along current lines, especially because their dysfunction has become self-reinforcing. The vicious circles into which these states are locked can be reformed only by strategies that break their path dependency—and by doing so also reengineer their formal institutions, sufficiently matching them to local conditions so that they can be adopted, driven, and sustained by local peoples. Such strategies would leverage traditional loyalties and latent capacities in the construction of the state—either by empowering them, by balancing them, by bringing them together in some form, or by forcibly redirecting them into productive activities. Slowly but surely, this process would integrate societies with the states that purportedly represent them—fostering the development of countries in the process.

Part II ———————————————————————

Prescriptions

4

A New Paradigm for Development

This chapter offers a new paradigm for fixing fragile states, a paradigm based on the analysis in the preceding chapters of why and how states develop—or fail to develop. Actually, it is not so much a single prescription as a set of guiding principles, one whose effectiveness depends upon it being customized to take account and *advantage* of local conditions.

States cannot be made to work from the outside. International assistance may be necessary but it is never sufficient to establish formal institutions that are legitimate and sustainable and that can provide the positive societal incentives necessary to jumpstart the development process. Instead of seeking to impose a Western-style blueprint unsuitable for local conditions,[1] international action should be first and foremost about facilitating local processes, about leveraging local capacities, and about complementing local actions, so that local citizens can create governance systems appropriate to their surroundings. States work effectively when they are a logical reflection of their underlying sociopolitical, historical, geographical, human resource, and economic environments, and when they are deeply integrated with the societies they purport to represent, able to harness the informal institutions and loyalties of their citizens.

The key to fixing fragile states is thus to legitimize the state by deeply enmeshing it within society. People in fragile states in Africa, the Middle East, Latin America, Central Asia, and elsewhere have enormous political, socioeconomic, and cultural resources built up over centuries that can serve as the foundation for political, economic, and social development. What these people and these countries need are state models and structures that can be adapted to take advantage of those resources. What they also need is international assistance—in a wide variety of forms (cash alone having limited usefulness in many cases)—that is concerned first and foremost with *facilitating local processes to enable them to foster the cohesive societies and widely accepted institutions necessary for societal governing systems to work effectively.* Only such conditions are likely to produce the political will and state capacity that the international community has so repeatedly said are the keys to development (see Chapter 1). Foreign money needs to complement and reinforce local capacities and institutions and be disciplined enough to avoid undermining or warping locally driven arrangements, which is all too common today, especially with the tendency of so many international programs to focus on financial aid targets, poverty reduction targets, and the importation of generic, typically centralized, state models. Countries must be built bottom-up, for they will rarely succeed top-down in such divisive environments. Helping underdeveloped countries should not be about propping up the state, but rather about connecting it—and making it accountable where possible—to its surrounding society. A country that cannot produce an institutional structure that its people regard as legitimate—because it represents their histories, desires, and realities—is unlikely to foster the conditions necessary for development. This basic concept needs to frame all analysis of state building.

This chapter offers ten guiding principles intended to assist international and local policymakers in fashioning a framework for the reform of fragile states. Each principle has the same overall goal: to produce a locally appropriate and self-sustaining governance system that can—within a reasonable amount of time—drive development forward. Not all principles, however, are applicable or equally applicable to all situations, and policymakers should select those principles that fit the circumstances prevailing in a given country. Of the ten principles, the first six focus on measures to make states work better, the next two deal with the role of outsiders, and the last two discuss the drivers and manner of change. Principles 1, 2, 3, and 4 emphasize the need to leverage or foster local capabilities, whereas principles 7 and 8 apply to situations in which outside help is required before local capabilities can be brought into play. Principle 5 combines local and outside capabilities. Principles 6, 9, and 10 are pertinent to almost all situations. The seven case studies that make up the rest of the book show how these guidelines can be practically implemented in various settings.

1. Adopt Local Models

States need to look inward for their resources and institutional models and adopt political structures and processes that reflect the history, complexity, and particularity of their peoples and environment. Far too many postcolonial regimes have looked outward for their governance models and resources, becoming dependent on foreign aid and effectively guaranteeing that their domestic roots will always be too shallow to support them. Robust states and formal institutions can develop only when political and economic systems are constructed according to indigenous governance models, patterns of behavior, needs, realities, and re-sources.

This does not mean that conventional, Western political models have no relevance to non-Western societies, but it does mean that those models need to be adapted to accommodate local political, economic, and societal customs and conditions. The goal should not be centralized states with Western-style laws and a democracy defined solely in terms of regular elections, but instead the promotion of capable, inclusive, participatory, responsive, and accountable governments no matter what form they take. Somaliland (Chapter 8), Botswana, and the Arab emirate-states, for example, have sought to root their political systems within a traditional paradigm that leverages widely accepted norms of governance.

As part of this indigenization, local languages need to be recognized for what they are, repositories of local peoples' sociocultural heritages and their "core abilities and creativity within their environments." Languages are "possibly the most crucial factor in the propagation and development of culture, science and technology based on known and historical foundations rooted in the practices of the people." While elites may often seek to block the diffusion of knowledge in local languages because it threatens their hold on power, any attempt to develop a society requires engaging its grassroots "by building on indigenous usages and knowledge bases."[2] Instead of forcing whole populations to learn foreign languages, much greater effort should be made to translate world knowledge into major indigenous tongues such as Arabic, Hausa, and Punjabi.

Far more emphasis must be placed on seeking locally appropriate solutions for problems of governance, land and resource management, and knowledge transfer if development is ever going to become locally propelled and thus sustainable. Certainly, no society that has successfully developed has depended as heavily on foreign resources, foreign political models, foreign languages, and foreign laws as fragile states typically do today.

2. Closely Integrate State and Society

States need to be deeply enmeshed within the societies they are meant to represent if they are to be effective tools of governance and development. While elections have their role in forcing a government to be responsive to its citizens, there are many other powerful tools that have played influential roles historically in ensuring that a state represents the needs of its people. Where societies tend to be divided, governments to be authoritarian, and elections to be manipulated—which is the case in many fragile states—these other tools are of tremendous importance.

As discussed in Principle 3, state institutions constructed around identity groups can duplicate some of the important features of nation-states, leveraging traditional approaches to problems of political and economic order. Although vulnerable in some cases to elite manipulation, cohesive identity groups are more likely to unify behind and discipline their own state structures (both formally and informally), ensuring that they work for the benefit of the group the structures represent. (Consider, for example, how much more effectively the Kurdistan Regional Government works for the Kurds of Iraq than the centralized Iraqi government does.)

In all cases, as an Organisation for Economic Co-operation and Development (OECD) report concluded, it is of "great importance to formulate policies that help to better link formal and informal institutions. Given the fact that it might be very difficult, impossible, or not desirable to change the indigenous social structure, there is an urgent need to know more on under which conditions the different levels of institutions... can be better linked."[3] Governments such as Bolivia (Chapter 9) and Mali[4] could, for instance, bolster their legitimacy and effectiveness if they were to recognize traditional land tenure arrangements (thus enhancing the security and usefulness of property rights) and document and formalize some aspects of customary law.

Taxes have an especially important role to play in integrating the state with society and ensuring the former is dependent on the latter. As has been the case with state building in Europe, bargaining over taxes can be the tool through which various interest groups within a society negotiate among themselves and with holders of state power over policy, constructing in the process a fiscal social contract and a new set of relations based on accountability, mutual rights, and obligations. The more that the elites who control the levers of government are dependent on their citizens for financing, the more likely they are to build up the organizational and political capacities of the state and tailor policy to meet the needs of taxpayers and citizens.[5] In contrast, the more that elites are able to harvest natural resource rents or foreign aid, the more likely they are to disregard the needs of society.[6]

Aid needs to be tailored to reinforce the role of taxation in connecting the state with society, rather than disconnecting one from the other.[7] Such an approach calls for paying more attention to enhancing the state's ability to levy taxes and to encouraging public debate on where revenue comes from and how it is spent, in contrast to the international community's current focus on setting aid targets and defining spending priorities. Money should be given on a matching basis and only in proportion to what governments themselves can generate, in order to ensure their dependency on local resources. Local governments should play a much greater role in revenue raising to increase their integration with local communities.

Where the state has showed itself unable to deliver even the most basic services to its people over a long period, many in the international development community prefer to work with nongovernmental organizations and to bypass the state completely.[8] "Aid had instituted the principle that much if not most development activity would take place outside of normal government channels.... Aid is increasingly substituting itself for the government."[9] In Afghanistan, for example, the initial international aid program planned after the 2001 war sought $1.6 billion from donors to be channeled through nonstate organizations but requested just $20 million to help the government function.[10] Although such an approach may be necessary in the short term because of an ongoing conflict or a humanitarian crisis, it does little to empower a society and jumpstart development. If anything, such an approach prolongs dependence on outside actors in a form of neocolonialism. If a state repeatedly resists efforts to help it function even minimally, which is the case of Somalia (Chapter 8), the Democratic Republic of the Congo (DRC, Chapter 6), and parts of West Africa (Chapter 5), something is probably fundamentally wrong in its structure.

3. Design Institutions around Identity Groups

If people are to make effective use of their own histories and customs in fashioning institutions and laws that best reflect their particular needs, then state structures must be better aligned with cohesive identity groups where practical. Such reengineering will naturally foster greater legitimacy of the state and make it better able to integrate informal institutions into formal structures while increasing the ability of groups to leverage their built-up imbedded social capital to improve economic conditions.

While Westerners steeped in liberalism and accustomed to living in cohesive states often espouse freedom of the individual as the key to reforming underdeveloped or tyrannical states, people in many places value a different kind of freedom, a collective "freedom of identity" for their suppressed identities. Such people yearn not for the personal freedoms of a multicultural country, but for the sense of belonging that comes from seeing their ethnic, religious, tribal, or other sectarian group actualize its many beliefs and govern its own affairs. "We call these loyalties 'primordial,'" comments Martin Kramer, a Middle East expert, "but they legitimately express a deep longing for security and a collective freedom from oppression."[11] These longings are universal human aspirations, though few countries in the developed world have firsthand experience with them because most states are nations and therefore absorb such aspirations naturally into state structures. However, where these longings are left unfulfilled, even rich countries can suffer from the resulting resentment. The Basques in Spain and, until recently, the Irish Catholics in Northern Ireland have both felt sufficiently dissatisfied with their status that they have fathered terrorist groups seeking secession. Many of the seemingly spontaneous local upheavals that have occurred in recent years from the Andes to the Balkans can be attributed to these unfulfilled desires.

Such longings argue for greater use of decentralized and federal state structures where the cohesive groups are conveniently separated into different geographical areas. In fact, as Alfred Stepan and Juan Linz, leading scholars on democracy and institutional design, have concluded, "virtually every long-standing and relatively peaceful contemporary democracy in the world whose polity has more than one territorially concentrated, politically-mobilized, linguistic-cultural majority, is not only federal, but 'asymmetrically federal' (Spain, Belgium, Canada, and India)."[12] In these cases, the state is "held together" by giving special institutional prerogatives to the decentralized political units in order that the individual groups may meet their identity aspirations and particular historical, linguistic, and cultural needs within the context of a unified polity. By contrast, most fragile countries are centralized in ways that accentuate their difficulties, such as is the case in Bolivia (Chapter 9), Pakistan (Chapter 10), and Iraq.

States that do not sufficiently respond to such demands risk not only losing whatever loyalty and legitimacy they have garnered but also inciting identity groups to mobilize and use violence to press for the actualization of their identity, security, and material needs. Stepan and Linz explain that "if citizens in a territorial region of a state define their primary loyalty as being exclusively to that region, and if they have almost no loyalty or identification with the central state, not only that federal system, but that state as well, is prone to disintegration—Yugoslavia by the early 1990s being the clearest case in point."[13] The Sri Lankan government's longstanding discrimination against the country's Tamil population and its continued rejection of a federal arrangement makes ending its war highly problematic.

The response of the international community to certain kinds of conflict might well change if social cohesion were to be regarded as a critical element in development. Instead of seeking to prop up states to which few people have allegiance, such as Bosnia-Herzegovina and Iraq, the international community could support creative forms of federalism—or, in rare cases, secession—that would give governments a better chance of fostering legitimacy and robust institutions and, therefore, of spurring development.[14] Although few Azerbaijanis want to see their country lose Nargorno-Karabagh (Chapter 11), some creative redrawing of borders with Armenia could make both states more cohesive and better able to deliver good governance and development. Bosnia-Herzegovina's continued need for outside supervision to keep the peace between its identity groups—more than a decade after a peace agreement was signed—shows the difficulties in attempting to build strong national institutions in the face of powerful intergroup animosities and subgroup allegiances. Similarly, by not constructing postwar Iraq's institutions around traditional identities, the United States has made intergroup frictions there much more intense than they might otherwise have been. The country will likely be highly dependent on outside forces to attain and maintain some semblance of unity far into the future.

4. Construct States Bottom-Up

In many cases, the best chance for leveraging local capacities and institutions and improving governance will be to focus on building up local governments and tying them as closely as possible to their local communities. While in some cases (especially in rural areas and small cities) this may mean leveraging traditional identities and institutions, including chiefs and village elders where they retain strong legitimacy, in the case of many large cities whose populations are diverse and increasingly divorced from their traditional roots, the best way to introduce accountability into state organs is to structure them around greatly empowered urban administrations.

While central governments (or, in some case, regional organizations) have important roles to play in ensuring a stable currency, promoting an extensive market for goods, constructing intercity transportation links, and setting basic banking, legal, health, and education standards, most state services that affect families and small companies are provided by local or district governments. They provide, for example, most education, health, and road construction services, and may even play a major role in judicial, police, real estate, and corporate regulation and oversight.

Although local governments will often be "afflicted by parochialism, factionalism, the danger of elite capture, inequity, and injustice" and will require "resources, support, and constructive initiatives from agencies (governmental and nongovernmental) at higher levels," downsizing government functions to villages, towns, and districts of each city can leverage the power of face-to-face interaction and more transparent and accountable forms of government. "The face-to-face relationships at the local level allow greater scope for establishing trust, accommodation, and a sense of mutuality than do the more anonymous relationships that exist at higher levels."

Given that fragile states are riven by identity, cultural, and linguistic differences, and that their different parts are weakly connected because of poor infrastructure, disadvantageous political geographies, and feeble administrative systems, locally based models of development are more likely to succeed than state-based models.[15] A locally based model would emphasize the construction of a series of competent city-based provincial bureaucracies built around relatively cohesive populations and based upon locally accepted institutions rather than trying to build a robust national government, especially in large countries such as the DRC (Chapter 6).[16] It would also ensure that local communities were not held hostage to the dysfunctionalities of a national government. If enough of these local administrations could make substantial progress on their own, they would be able to reorient the state into a truly bottom-up arrangement.

Giving local—and provincial—governments greater authority to raise revenue and helping them build up their capacity to generate and collect taxes should make them more dependent on local companies and other taxpayers. Establishing various forms of iterative accountability loops (Chapter 6) and decentralized democratic bodies such as oversight committees, deliberative forms of public participation (both in Chapter 9), and traditional forms of consultation (Chapter 8), can institutionalize processes whereby the state is tied more closely to society, thereby making it more legitimate, more accountable, more reflective of people's needs, and more effective in the delivery of public services. "Participatory mechanisms can provide access for poorer groups to policymaking processes. This puts the focus on the iterative relationship, over time, of state and society, rather than on 'strengthening' civil society vis-à-vis the state . . . the detailed design of institutions and programmes needs to be locally agreed, and adapted to a particular context."[17]

5. Exploit the Advantages of Regionalism

In regions (such as in West Africa [Chapter 5] and Central America)[18] populated by multiple pintsized fragile states, regionalism offers the best chance to overcome the poisonous and self-reinforcing nexus of identity divisions, weak administrative capacities, undersized markets, and limited human resources. Regional associations of small, poor countries—if allowed to fully leverage region-wide capacities and outside assistance, and if empowered with the necessary authority and staffed by team of competent managers—could gradually transform the institutional environments and economic prospects of their member-states.

These regional organizations could do much to overcome institutional dysfunctionalities. They could, for example, introduce and enforce measures to unite markets, reduce corruption, increase competition, render judiciaries more effective, make border checks and customs procedures more efficient, develop transportation infrastructure between population centers, and promote investment. The regional bodies could recruit executives from the region with experience in working in the developed world or in multinational companies to manage the organization's administrative and governing organs; with such people on staff, a regional organization would likely outstrip any member-state in terms of the quality of its personnel. Furthermore, foreign technical assistance could be directed at this one umbrella entity instead of divided among far too many, far less capable entities.

Regionalism would also sharply reduce the intergroup tensions that poison the institutional environment of fragile states by lessening the importance of the root cause of intrastate conflict—the dysfunctional state and the opportunities for whomever controls it to exploit and plunder its resources. Robust regional structures would, in fact, do much to improve state structures both through the standards they set and enforce throughout their territory and through the example they would set in regions with few good institutional models to follow. In time, institutions would reinforce each other, strengthening governance throughout a region, the opposite of what happens today in regions where weak states undermine each other's attempts to advance.

6. Unify Disparate Peoples

As state cohesion is a major predictor of state effectiveness, more emphasis should be placed on measures that unify disparate peoples in fragile states. This is especially important in countries where multiple identity groups are not concentrated in particular areas but are spread throughout the country, making it pointless to introduce federalism and other territorially based institutional arrangements. In such countries, programs should be adopted that create stronger social and cultural bonds across groups, that institutionalize cooperation, and that promote reconciliation where there has been a history of intergroup hostility.

Some states have found a unifying force—such as Swahili in Tanzania, a unique Islamic heritage in Senegal, a state-backed ideology in Syria (Chapter 7), or a charismatic leader as Félix Houphouët-Boigny in Côte d'Ivoire—to bridge their geographical, historical, and identity divides. But the unity based on such forces can prove fleeting, whereas the process of institutionalizing a sense of common identity and common formal structures can take generations. Thus, for instance, despite Houphouët-Boigny's popularity in his day, Côte d'Ivoire descended into civil war in the years after his demise.

In states containing combustible mixes of identity groups living side by side, such as Syria (Chapter 7), formal bodies should be designed to institutionalize cross-group cooperation and to minimize the potential for ethnic, religious, tribal, or clan divisions sparking verbal or violent conflict that undermines the state. Instead of promoting unfettered democracy and freedom as the keys to progress, which the West typically does, divided countries need to create a secure and unified environment before introducing significant change (see Principle 10's discussion of gradualism). Iraq shows what can happen when cross-group trust completely breaks down; Bolivia (Chapter 9), Pakistan (Chapter 10), Azerbaijan (Chapter 11), and Lebanon also stand as cautionary tales.

There are various ways to institutionalize cooperation in these settings. A national security council, modeled on Turkey's (Chapter 7), could bring together leaders of each major group within a state to make major decisions and to police the media, schools, politicians, and religious figures to ensure that no inflammatory language or action threatened intergroup peaceful coexistence. Various forms of political engineering could also help. For instance, political systems could be designed to ensure that parties are large, inclusive, and broad-based (that is, they bring together various interests and identity groups) by limiting their number and requiring that each secure a certain minimum level of support in each province, as Somaliland has (Chapter 8), or by requiring that they establish branches in a certain minimum proportion of provinces and garner a minimum number of seats in legislatures, as Indonesia has. Forms of consociational government, such as those in Switzerland, Belgium, and Burundi, could mandate coalitions of all groups and wide representation in cabinets, civil services, legislatures, and the military, reducing tensions by lessening or eliminating actual or perceived imbalances. Similarly, apportioning the profits from natural resources in a fair and transparent manner, ensuring that social spending is impartially distributed, and reducing economic inequities between rival groups would dispel some of the potential for friction in divided polities.

Celebrating each identity group's distinctiveness while attempting to build a "nation of nations" is more likely to succeed than trying to build a state on the "negation of social identities," that is, a "nation against identities."[19] Fostering strong "we" feelings through various educational, sports, and cultural programs can foster complementary or multiple cultural identities that strengthen national bonds, diminishing intergroup frictions in the process. South Africa, for example, has creatively used sports since the end of the apartheid era to unite its fissiparous peoples. Greater access to television can help foster a sense of unity by promoting a common national popular culture while showcasing differences with other states. Programs that helped reconcile long-festering intergroup wounds, such as South Africa's Reconciliation Commission, Guatemala's "Why Are We the Way We Are?" traveling exhibition, and Burundi's leadership training programs, either by instigating a national dialogue to work out differences or by bringing top opinion-makers from each group together, have proved valuable in many countries.

Settling border disputes would help to bolster national identities by strengthening citizen loyalty to the state. Many fragile states resist finalizing their boundaries because they are unwilling to accept the territorial status quo, but this only weakens their cohesion while strengthening irredentist and secessionist tendencies on both sides of the frontier. Syria (Chapter 7), Bolivia (Chapter 9), Pakistan (Chapter 10), and Azerbaijan (Chapter 11), among many others, have unsettled borders and disputes with neighbors that prevent them from consolidating their identity as states.

7. Supplement State Capacity

In many cases, states are unable on their own to create and sustain some of the capacities necessary for them to promote stability and development. Where institutional reengineering and other creative mechanisms are unable to overcome these deficiencies, outside assistance might be more helpful if it was directed at supplementing capacity rather than providing more cash or technical assistance.

As discussed above, regionalism offers a chance for states that have few and meager capabilities and resources to work together in a partnership with developed countries to generate indigenous solutions to their problems. It also provides a far better platform from which to leverage outside technical assistance than many individual states can command.

Countries with long histories of internal strife may need an outside security guarantee or security force to maintain peace and security. Where they contain easily exploitable natural resources, such as is the case with Sierra Leone and the DRC (Chapter 6), any attempt at state building will likely be endangered by the ease with which various criminal gangs can corrupt the government to gain access to the country's wealth. In Sierra Leone, peace was restored by a "modest" British military intervention, "quite possibly . . . the most cost-effective major instance of British assistance to Africa." Since the force has been withdrawn, ongoing security has been ensured by "a ten-year 'over-the-horizon' security guarantee." Before 1994, France provided a similar, though less explicit guarantee to Francophone

Africa, reducing "the incidence of civil war by around two-thirds, again a cost-effective form of assistance." In many cases, "during the first decade of peace an external military presence or guarantee is the only reliable option."[20]

Foreign corporations, as well as foreign states, could similarly lend a hand. Multinational companies could be mandated to provide security and education, health, and infrastructure improvements to local citizens in areas where those companies prospect for natural resources if a weak state is unable to do-so (see Chapter 6). In such cases, contracts would ensure a steady flow of royalties to the government while directing corporations—which typically have much greater administrative capacity than most fragile states—to tame the lawless areas around major mining sites and to ensure that people living nearby reap the benefits of their geography. In these cases, large firms with excellent labor and community relations reputations would be invited to participate in public, transparent bidding processes, and the winning firm would then be monitored by domestic and international oversight committees to make sure it did not abuse its position.

Intergovernmental organizations and regimes could likewise help to plug the gaps in the domestic capacities of fragile states. Kosovo and Bosnia-Herzegovina have both operated under forms of conditional sovereignty, with a UN or EU special representative holding proconsular powers in order to prevent ethnic differences from reigniting a violent conflict. Liberia was forced to accept an intrusive and transparent revenue collection regime in which foreign nationals worked with Liberian counterparts to introduce systems to prevent corruption.[21]

Forms of shared sovereignty, whereby a weak state partners with a more developed country on some aspect of its country management, could prove more useful than simple technical assistance. The provision of security guarantees is just one example of this approach. To take other examples: A country with a highly developed legal system could provide a "judicial blanket" for a fragile state in the form of a series of courts to adjudicate major cases and supervise lower courts. Natural resource revenue could be placed into an international escrow account comanaged by a foreign country or international body. Monetary policy might be delegated to an outside authority, as already happens in the fourteen African states that use the CFA franc.

All of these measures would be much more cost-effective means to help fragile states than simply disbursing aid, even if the arrangements were meant to continue indefinitely, which might be necessary in many instances. Moreover, creating models of good governance in some functional areas would spur improvements in other areas. Greater security and better revenue collection schemes, for instance, would reduce corruption and lawlessness throughout a country. As in the case of the British intervention in Sierra Leone, they are generally likely to be well-received by citizens in the affected countries, though some elites might be more reluctant to embrace them, because such measures do much to curtail abuses of power.

8. Reinforce and Complement Local Processes

At present, "much external action either undermines (local) governance structures or puts in place structures that are unsustainable."[22] Instead of continuing to promote one-size-fits-all prescriptions, Western aid agencies and governments should make much more use of nonfinancial aid, put more emphasis on institutional reengineering, devote greater effort to reinforcing local processes in a bottom-up fashion, and work harder to ensure that the assistance provided actually helps local efforts to spur development.

For a start, aid agencies need to broaden their missions beyond dispensers of aid and advice into comprehensive facilitators of development, with access to a wider set of policy instruments. Shortages of money in fragile states need to be seen as rooted in the dysfunctional institutional environments that discourage investment of any kind, not as mere shortfalls in financial plans.

Assistance should be seen primarily as a way to reinforce a process that is firmly rooted in local society and, ideally, in local institutions (Chapter 8). Aiding states in this way requires far greater sensitivity to local sociopolitical climates and much deeper analysis of how aid affects the state-society relationship. Any project should be evaluated in terms of how it impacts relationships, especially between state and society and between members of a single national or local community, and how it improves local capacities, rather than being judged purely on whether it improves some quantitative measure of well-being (such as the United Nations' Millennium Development Goals). Financial assistance, the most fungible of all aid, must be disbursed with special care to ensure that it does not distort institutions that must remain firmly embedded in, dependent upon, and accountable to local societies to be effective. Except where there is a dire humanitarian crisis, aid to governments should be given only in a reasonable proportion to a state's own revenue-generation capability, so as to minimize disruption to the state-society relationship, even if this means sacrificing some of the effectiveness of programs in the short-term. Matching funds, for example, would encourage governments to increase public services to local companies and citizens. Fostering self-reliance and self-help initiatives by aiding community-initiated projects, where modest assistance could prove decisive, should be a greater priority than now, when top-down initiatives dominate the agendas of most NGOs and donors.

Technical assistance should focus on the systematic transfer of knowledge to local officials, such that it builds local capacities that should in time reduce the need for outside help. Implanting foreign nationals in key positions in fragile state administration (especially in revenue management functions, where corruption is notorious), offering many more opportunities for government ministers and managers to take lengthy training courses in developed countries (Chapter 11), and investing in the creation of regionally based academies that could train thousands of administrators in the arts of governance (Chapter 5) are all examples of this approach. Regional organizations—which have a better understanding of local conditions than do Western organizations—could certainly play a major role in the process of transferring governance know-how downward to state governments.

9. Foster Private Investment and Competition

Although they generally receive scant attention from the development community,[23] businesses and private investment are actually the main engines of development and should be prioritized as such. Only companies can drive the self-sustaining wealth-generating process underpinning development forward; provide work to the armies of unemployed in the underdeveloped world;[24] efficiently transfer better work skills to large numbers of people; increase productivity throughout an economy; lower the price of goods consumed by poor people; and provide the revenue necessary to fund education, health, and other public programs and to wean governments off of foreign aid. Indeed, every successful developed country has depended, in large measure, on private investment to generate its wealth. Measures that improve the investment climate and encourage greater competition have multiplier effects throughout a society and country.

But promoting a business-friendly climate is a multifaceted endeavor, often involving many more elements than generally appreciated. Investors mainly act to earn profits, thus governments must make changes that either lower the risks or increase the returns of businesspeople in order to see more companies and individuals take chances with their money, time, and reputations. As increasing productivity—the key to sustaining growth rates and income rises over a long time—depends on amplifying competition throughout an economy, efforts should be concentrated on measures that lower barriers to entry, enlarge markets, simplify government procedures, reduce crime and corruption, enhance the effectiveness of commercial courts, and eliminate the scope for favoritism among officials. Regionalism, with its larger markets, common standards, and, ideally, better governance, has an important role to play for small economies (Chapter 5). Improving transportation links and taking measures that directly tackle roadside corruption will reduce the cost of goods across larger areas, thus also enlarging markets and competition.[25] Establishing new bodies that specifically promote and manage the approval process for investment, facilitate trade, register and enforce property rights, and reduce corruption should all be priorities of governments and are areas where foreign assistance could play major roles in improving economic conditions at relatively low cost. Privately managed export-processing zones (EPZ) could provide incentives for investors to build the infrastructure and service arms necessary to attract investment into countries that lack some of their own capacities to do so.

Although foreign direct investment (FDI) should play just a supplemental role in most countries, its unique role in transferring advanced skills and standards to developing economies make its promotion an essential element in any business-friendly development strategy. FDI has powerful spillover effects in developing economies because of how it transfers management know-how (such as quality-control procedures, project management skills, and customer relations tools), improves the capabilities of suppliers, and disciplines governments. Indeed, the most striking economic transformation of the past twenty-five years—China—has been significantly driven by FDI, which produces a majority of its world-beating exports and the lion's share of its technologically advanced goods. In 2004, developing countries received five times as much FDI as financial aid.[26]

Measures that hold companies more accountable in corruption-prone environments, such as weak states containing plentiful natural resources, are also essential to ensure that the more unsavory, even criminal enterprises that often operate in such places do not receive unfair advantages over the more socially responsible firms that help poor countries simply by their regular participation in the local marketplace as fair investors, merchants, and competitors. Initiatives such as the Extractive Industries Transparency Initiative (EITI), a British-led initiative to improve the transparency of primary mineral revenues (Chapter 11), could be expanded to include more industries (such as construction, also often plagued by corruption). Strengthening safeguards against corruption in national export credit guarantee agencies and taking tougher stands against bribery and money laundering would also help improve corporate behavior.

10. Creatively and Gradually Increase Accountability

In states where rapid change may be detrimental to stability or may be obstructed by elites, emphasis should be given to encouraging gradual, incremental reform that introduces a variety of mechanisms to hold governments more accountable, to integrate them more closely with their societies, and to make them more dependent on their citizens. While elections are an important tool in ensuring that leaders and governments work to benefit their populations, they have been overemphasized at the expense of other instruments that could encourage better governance—and that are more likely to be practical in the short and medium term, given the political conditions in many states.

As the Iraq experience vividly shows, dramatic change—including abrupt moves to fully competitive elections—in states with weak cohesiveness, fragile institutions, and a history of intergroup animosity can be highly explosive, leading to instability that severely undermines the whole reform agenda. "Even 'adversarial' Western democracy, in short, depends as much upon cooperation as it does upon competition; it rests not only on the jostling of diverse interests, but also on the recognition of the common ground upon which all members of the national community stand. By contrast, many culturally plural states today have an uncertain concept of nationhood ... different ethnic groups often see each other as hostile, alien entities with fundamentally opposed interests.... A sense of communal interdependence and trust among group leaders are often notable by their absence."[27] In countries such as Iraq and Syria (Chapter 7), rapid democratization is likely to be counterproductive, increasing divisive competition between groups that the state's feeble governing structures find hard to accommodate. It is better to make unity and security one's top priorities and to introduce more far-reaching reforms only gradually, as the evolving institutional and sociopolitical context allows.

In most cases, the ruling elites that plunder weakly rooted state structures need to be engaged on some level and even rewarded in some fashion before they will consent to any major change that may reduce their authority. (Local elites, who gain their authority from the traditional institutions of identity groups, are, in contrast, more likely to play positive roles in helping their particular communities.) The ability of the international community to influence members of a ruling clique will depend on the incentives it can deploy, including money, international opportunities for travel and education, invitations to prestigious meetings, and contracts for elite-owned companies. Introducing change slowly, in ways that do not dramatically threaten the status quo and that encourage the more reformist elements within a controlling clique, is crucial if progress is to be made (Chapters 7 and 10). Where ties between elites help bind diverse identity groups together, institutionalizing those elites' positions might encourage their support for reform.

Gradualism is not a call for sequentialism—that is, for putting off serious reform until the distant future.[28] Gradualism is an attempt to introduce reforms in a way that does not explicitly threaten the status quo yet creates an iterative and self-sustaining process, a process of change that seeps through a system, affecting society and the state on many levels and transforming their relationship over time. Such an approach aims to root the state more firmly in society and to hold elites more accountable to their populations through various instruments. Initiatives that improve the fiscal relationship between governments and their peoples— such as increasing the transparency and conduct of budget-making procedures,[29] bolstering the capacity of watchdog NGOs, boosting the proportion of revenues coming from taxes—all promise to make leaders more attentive to their citizens. Improving the rule of law and the capacity of the judiciary and various other organs of the government should improve their responsiveness to citizens. Making an elite more representative of its country's diverse population will increase stability, laying the groundwork for other measures.

On a broader level, increasing the breadth and depth of relationships with the international community and between various groups within the state promises to increase state stability, cohesiveness, and readiness for change. Restructuring a state's economy and trade regime is likely to augment the mixing of people across groups, the importation of new norms of behavior, the number of stakeholders in reform, and the pressure for better stewardship of the country on many levels. International training, education, and exchange programs will raise the professional standards of administrators, public watchdogs, and the next generation of leaders.

THE WAY FORWARD

Taken together, these ten guidelines amount to a significant reconceptualization of the causes and problems of fragile states and of the best way to fix them. Obviously, neither local leaders nor members of the international community are likely to embrace this new diagnosis and prescription immediately or entirely. However, there are at least four reasons to be cautiously optimistic that the guidelines advanced here may, gradually and incrementally, enter the development debate. First, few people, whether inside or outside the development community, pretend that past attempts to fix fragile states have succeeded (see Chapter 1) or that new approaches are not needed. Second, as the intensity and seriousness of the problems posed by fragile states grow—spawning concerns about international security, political instability, and human misery far beyond their own borders—so, too, does the number of people and organizations that have a vital interest in seeing these countries' dysfunction ameliorated. Increasing apprehension over terrorist activities, criminal networks, illegal immigration, and the security of mineral supplies is steadily raising the profile of fragile states in Western foreign policy agendas. Third, the new paradigm presented in this book harmonizes to some degree with other initiatives to devise an effective means of understanding and remedying state fragility. For instance, the United Kingdom's Department for International Development (DFID) has embraced a "drivers of change" analysis, "whereby DFID country offices commission work to understand countries through nontraditional aid lenses: history, culture, power dynamics, political landscape, incentives analysis and institutional analysis."[30] Similarly, the U.S. military has increasingly emphasized the importance of understanding and working with local institutions and local social structures in trying to stabilize Iraq and Afghanistan.[31] The significant reduction in violence in Iraq in the second half of 2007 was based largely on "four years of hard-won knowledge of Iraq's complex tribal and sectarian politics" that allowed local commanders to follow "a template for governance in Iraq that has existed for centuries and which even dictators like Saddam Hussein had to rely on."[32] Fourth, the prescriptions presented in this chapter are eminently practicable if carefully customized to fit local conditions. The following seven case studies offer concrete examples of how, individually and collectively, these ten guidelines can be used to resolve a broad array of problems in an equally broad range of fragile states.

Of course, these prescriptions cannot be expected to achieve a sudden transformation given both the nature and the scale of these countries' current problems. The obstacles to fixing fragile states are formidable and setbacks are inevitable. But if we persist with current policies—if we continue to work with an unnecessarily narrow array of instruments and to ignore some of the most important ingredients necessary for success—failure is guaranteed. The analyzes and prescriptions in this book offer a better model to use in formulating an appropriate strategy for these troubled, yet important places. Only by learning from the mistakes of the past and formulating polices that recognize and respond to local conditions can we construct a brighter future for the unfortunate citizens of fragile states—and bring greater security, stability, and prosperity to all the world's citizens.

Part III _____

Application

West Africa: Stitching a Fragmented Region Together

Africa has drifted on and off the international agenda for years, with evanescent attention usually being tied to equally transitory media coverage of manmade and natural disasters. Since 9/11, however, Africa has received far greater and more sustained attention. Dismayed by the continent's slow rate of development and alarmed at the evils—including terrorism—bred by its fragile states, Western leaders committed themselves during the 2005 G-8 Summit in Gleneagles, Scotland, to a renewed effort to lift the region out of poverty and help it to jumpstart growth. Among other things, the major industrialized countries agreed to double aid to the continent and forgive the debts of its poorest states.

Of the countries targeted for assistance, many are located in West Africa, an area containing an extraordinary number of fragile, underdeveloped states. Of the region's fifteen countries, a dozen have been troubled by war, ethnic or religious clashes, political unrest, famine, or serious economic dislocation in recent years. Even if the industrialized democracies redeem their 2005 pledges in full—and there seems little chance of this actually occurring—they will do no more than help to attenuate the symptoms of West Africa's ills; by themselves, the debt deal and increased aid cannot cure the region's many troubles. Meanwhile, the continent has slipped out of the international spotlight, with the G-8, under new leadership, emphasizing other priorities.

There is far more than altruism at stake here. West Africa is an increasingly important source of oil and other energy resources. The fragile states that dominate the region provide lawless sanctuaries where terrorist gangs (including al Qaeda) and crime syndicates organize, recruit, buy weapons, or simply hide.[1] The instability bred by these groups spreads across borders, with consequences far and wide. The cost to stabilize these states is far greater than the modest expense to underwrite a new way to approach the problem.

Instead of simply continuing to pump billions annually into the region's many dysfunctional regimes, the developed world should focus more on a regional program, where a modest investment could help shore up a set of weak states simultaneously. Across Africa in recent years, a new generation of leaders itself has promoted regionalism as a crucial element in solving the continent's myriad security and economic problems. Cross-border cooperation since the mid-1990s to handle crises in Liberia, Côte d'Ivoire, and elsewhere are initial indicators of this strategy. Beyond those ad hoc cases, this generation has launched new organizations such as the African Union (AU) and invigorated dormant associations such as the Economic Community of West African States (ECOWAS), challenging old assumptions about local capabilities and offering new ideas for fixing broken countries.

Only a sustained campaign, supported by the West but driven by local leaders, to build regional institutions can hope to set West Africa firmly on the road to recovery. Regional integration may offer the only way to craft the commercial environment necessary to attract investment—without which no development can occur or be sustained—and wean countries from their chronic dependence on aid. By circumventing the maladministered state bureaucracies that squander aid and smother reform, regionalism could dramatically improve business conditions. A unified market offers the best way to overcome the prohibitively high cost of doing business in economies so small that few investors have any interest beyond exploiting primary materials for export. If ECOWAS and the West African Economic and Monetary Union (UEMOA) were to be merged and adequately empowered, the resulting organization would improve security and raise governance standards. Its multinational mandate would help it overcome the two greatest problems facing national regimes: their peoples' weak sense of statehood and the critical shortage of capable, honest officials.

Helping long-troubled regions such as West Africa requires nothing less than embracing a new approach toward development. Instead of trying to fix a plethora of dysfunctional governments one by one, efforts should be concentrated on building up a strong regional organization. Suitably reinforced, this organ could over time help overcome many of the difficulties that have defeated individual states and play a far greater role in engineering growth than previously envisioned.

A BROKEN REGION

West Africa, the fifteen countries stretching from Senegal to Nigeria that are members of ECOWAS, has been racked by some of the worst problems facing the developing world: pervasive intergroup conflict, corrupt officials suffocating vacuous institutions, a dearth of skilled workers made worse by a prolific brain drain, poor investment climates, and the AIDS epidemic.

Common problems obscure immense diversity among the hundreds of different groups that populate the area, between northern Muslims and southern Christians, between deserts and rain forests, and between countries. The French and British colonized most of the region in the nineteenth century, dividing it linguistically, economically, and politically into one large country, Nigeria, and fourteen small fiefdoms. These boundaries did not reflect the strong cultural traditions of the Igbo, Hausa, Asante, Wolof, and other indigenous peoples (see Map 5.1), and thus the legitimacy of these states was undermined from the outset, leaving divided populations to see any competition for power as a zero-sum game and enabling elites to exploit identity divisions for personal gain. When they became independent (mainly in the early 1960s), few of West Africa's states had the cohesion and critical mass of effective administrators necessary to build the strong national institutions—such as regulatory bodies, central banks, and courts—that could in turn ignite growth.

No West African country has been able to overcome its problematic circumstances in over four decades of independence. The United Kingdom's Department for International Development considers ten of the fifteen countries "fragile."[2] Nine of these fifteen scored a "D" or "F" on the World Bank's "Country Policy and Institutional Assessment" (CPIA) system for rating the quality of institutions and policies.[3] In essence, 75 percent of the area's people live under governments that cannot deliver even the most basic services—including, in many cases, security. The area contains five of the world's seven most impoverished territories,[4] and over one-half of the overall population lives in absolute poverty, meaning they are unable to afford the most basic human needs.[5]

Aid has yielded mixed results at best. Despite receiving close to $5 billion a year from foreign governments (and increasing debt levels fivefold), the region's GDP per capita was lower in the early 2000s than it was twenty-five years before.[6] Notwithstanding spending hundreds of billions of dollars over the past quarter of a century, few governments have significantly enhanced economic prospects. Even the few states that have made progress live a precarious existence. Senegal and Ghana, both of which have often been held up as success stories in recent years and have performed well on recent CPIA assessments, sought over twenty adjustment loans from the World Bank and IMF during the 1990s, three times the average for developing countries.[7] They remain heavily dependent on outside money—almost one-half of Senegal's government budget is financed by aid—and their comparative stability is ceaselessly threatened by spillover conflict and corruption. Senegal has been fighting an insurgency in its south since 1982; Ghana is threatened by the civil wars of its neighbors.

Inhabiting a bad neighborhood where almost all countries share analogous weaknesses multiplies the difficulties facing individual states. Were any country to significantly outpace its neighbors, it would immediately be burdened with an influx of people seeking a better life and of criminal elements tempted by its relative prosperity. Côte d'Ivoire, once West Africa's economic star, caused suffering throughout the region when it succumbed to a civil war rooted in identity

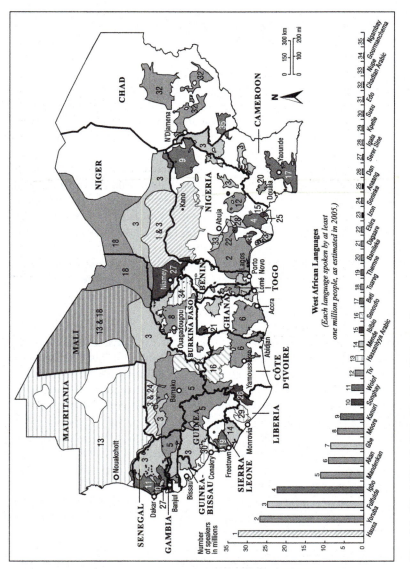

Map 5.1. West Africa's Ethnolinguistic Demography
Source: Sahel and West Africa Club/OECD.

tensions exacerbated by these factors and by the destabilizing impact of neighboring Liberia, whose macabre and bloody conflict infected a wide slice of the area. Millions of migrant workers were forced to flee, reversing the flow of remittances; trade relations were disrupted, shrinking markets; and criminal activity increased, disrupting legitimate businesses.[8] More than 25,000 peacekeepers are needed to maintain a fragile peace in the region's simmering war zones.

Pint-sized, expensive markets keep most states isolated from the dynamic changes globalization is bringing elsewhere. The region's aggregate GDP is less than half of Norway's.[9] Although infrastructure costs are among the highest in the world—electricity averages 4.5 times and international telephone calls four times the charges in OECD countries[10]—the systems are woefully inadequate and unreliable. The regulatory burden forces all but the largest businesses underground. In Niger, for example, it takes eleven steps and costs four times the average income just to register a business.[11] Much of the sparse road network is in poor condition[12] and frequent checkpoints—one every fourteen kilometers on the road between Lagos and Abidjan[13]—shrink markets. The onerous business climate makes aid the only growth industry: over 70 percent of gross capital formation consists of donor money, five times the level of foreign investment.[14]

These conditions discourage most ventures outside the extraction of raw materials such as oil, rubber, and gold. As a result, roughly 90 percent of the region's exports come from a handful of commodities, often produced in protected enclaves that limit exposure to embezzlement and violence.[15] Few are tempted to invest in any add-on business activity that would increase the value of goods produced locally. This flawed environment hinders corporations from contributing to local economies: few managers are trained, hardly any companies learn how to supply internationally competitive products, and governments are not challenged to upgrade standards.

Calls for more aid from the United Kingdom's Commission for Africa, the United Nations' Millennium Development Report, and the World Bank miss the point. Most West African countries are so disadvantaged in their current form that only rethinking the state-led development paradigm offers a way out of their current malaise.

A DECREPIT MODEL

Despite significant evidence that the state-based development model is not working, almost all assistance continues to be funneled to governments. The modest redirection that might improve an uninspiring record continues to be held back by institutional rigidity and entrenched interests. Historically, donors have not been organized to initiate or even consider funding regional programs. The World Bank and its sister multilateral organizations are structured around country teams that produce state-based statistics, expertise, and professional incentives, and predominantly loan to individual governments that are henceforth responsible for repayment.

Yet the World Bank's conservative hierarchy warps its own analyses of the region's problems. Despite arguing that "it is reasonable to expect that, particularly in the case of West Africa, regional integration will contribute to accelerated growth," it still sees any multistate initiative "as a means of reinforcing and enhancing country performance and the effectiveness of Bank country assistance"[16] and continues to maintain that "the bulk of financing to support regional integration efforts is required at the country level."[17] From 1976 to 2000, the bank financed only thirteen multicountry projects, totaling about $300 million—roughly 1 percent of total lending to West Africa.[18] Indeed, the Bank's own Independent Evaluation Group concluded in a 2007 report that "regional development programs have a huge, yet under-exploited potential to advance economic growth and reduce poverty" and that "bank incentives and capacities, which are geared to country programs, are not optimal for the support of regional programs."[19]

Governments have not been more discerning. The United States, for example, invests almost no money in enhancing regional capacity: of the $3.37 billion requested by the George W. Bush administration for Africa-related aid projects in fiscal 2005, only a paltry $14.4 million—0.4 percent of the total—was allocated to programs that strengthened West African institutions.[20] Donor reforms emphasizing accountability and "ownership" actually accentuate these trends by excluding regional projects from consideration. The Millennium Challenge Account, an innovative program that attempts to improve the effectiveness of aid by tying disbursements to government performance, focuses only on states. The mechanisms to track progress toward the United Nations' Millennium Development Goals similarly imply a country-driven approach.[21]

This underinvestment in regionalism has prevented all kinds of cross-country public projects—highways, hydroelectric projects, cross-border regulatory agencies—from receiving adequate support. It also furthers economic dependence: only 10.3 percent of ECOWAS exports go to member countries[22] (over 60 percent of EU exports were intraregional before the 2004 enlargement) whereas almost two-thirds crosses oceans to Western customers.

REGIONALISM: A CATALYST FOR CHANGE?

Of course, the absence of any credible regional organization has given donors an easy excuse to avoid encouraging a regional approach. Donors are hardly likely to play venture capitalist. Until relatively recently, few supranational organizations mattered; international relations were conducted bilaterally between wholly sovereign governments. The ability of any country to advance itself depended wholly on its own capacity to deal with whatever challenges confronted it. As a result, states had to manage the delicate development process, including upgrading education, expanding infrastructure, and reforming institutions, on their own. Over the past forty years, however, an alternative model has evolved. Regional organizations such as the European Union have redefined international relations, sovereignty, and development, showing how a centralized, multicountry bureaucracy might play a significant role in shaping state behavior, standards of governance, and even societal evolution.

Although West Africa faces a unique concoction of problems, some of the functions performed by other regional organizations such as the European Union promise to be of great benefit if tailored to local needs. Imagine, for example, what might be achieved by a centralized commission with a long-term commitment to stabilizing, modernizing, and enriching West Africa; able to provide practical help and incentives to foster solid institutions, sound economic conditions, and democracy; staffed by executives intimate with local conditions; and empowered to seek regional solutions for what are, in essence, regional problems. If such a body could be created with the mandate to raise governance standards, merge economies, establish one set of rules for doing business, and integrate transportation systems, the new dynamism would not only unleash the caged entrepreneurism of West Africans but also draw multinational corporations from around the world. (Foreign direct investment, it should be noted, is worth five times more than foreign aid to the developing world.)[23] Considering current conditions, this organization would substantially improve the business climate even if it started with a far narrower agenda than the one envisioned here.

By superseding national institutions in a few crucial domains, the new organ would help circumvent some of the most deep-rooted problems holding the region back. As a new entity, it would not inherit the troubled legacies of state governments, including illegitimacy spawned by discredited policies, toxic relations with identity groups, and legions of corrupt bureaucrats. By recruiting top-flight managers with the right mix of incentives, the new organization would swiftly become the region's most competent public body, capable not only of devising common policies but also of helping transform state bureaucracies. If it could remove the worse excesses of local malfeasance it could profoundly alter the dynamics of local identity conflict by withdrawing lucrative instruments of administrative patronage. Outsiders could concentrate their limited resources on supporting this one proficient organ instead of trying to fix fifteen dysfunctional bureaucracies.

To be sure, efforts to construct a regionwide organization face significant obstacles. Past initiatives to create such a body have been plagued by rivalries between states, by a reluctance to compromise national sovereignty, by internal instability within key states, by resistance from officials who profit from disparate national policies, and by a general lack of capacity and political will to move forward. Attempts at *economic* integration have met with especially stern opposition from the powerful vested interests. Rent-seeking traders and their government patrons stand to lose much business if formal and informal barriers to the effective coordination of policy are reduced.[24] Even officials concerned not so much for personal gain as for the well-being of their country as a whole have been unwilling or unable to implement protocols regarding integration because of the threat of revenue losses from reduced tariffs and of job losses from diverted trade.

Donors—whose money influences policymaking in aid-dependent, impoverished countries—have also held back states in some cases. World Bank and IMF structural adjustment and trade liberalization schemes aimed at individual countries make policy coordination and moves toward a regional trade strategy problematic.[25] The lack of funds for integration efforts at both a regional and national level also deterred action.

Wide Recognition of the Need for Regionalism

Despite these obstacles, regionalism has repeatedly been proposed as a solution for many of the economic and political problems that bedevil both West Africa and the continent as a whole. Indeed, Africa's postcolonial history has been marked by numerous bold initiatives aimed at integrating states. Unfortunately, few of these plans have delivered as promised (for the reasons just mentioned), and advocates have learned to emphasize that regionalism is no panacea and works best when complemented by local and national initiatives in areas such as education and health. But, as regionalism's proponents rightly point out, plans that ignore the regional aspect of many of West Africa's problems are just as likely to fall short of their objectives.

This argument appears to resonate among Africans at all levels, who recognize the potential for regional initiatives and who, in many cases, are well accustomed to working alongside their neighbors. West Africans, for example, have traveled and traded throughout the region for centuries. Coastal states harbor large numbers of immigrant workers from Sahelian countries (that is, countries located between the Sahara and the more fertile region to the south), in some cases reaching as high as 25 percent of the labor force.[26] Bustling cities such as Abidjan, Accra, Dakar, and Lagos contain significant communities of residents from elsewhere in the region. Meanwhile, informal transborder trade proliferates.

Renewed efforts at cross-border cooperation are far more hopeful than before because of a greater understanding of the need for regional integration, the proven failure of alternative models, the presence of a new generation of better-educated and more enlightened leaders, the desire of post-apartheid South Africa to play a constructive role on the continent, and the positive regional influence of a better led Nigeria. Continental initiatives since 2000 such as the AU and the New Partnership for Africa's Development (NEPAD) have had some success overcoming past mistakes by adopting a more realistic agenda, embracing a closer partnership with developed countries, and exerting stronger peer pressure on uncooperative neighbors. Some heads of states have even pushed for a far faster pace: calls from a few of these to form a pan-African government made the topic of a continentwide administration the main item on the agenda of the 2007 AU summit in Accra. A

2006 AU report on the subject recommended phasing in integration step-by-step in seeking such a goal by 2015.[27]

Thabo Mbeki of South Africa and Olusegun Obasanjo of Nigeria have played major roles in the changing climate, both contributing significantly to these endeavors and both offering hope that more is to come in the future. President Mbeki has taken advantage of South Africa's swift transformation from global outcast to regional hegemony to lead initiatives to settle wars and strengthen governance across the continent. Obasanjo, Nigeria's first democratically elected head of state in over two decades, contributed to peace efforts within the region as well as in Sudan and has made fighting corruption a major priority of his administration. Obasanjo stepped down from the presidency in 2007 and would be a leading candidate to play a major role in any newly empowered regional organization, especially in West Africa. His support for closer regional ties is unequivocal; as he himself wrote in 2001, "We must resolve . . . with full commitment to establishing a viable ECOWAS that will be a major plank for progress, peace, security and development in our subregion. Given our strong commitment to the vision and objectives of ECOWAS, we urgently need to initiate strategies aimed at accelerating the process of regional economic integration and peace consolidation."[28]

Obasanjo and Mbeki are not alone in seeing the importance of regionalism. For instance, the United Nations' Economic Commission for Africa (ECA) declared in 2004 that "revitalized regional integration offers the most credible strategy for tackling Africa's development challenges, internal and external. Why? Because of the many weaknesses that overwhelm the limited capacities and resources of individual countries. Collective efforts, with dynamic political commitment to integration, can help overcome the daunting challenges."[29] The ECA executive secretary, K. Y. Amoako, elaborated: "I want to see intra-African integration not because we will garner some utopian share of world commerce, but first and foremost because it will improve our lives here. It will free up the time of African businesspeople to do business here. It will lower costs. It will make the African consumer's plight so much more hopeful. We must build for ourselves. If we do that, others will come."[30]

Customizing Regionalism for West Africa

Essentially, West Africa needs what its states do not have the capacity to establish on their own: institutional and management depth, an effective judiciary, interstate infrastructure, and a secure living and working environment. Must, then, the creation of a West African regional organization wait for the development of strong West African states? Fortunately—for the wait would be long indeed—the answer is no. What needs to be done is to create an organizational framework customized to fit West African conditions, leveraging limited resources across a broader horizon. The full benefits of such an endeavor would not be felt for decades,

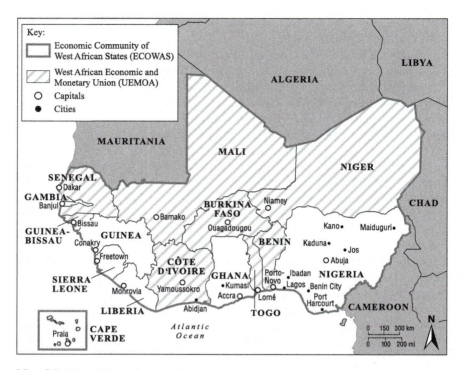

Map 5.2. West African Regional Organizations
Source: Sahel and West Africa Club/OECD.

but the citizens of West Africa would appreciate some tangible advantages—improved governance, better business conditions, and enhanced links between countries—within just a few years.

The example of the Franc de la Communauté Financière Africaine (the Franc CFA is a West African currency shared by seven of France's ex-colonies and Guinea-Bissau) shows how this might work. Legal tender in UEMOA's eight countries (see Map 5.2), the CFA, originally created in 1945 as a means to consolidate French Africa's economies, is issued by a central bank in Dakar, Senegal, and backed by an external guarantee from the treasury in Paris. Although the role of France in this North-South partnership is controversial at times, the CFA has delivered currency stability, lower inflation rates, reduced administrative costs, budgetary discipline, and a less risky business environment for investors.

On a broader level, since its founding in 1994, UEMOA has advanced stable macroeconomic management and regional integration. A multilateral surveillance system supervised by community authorities has helped members in "reducing fiscal deficits, eliminating payment arrears, decreasing the public wage bill, raising the investment financed from domestic resources, raising the government revenue as a ratio to GDP, and lowering the external current account deficit."[31] UEMOA completed a customs union in 2000 and has made significant progress harmonizing business laws. It has improved the stability of central organs by imposing a levy on all imports entering the zone from third countries, and introduced a mechanism to compensate countries from the revenue loss of lowered tariffs.

ECOWAS, a much looser grouping, has also contributed to the new regionalism by playing a growing role in security since establishing a peacekeeping force in 1990. The association's capacity to mediate and enforce peace agreements has grown steadily. Its ability to provide tangible incentives and threats to armed factions were crucial in advancing negotiations in both Liberia and Sierra Leone, and it has dispatched troops to Liberia, Sierra Leone, Guinea-Bissau, and Côte d'Ivoire.

STEPS TOWARD A NEW ORIENTATION

Only a true partnership uniting West African leadership with Western resources can construct a regional organization able to substantially change development prospects. Although the process will take years or possibly even decades, the steps that need to be taken initially are already clear.

The Local Agenda

The leaders of the most influential West African states—Nigeria, Ghana, Senegal, and, if stable enough, Côte d'Ivoire—should start by agreeing on a joint program. Supported by the continent's major players—most notably South Africa and NEPAD, both of which have made strengthening regional organizations a priority and have resources that can be applied to the effort—these states need to present a realistic plan that can gain the support of other West African countries and the donor community. Although the current UEMOA and ECOWAS agenda is ambitious, some goals are misdirected and capacity lags far behind needs. In particular, far more must be done to reduce the red tape, corruption, and other obstructions that discourage legitimate moneymaking.

As a start, West African leaders need to merge the two organizations, thereby concentrating all resources in one body and ending unnecessary duplication between the UEMOA Commission and the ECOWAS Secretariat. The most sensible way to achieve this would be to merge the ECOWAS security apparatus with the UEMOA economic team, and to have non-UEMOA countries join UEMOA's customs union and currency. Yet the region must first overcome historical divisions, differing economic strategies between the French- and English-speaking zones, and the fact that Nigeria's larger market, fiscal recklessness, and oil-dependent economy make it an uncomplementary partner. A more realistic approach would be to adopt a modified version of this strategy, allowing the six smaller non-UEMOA countries to join its multiple programs at their own pace and forming a limited association with Nigeria that focused on trade integration and security cooperation.

The region's leaders should then focus this new organization—let us for present purposes call it the West African Union (WAU)—on building the capacities necessary to ameliorate the wretched business environment. Current projects that assist countries in fiscal management should be enhanced, as is planned. But the WAU should extend UEMOA convergence standards to encompass all areas that influence commerce, establishing clear guidelines on such activities as starting and closing companies, enforcing contracts, registering property, public procurement, hiring and firing workers, and getting credit.[32]

Strong regional powers to combat corruption, promote competition, and facilitate trade would do more than anything else to break the logjams preventing faster growth. Most national institutions are too compromised or ineffectual to tackle these issues alone. A new anticorruption directorate could send its own inspectors throughout the region, working with local police to track down suspects and then trying them in its own special courts. A competition promotion office would not only help to break up the region's many monopolies but also ensure that the benefits of commercial competition are spread as widely as possible. Properly empowered, it could force governments to change regulations to encourage commercial activity, not deter it, as is too often the case now.

A trade facilitation agency would tackle the myriad causes of high transaction costs, quickening the movement of goods by enacting unified, simplified, transparent procedures for customs clearance and payments and by dispatching its own people to remove the many blockages—such as the reams of official paperwork at border crossings and the fees exacted at unofficial road blacks—that act as a tax on trade. For goods conveyance, the agency would unify technical standards, enforce reduced transit charges, and encourage competition between multiple providers. Establishing a regional customs authority would dramatically improve export conditions.

These strengthened capacities would enable West Africa to better meet developed country demands in areas such as intellectual property protection, port security, and agricultural produce health standards.

Efforts to improve infrastructure should be focused on measures to enlarge markets. Channeling money into improving the fragmented highway, railroad, and waterway connections between countries, and improving ports would reduce transport costs and expand the reach of factories, making the local production of a wide assortment of goods profitable and spurring investment.

Accelerating current plans to expand ECOWAS's security capabilities is essential to implement such an agenda. The instability caused by the fighting in Côte d'Ivoire and elsewhere affects the whole region, endangering any effort to deepen integration. The WAU needs permanent access to analysts, diplomatic officers, and well-trained soldiers and police officers to analyze incipient threats, mediate conflicts, and intervene where necessary to maintain or enforce peace.

All these proposals require a strong central secretariat, especially as empowering the WAU will come at the expense of existing institutions and will surely provoke considerable opposition from those whose power or earnings will be diminished. Government officials and businesspeople whose authority or wealth is tied to corrupted bureaucracies and informal cross-border trade will hide behind national structures and seek to undermine or circumvent the new organization's authority. The WAU secretariat's portfolio of rewards and penalties will have to be expanded to ensure compliance with its directives by governments, companies, and individuals, an area where donors could prove especially helpful. Of course, these will be more effective if backed by a combination of enlightened national leaders providing the appropriate peer pressure on recalcitrant colleagues and a selective use of financial inducements to ensure elite compliance.

A strong secretariat must, of course, be staffed by high-caliber personnel. This will require hiring on the basis of merit rather than nationality or political connections. By offering the right mix of prestige and pay, the WAU could attract experienced executives from Africa's immense diaspora, leading multinational investors, major local companies, and the continent's few well-functioning governments. Establishing a West African Governance Institute to train officials, politicians, and judges and propagate best practices would help these fortified structures have a multiplier effect throughout the region. Devising a financing plan based on tariffs, customs fees, transport charges, and payment surcharges independent of both donors and governments would make the secretariat robust enough to support this ambitious agenda, especially given the fact that ECOWAS members paid only about two-thirds of required contributions in 2002.[33]

The Role of the West

In turn, the developed world has begun to recognize the potential benefits of supporting African continental and regional associations, at least in the area of security, where the West has an obvious self-interest. The G-8 agreed in 2003 to help the AU establish an African Stand-by Force, which is expected to reach 15,000 soldiers by 2010.[34] Under the Global Peace Operations Initiative (GPOI), proposed by President Bush at the 2004 G-8 Summit, the members of the G-8 are training 40,000 African peacekeepers over five years.[35] Regionally, Germany, Britain, Italy, Canada, and the Netherlands funded a new peacekeeping center in Accra, Ghana, to train ECOWAS soldiers for both UN and local duties. The European Union has set aside €350 million for African-led peacekeeping operations during 2006–2010.[36] The Bush administration dedicated $100 million in fiscal year 2006 for the GPOI.[37]

Outside the sphere of security, however, external support has been far more restrained. Although the European Union—and, to a lesser extent, the multilateral banks—has supported the UEMOA Commission since its 1994 launch and is helping the ECOWAS Secretariat, funding levels remain modest.[38] Furthermore, the European Union's own geopolitical and economic agenda has meant that trade liberalization, macroeconomic reform, and regulation alignment have been emphasized at the expense of the development of the institutional capacity that could overcome the biggest on-the-ground impediments to investment.[39] Other Western players, including the United States, have done even less.

The West should make regionalism a much higher priority and encourage local leaders to push forward an ambitious agenda. Once that agenda has crystallized, the West should back plans in three ways: reallocating aid money, ratcheting up technical assistance, and providing the incentives necessary to ensure that policy commitments to the WAU are honored.

The financial needs of an expanded regional organization are distinctly modest compared to current donor-funding levels. In 2001, the combined budget of the ECOWAS and UEMOA central bodies was less than $25 million, of which only about $5 million was covered by aid—just 0.1 percent of commitments to the region.[40] Donors could together sponsor a five- to ten-year plan of grants to systematically enhance regional capabilities. Funding could increase by $20 million annually as the secretariat expanded its work, subject to members meeting certain obligations and the organization passing regular performance audits; local funding from tariffs and other fees would also rise progressively. A long-term commitment that leveled off at $100 million annually would go a long way toward creating the momentum necessary to accelerate regional designs. Additional support, training, and logistical help could be directed at improving security capabilities.

Bilateral support could be reconfigured to match the regional agenda by prioritizing infrastructure projects that linked countries and adding a regional component to programs that tied aid to improvements in governance. Benefactors could also fund the creation and operation of national integration ministries responsible for interfacing with the WAU, pay the dues of the most disadvantaged states, and compensate for some of the revenue lost by governments as a consequence of relinquishing control over sundry charges such as tariffs and customs revenue. Much of this funding could come from existing resources if money was spent more judiciously. (As much as 50 percent of current aid budgets are spent on expensive consultants and administrators. Of $52 billion of aid disbursed to developing countries each year, only half is spent in recipient countries.)[41]

Technical assistance could be dramatically increased. French and EU support has been vital in building up UEMOA's in-house macroeconomic and trade capacities, and has helped in areas such as legal harmonization, statistics collection, public finance management, and conflict prevention. Similar assistance would be no less crucial to both developing WAU's capabilities and ensuring that national bureaucratic malfeasance was not conveyed to the regional level.

The international community also has an important role to play in ensuring that commitments are fulfilled. Agreements that provide a lock-in mechanism with penalties, such as the 1999 UEMOA Convergence, Stability, and Growth Pact, would be more robust if backed by the carrots and sticks available to the

West. Bilateral grants, loans, and debt relief should all be conditioned on meeting regional commitments. The G-8 should also provide a diplomatic shield to insulate the secretariat from political pressure in the areas of recruitment and adjudication of members' compliance with the organization's rules.

Even if the WAU shows some of the same flaws that disfigure national governments and faces stern resistance from some corners, it can still substantially improve local conditions if the West makes a concerted effort to strengthen the organization's capabilities, provide effective checks on corruption, and work behind the scene to overcome opposition.

THE VALUE OF REGIONALISM

Strengthening regional organizations may be one of the best ways to tackle the problems that plague fragile states in Africa and elsewhere. It can invigorate development prospects by transforming business climates. It can change societal dynamics by empowering people, unshackling them from the restrictions imposed by ineffectual governments. It can even reduce the intensity of intergroup rivalries by creating a supranational umbrella under which all groups are forced to compete on an equal footing.

Development is a complex process that can succeed only when societal dynamics create a self-propelling momentum for positive evolution. Decades of searching for a way to jumpstart this process in places such as West Africa have proved fruitless because previous attempts were not only targeted on individual states but also bolstered their status—and with it the corruption, maladministration, and frictions they nourish. Reconsidering how to harness people and institutions to drive development, and what can and cannot be achieved with existing structures, shows that regionalism offers a remarkably effective way to proceed in some of the most troubled regions.

The Democratic Republic of the Congo: Constructing the State Bottom Up

No one can doubt the need for a bold approach to reforming the apparatus of government in a country that has been described by one UN official as "the world's deadliest humanitarian catastrophe."[1] The Democratic Republic of the Congo (DRC) is roughly the same size as Western Europe, but its state has withered away almost entirely, leaving an increasingly despairing population to fend for themselves within a Hobbesian nightmare of chaos and violence (see Map 6.1). Between 1998 and 2007, some 5.4 million Congolese were killed by violence, disease, and malnutrition,[2] while armies, warlords, and assorted gangs pilfered hundreds of millions of dollars in gold, diamonds, and coltan.

The collapse of the DRC not only affects its unfortunate citizens but also destabilizes states throughout the continent, at least half a dozen of which have been drawn into its civil war in recent years, spawning Africa's first "world war." Its subversive impact extends more widely still, for the United States and other Western nations are acutely conscious that the anarchic conditions within the DRC nourish terrorists, arms traffickers, and criminal networks hostile to international security. Reports that Iran has been smuggling uranium out of the DRC have only exacerbated Western fears.[3]

In short, the DRC represents the world's greatest humanitarian and governance challenge, with direct implications for hundreds of millions on the most impoverished continent and indirect implications for the security and well-being of people everywhere. In recognition of this, the international community invested billions of dollars between 2002 and 2006 in restoring security and government in the DRC, including over $500 million in drafting a new constitution and electing a new administration.[4] Sadly, however, this effort to usher in stability, accountability, and democracy has already begun to fail; indeed, it was always doomed to failure because its success depended on a formula inappropriate to the country's conditions. This latest international effort to fix the DRC prescribes conventional remedies for failed states—elections, economic liberalization, and security reforms—all of which are desirable but none of which will make a significant difference unless coupled with an ambitious plan to counteract the systemic roots of the country's profound dysfunctionalities. If the DRC is to develop homegrown capacities that can eventually overcome the state's problems, the country's institutions must be redesigned so that they better reflect its political geography, limited governance capacities, dearth of infrastructure, and abundant mineral wealth. Above all, this means giving local leaders a genuine chance to effectively serve the population.

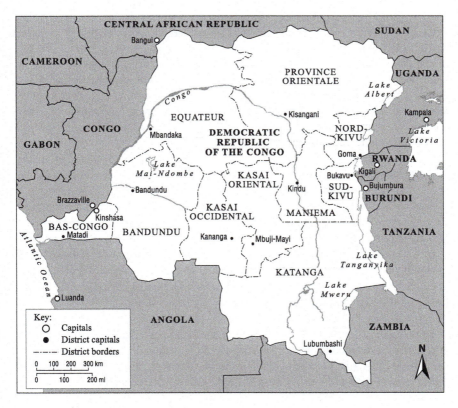

Map 6.1. Democratic Republic of the Congo, Political Map
Note: The DRC's eleven provinces are being expanded to twenty-six under the new constitution.
Source: United Nations.

THE BURDEN OF HISTORY

The country's current deplorable condition is in many ways a product of its history. In the late nineteenth century, the Congo Free State suffered appallingly from colonial misrule, with as many as 10 million Congolese killed within a single generation.[5] Such brutality diminished in the twentieth century, but a kind of apartheid took its place. On the eve of its independence in 1960, the DRC (or Zaire, as it was known for much of its postcolonial life) was woefully unprepared for self-rule, because Belgium had made every effort to prevent Africans from acquiring the knowledge to manage their own affairs. In January 1959, one year before Belgium pulled out, there were only three African civil servants among the country's 4,600 top officials and no African doctors, dentists, pharmacists, professional lawyers, engineers, or even veterinarians.[6] In all, only seventeen Congolese had earned a university degree before independence.[7]

What limited governance capacity existed at its birth was undermined within days by domestic infighting and foreign scheming. In a sign of things to come, initially Belgium, and later the United States, intervened to ensure that this country, strategically positioned at the core of Africa and richly endowed with mineral deposits, would not fall out of its sphere of influence. The anarchy that engulfed the country prompted most Europeans, without whom neither industry nor government could function, to flee. An ambitious UN intervention eventually ended the violence, but it would be five years before a coup d'état by Joseph-Désiré Mobutu restored stability.

Mobutu's reign, which lasted from 1965 to 1997, initially brought a modicum of functioning government to the country, but that progress was short-lived. By the mid-1970s, the country was being plundered for the benefit of its leader and patronage network, steadily emasculating the state's ability to govern the country's vast territory. Even under colonial rule, the state had never achieved hegemony over all its territory, but after independence its writ progressively retreated, especially after Mobutu realized that his continued rule depended on co-opting regional elites by giving away state control at the local level. Government was transformed into an institution for the distribution of cash, assets, and special rights to favored parties. Only Western largesse aimed at shoring up this anticommunist bulkhead masked the growing problems. But after the fall of the Berlin Wall, foreign assistance became increasingly conditional on governance standards that the DRC could not meet even if it wanted to. Mobutu resorted to increasingly desperate measures, and by the end of his rule he was involved in clandestine trade, tax avoidance, passport sales, money laundering, and drug trafficking.[8] In all, his regime siphoned off between $4 billion and $10 billion during its time in power.[9]

Meanwhile, any semblance of a state disintegrated. As early as 1978, Mobutu needed troops from France and Belgium to quell a rebellion because his own security forces were inadequate to the task. By 1993, income levels had shrunk to 35 percent of their preindependence level.[10] Inflation reached 23,000 percent in 1995.[11] Foreign debt ballooned to $14 billion.[12] Only 15 percent of the roads inherited in 1960 remained passable.[13] By 1994, former U.S. Assistant Secretary of State for African Affairs Herman Cohen could observe, "To say that [the DRC] has a government today would be a gross exaggeration."[14] The regime by then had only a tenuous grip on Kinshasa, the remote presidential palace in Gbadolite, and the central bank. The World Bank no longer included the country in its data tables and the International Monetary Fund expelled it.

The DRC's condition, it seemed, could get no worse. Amazingly, it did. In the years following Mobutu's departure, the DRC experienced almost nonstop violence, including multiple foreign interventions, numerous rebellions, and the assassination of one of its presidents. By 2003, GDP per capita had fallen to only 28 percent of its level at independence.[15] One-third of the country's 54 million people faced disease, malnutrition, and homelessness because of the fighting.[16] An astounding 75 percent of children under five years of age were malnourished.[17]

Although the international community has made a Herculean effort to help the country in the years since the civil war ended in 2004, markedly improving conditions in many places, the DRC remains highly unstable and seriously misgoverned. In January 2008, the *New York Times* reported, "The rate at which people are dying in the country remains virtually unchanged ... the mortality rate is 57 percent higher than the rest of sub-Saharan Africa."[18] Despite the presence of 17,600 UN peacekeepers, violence continues in parts of the eastern provinces. *Foreign Policy* identified the DRC as the second most unstable country in the world after Sudan in its "Failed States Index," published in May 2006. The World Bank rated the DRC the fourth worst administered state in the world in 2005, ahead of only Somalia, Iraq, and Myanmar.[19] Its "human development index value"—a comprehensive measurement of the quality of life calculated by the UN Development Programme—was lower in 2005 than it had been in 1975.[20]

THE BURDEN OF GEOGRAPHY

Most African states have had to face the challenge of building stable polities despite arbitrarily drawn borders, splintered identities, and weak governing capacities. In the case of the DRC, however, the scale of these problems has been magnified by its tempting natural resources, vast size, disadvantageous political geography, and meager infrastructure.

The DRC has a wealth of mineral deposits. It was once the leading source for industrial diamonds worldwide, and it has one of the world's greatest concentrations of copper, cobalt, and coltan (10 percent, 33 percent, and 85 percent, respectively, of global reserves).[21] Uranium for the first U.S. atomic bomb was mined in the territory. But instead of acting as the country's economic engine, this natural resource base is fueling today's conflict. Local militia and foreign armies plunder vast amounts, which they smuggle out of the country and onto the international market. An estimated $400 million in diamonds and gold alone have been smuggled out of the state annually in recent years.

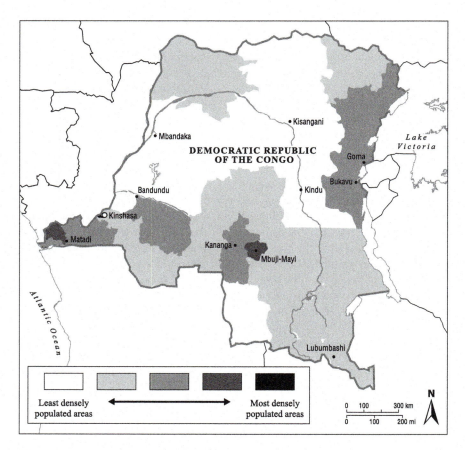

Map 6.2. Democratic Republic of the Congo, Population Distribution
Source: Jeffrey Herbst, *State and Power in Africa: Comparative Lessons in Authority and Control* (Princeton, NJ: Princeton University Press, 2000), 148.

The country's population is divided into a number of pockets of high density hundreds of miles apart from one another, generating centrifugal forces that continuously threaten to pull the country apart (see Map 6.2). Before colonial powers redrew Africa's map, each of these pockets had its own political economy bolstered by strong cultural and societal ties and a network of trading links with the surrounding area. The colonial mapmakers ignored central Africa's sociocultural realities, creating a state where, even more than a century later, many of the residents of these widely separated regions still have much more in common with their neighbors on the other side of the national border than with their fellow citizens on the other side of the country. Indeed, given the difficulties crossing the sparsely populated spaces that separate the DRC's different regions, there is little economic rationale for these districts to trade with one another; the costs of

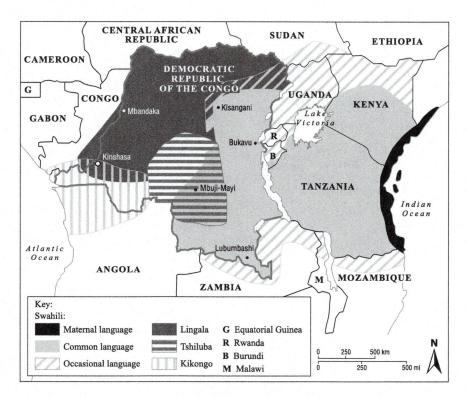

Map 6.3. Democratic Republic of the Congo, "National Languages"
Source: Organisation for Economic Co-operation and Development (OECD).

doing business with neighboring areas across international borders—not only the costs of transportation, but also the costs of overcoming cultural and linguistic differences—are much lower (see Maps 6.3 and 6.4). As a result, the country's population distribution severely complicates all attempts to construct national governing bodies, interlinked institutions, and a unified identity.

These difficulties are compounded by the DRC's extremely limited transportation and communications infrastructure. There is only one well-paved road in the whole country—between Kinshasa and Matadi, the DRC's only ocean port.[22] Not even one person in a thousand has a mainline telephone line, and only one in ten thousand is an Internet user, putting the DRC last on a list of 175 countries for both categories.[23]

With substantial areas of the country effectively cut off from the capital and even from regional urban areas, major cities find it easier to compete than co-operate. As Jeffrey Herbst notes, "much of [the DRC's] history can be read not only as a dispute between the east, north, and south, but also a battle between the capital of Kinshasa and the far away cities of Kisangani and Lubumbashi."[24]

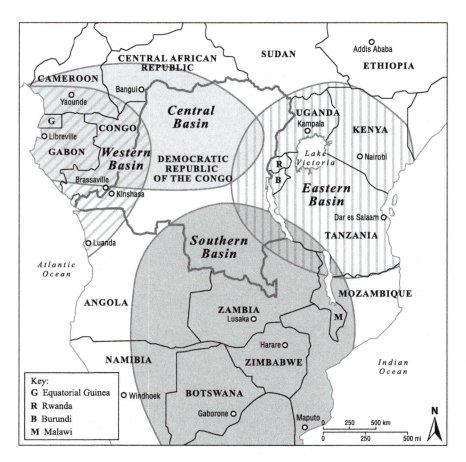

Map 6.4. Democratic Republic of the Congo, Regional Basins
Source: Organisation for Economic Co-operation and Development (OECD).

"Many provinces," Herbst remarks, "have informally seceded."[25] The majority of uprisings throughout the country's history have been in the territories farthest from the capital in the east, such as Kivu, Katanga, and Kasai, where the writ of the central government is weakest and the consequences of state dysfunction the greatest. Attempts at democratization have always yielded political parties with strong ethnic and regional roots. The 1960 elections were contested by 120 political parties, only one of which could be considered national in scope.[26] More than 250 parties registered for the July 2006 elections and more than seventy of them made it into the new National Assembly, where most of them represent regional or individual aspirations, not a national agenda. Regionalism also played a significant part in the 2006 presidential elections, with the linguistically distinct eastern and western regions favoring different candidates.

THE INTERNATIONAL RESPONSE: THE WRONG PRESCRIPTION

The international community's prescription for fixing the DRC continues to rely heavily on the standard prescription for fixing failed states: a new constitution, elections, economic liberalization, and security reforms. These measures, however, have yielded at best only mixed success in other failed states and are profoundly inadequate to the scale of the challenge in the DRC. The West has generously pumped billions of dollars into humanitarian programs and supported a large deployment of UN peacekeepers, but it has not seriously examined whether its strategy for the country will deal with the root causes of its dysfunction, making it likely that the DRC will remain a victim of its inappropriate institutions.

International efforts at reformulating the country's flimsy and scanty governing structures in a new constitution have rightly concentrated on decentralization, but they have not gone nearly far enough in reallocating power so as to overcome the bureaucratic weaknesses that will undoubtedly plague any state body. Indeed, all national government bodies have historically been unable—or unwilling—to project their authority much beyond the capital, as evidenced in a whole slew of health and education indicators. For instance, Kinshasa's residents live as much as thirteen years longer than citizens in some other parts of the country; and whereas 89 percent of Kinshasa's population has access to healthy drinking water, the average countrywide is only 46 percent and in some provinces it is as low as a quarter.[27] The new government bodies set up during and after the transition show little improvement, remaining "weak and abusive or non-existent."[28]

The new constitution that was approved in a nationwide referendum at the end of 2005 has given provincial governments greater power and greater control over revenues; they now have their own governors, ministers, and assemblies. The newly established right of regional governments to directly access local tax revenue should prove particularly important in increasing regional government capacity and responsiveness. But the presidency retains immense executive authority, and, with a splintered electorate and weak political parties, will continue to dominate the country's political space and formal institutions, thereby inviting a repetition of the monarchial pretensions and corrupt practices of past presidencies.[29] The new constitution thus makes no break with the zero-sum nature of Congolese political calculations and seems guaranteed to perpetuate the kind of divisions that have bedeviled the country since independence. In fact, eastern and southern domination of the new government has fomented resentment and civil unrest throughout the western provinces, precipitating a brutal crackdown against the opposition, with hundreds being killed in clashes during a March 2007 confrontation in the capital and the runner-up in the presidential election being forced into exile in Portugal. By the summer of 2007, the eastern region, too, was once again becoming increasingly violent, uprooting more than 400,000 people in the process. The only way to break this cycle of violence is to empower regional governments to a much greater degree, thereby giving most of the many mutually antagonistic factions a large enough stake in the new order to pacify them. The new constitution has, in effect, bought short-term peace—and the consolidation of a national government favorable to Western political and business interests[30]—at the expense of the chance for stability throughout the country and genuine development over the long term.

Similarly, despite emphasizing the need to improve administrative capacity, particularly at the regional and local level, little international funding has been allocated to accomplish that goal. Projects aimed at improving electoral laws, bolstering investment legislation and environmental protection, strengthening political parties, and empowering local NGOs receive far higher priority than those aimed at upgrading the ability of public servants, especially those outside the capital, to manage their tasks, even though the latter will be far more important in ensuring that the government serves the needs of its people in the years to come.

The World Bank, the DRC's largest overall donor, allocated only $15 million specifically for "institutional strengthening" from a total of $1.4 billion it dedicated to ten projects in 2004. The Bank's *Transitional Support Strategy* for the Congo instead emphasizes improving governance "through both advisory services and adjustment operations," with a focus on "economic reforms," "analytical work to . . . prepare for new lending operations," poverty reduction, and "preparatory . . . work on external debt,"[31] most of which require national government action and are at least partly aimed at serving the Bank's own needs. Bilateral donors are similarly reluctant to fund improvements in the institutions and performance of government: of the $1.3 billion in support committed by bilateral donors in recent years, only $10.5 million targets "governance" and "institutional strengthening." (In contrast, almost $170 million was earmarked as "support to NGOs," "civil society," and "support to political processes.")[32] The United States Agency for International Development (USAID) planned to spend just $500,000 of its $71 million aid for the DRC in 2005–2006 to "support democratic local government and decentralization."[33] The pronounced focus on NGOs, especially foreign-managed NGOs, at the expense of government institutions, especially in regions that have historically been underserved by the state, is likely to prolong the country's inability to manage its own affairs.

Meanwhile, Western governments are trying to improve the DRC's decrepit armed forces, recognizing, as the International Crisis Group has noted, that this "is one of the most important tasks of the transition"[34] and the key to both protecting the country's mineral wealth and reintegrating the various militias into society. That task is formidable, to say the least. Bands of assorted soldiers, rebels, and gangsters roam the eastern hinterlands, killing, raping, stealing, and smuggling; as many as 320,000 fighters and ex-fighters are in the country.[35] Just a handful of the eighteen army brigades planned by the transitional government have been set up, and all of them are underpaid, underfed, underequipped, and underarmed.[36] These units have not only shied away from engaging rebel groups, but have become the "worst human rights abuser" in the country, looting, killing indiscriminately, and committing various other acts that are fueling ethnic tensions, threatening to ignite another major crisis in the east.[37] "Natural resources still fuel the conflict and there is no real end in sight," said a Western diplomat in Kinshasa in early 2006. "Rebels may be pushed out, but the army then comes in and continues the mining. The prospect of short-term gains for local chiefs and the military still outweigh the long-term plans anyone has."[38]

The international community has attempted to improve the security situation in a number of ways, though with limited success. Various parties have funded demobilization, helped create integrated army brigades, and trained both army and police units. The international community has also mustered the funds and political will to deploy 17,600 blue helmets at an annual cost of some $1 billion.[39] Yet, "Large parts of the national territory remain lawless."[40]

THE RIGHT PRESCRIPTION: SECURING NATURAL RESOURCES

Instead of hoping that the DRC's systemic weaknesses will disappear given the right constitution, political leadership, and economic policies, international efforts should be directed at constructing institutions that actually suit the country's on-the-ground conditions. This would involve making decision makers much more beholden to populations, leveraging what limited governing capacities exist in ways to improve the management of public bodies and natural resources, and nourishing the homegrown capabilities necessary to eventually strengthen the state and wean the country off foreign assistance.

First, however, something has to be done to help the DRC protect its major mineral sites from being plundered, for until it can do so, the country will remain hostage to the armed groups that continue to pillage its natural resources and use the wealth they accrue to undermine its institutions. The state's security forces cannot be expected to perform this task anytime in the near future, so the DRC must depend on some sort of international presence to protect its natural resources. Maintaining a greatly strengthened foreign deployment of some kind might be the best solution, but the cost of doing so would far exceed the West's generosity. (Prior to 2008, the UN presence consumed one-quarter of the entire UN peacekeeping budget.) It would also demand the kind of sustained commitment that the international community, which has more pressing concerns elsewhere in the world, simply cannot muster when it comes to Africa. And, at least for the foreseeable future, no African Union force could perform the task, given the organization's still limited competencies and budget.

There is, in fact, only one player with sufficient incentives and capabilities to establish security and good governance in resource-rich areas, and to do so in a way that would benefit both the state and the people of the DRC: multinational natural resource companies.

The DRC government, with assistance from the international community, should negotiate new contracts with such companies. Those contracts could not only lay out a royalty structure that would generate profits for the firms and provide a steady flow of revenue to the state (something it has not enjoyed for years because of the insecure environment and the "widespread use of unfair, illegal, or unclear contracts"[41]), but also insist on faithful observance of the most stringent international conventions on transparency, thereby combating corruption and building public trust. Furthermore, the contracts could mandate the corporations to undertake and be accountable for an array of security and social programs that could tame the lawless areas around major mining sites and ensure that citizens living nearby reaped the benefits of their geography.

For example, agreements could include detailed provisions for policing deposits, facilities, roads, and a zone around these areas, forcing firms to deploy their own guards to secure these sites. Companies could be obliged to pave roads, build schools and hospitals, and fund teachers and doctors, giving tens of thousands of people around their facilities access to at least a minimum standard of education and health care. Agreements could not only specify what percentage of revenues garnered from production would be allocated to social and security programs, but also set a long list of performance indicators and disclosure requirements to ensure companies meet their obligations and are seen to do so. In effect, companies would be promising to deliver a series of services to the country in addition to paying the government for exploiting its resources.

No doubt many people would recoil at this idea. Most Congolese and, indeed, most Africans would shudder at the echoes of a brutal colonial past. Outside Africa, many others—including those donors with an instinctive distrust of corporations—would likewise expect the companies to abuse their authority. These concerns are partly rooted in the conduct of foreign businesses in the country during the colonial period: King Leopold's Congo Free State was operated as a for-profit concern in a grotesquely brutal fashion and the Belgians outsourced the governing of large swathes of the country to mining companies such as the Union Minière du Haut Katanga (UMHK). The better-run firms did, however, provide free housing, medical care, education, and retirement pensions for thousands of families, doing so partly out of paternalism and partly out of a recognition that improving employees' welfare yielded higher profits. The greater transparency of corporate operations today, combined with the sensitivity of large Western firms to public criticism of their conduct, makes abuse far less likely than in the previous era. These concerns could be further alleviated by restricting the bidding process to large, internationally reputable firms with excellent records in environmental protection and labor and community relations. Corporate performance could then be monitored by the national and local government and by a newly created international watchdog made up of DRC officials and citizens, representatives of organizations such as the World Bank and the African Union, and possibly even NGOs such as Human Rights Watch and Oxfam. Failure to meet performance standards would be punished by a range of penalties, including large fines and the revocation of certain rights granted in the original contract. Given that multinationals are accustomed to running highly efficient operations, have wide experience managing security in diverse settings, and regularly outsource and monitor outside vendor performance in some of the world's most challenging environments, the corporations would likely do an excellent job. Indeed, the zones they managed would probably have far better public services than other parts of the country. The DRC state would be able to concentrate its limited resources on tackling less vulnerable areas elsewhere.

Although critics might point to the failure of multinational corporate projects to deliver benefits to local populations in places such as Nigeria and Chad, it should be noted that contracts elsewhere have not mandated detailed service requirements nor have they made companies answerable to international organizations. Investors have rarely been asked to do more than extract natural resources and pay royalties. It may also be noted that there are impressive examples of multinationals working successfully with developing country governments on major projects aimed at improving the quality of life of local populations. For instance, Rio Tinto, a British mining corporation, has created foundations to serve as development agencies in countries ranging from Namibia to Indonesia. In Papua New Guinea, companies receive tax offsets in exchange for the construction of roads and the delivery of health care and education services. International companies have been at the forefront of efforts to combat AIDS, reduce the incidence of malaria, and improve education standards in many countries in Africa.

Unfortunately, the DRC's unstable conditions and corrupt government are deterring socially responsible multinational companies such as Rio Tinto from operating in the country, creating a vacuum that is being filled by firms that care little or nothing for notions of corporate social responsibility. Most mining activity in the country since the end of the civil war has been carried out by small firms with links to the elite surrounding the president. In September 2007, the government announced that China would lend $5 billion to the country in return for mining concessions and infrastructure toll revenue.[42] Neither China nor the small firms are likely to invest in social development projects near their mining operations.

THE RIGHT PRESCRIPTION: PROMOTING HORIZONTAL DEVELOPMENT

Efforts to develop the DRC state vertically, along the lines of the Western model of top-down governance, seem once again to have failed. But such efforts were misguided in the first place, for the DRC is a vast country without nearly enough competent administrative staff to overcome its distances and fractured nature. Instead of treating the DRC's inability to imitate Western-style state building as a sign of its inability to modernize, the international community should be advocating a far more horizontal model, in which the main governing structures are shaped around cities and their surrounding rural areas, with the central administration's powers and responsibilities sharply reduced and programs adopted that build capacity from the ground up, not from the top down. This truly decentralized configuration would allow local societies to reclaim government as their own, harnessing where possible the informal institutions that have replaced the state in most places, making officials far more responsive to their constituents, while giving the population real "ownership" of formal bodies for the first time.

Foreign aid agencies have implicitly recognized the need to organize the state in this way by their use of decentralized programs, by distributing the great majority of their funds to district-level endeavors, and by their repeated circumvention of national bodies. For example, the European Union Humanitarian Aid department (ECHO), the DRC's largest source of humanitarian aid, allocated only 11 percent of its €39 million 2003 budget for national issues and spent the majority of its funds in the country's most disadvantaged provinces.[43] USAID works at the "health zone" level, with the country divided into no fewer than five hundred such zones, each with a population of approximately 150,000 people.

A looser, more horizontal governing structure, in which municipal governments had full control over their budgets and full responsibility for most programs would make individual units far more effective, especially if outside assistance focused on improving their management, transparency, and accountability (as described in the next section). These greatly empowered local bodies would—where practical—encompass populations with a common sociocultural background, and the physical proximity of officials and politicians to their constituents would make the former more attentive and responsive to the needs of the latter. Even the current Kinshasa government is obliged to do a far better job of serving those living in or near the capital than those in other parts of the country (as discussed above). International donors would also gain far more flexibility in rewarding competent regional and local governing organs without penalizing the whole country. Competition between areas for outside assistance and investment could spur further reform, replicating some of the processes that drive improved government performance in better functioning states.

In this model, the national government would work as the head of a loosely confederated state, confining its ambit to foreign affairs, monetary policy, the judiciary, customs, interregional infrastructure, the coordination of policies across regions, and various endeavors (such as mandating anticorruption budgetary measures) that strengthened competition in the national marketplace and made local institutions more robust. It would have limited involvement in the organization of social programs and local infrastructure investments, the areas of government that most affect individual citizens. Local units could be designed around the country's twenty-one major cities,[44] enabling foreign organizations to focus their efforts on improving governance and service delivery locally, substantially increasing their reach into the country's heartland.

Needless to say, such a far-reaching program of decentralization would face many obstacles, not least opposition from the kleptocratic regime in Kinshasa. Fortunately, several factors favor a bold approach. In the first place, the central government is so weak and discredited that it could do little more than verbally protest its loss of authority. (Reassuring national leaders that they would maintain the prestige and benefits of their positions would probably satisfy some of these complaints.) Second, the widespread endorsement of the new constitution indicates a readiness among many Congolese to embrace a profound revision of the DRC's political structure. Third, donors could use their control over grants, loans, and the income from corporate investments to ensure that most of the money, and the authority to use it, goes to the bottom rungs of the government instead of the top.

THE RIGHT PRESCRIPTION: MAKING GOVERNMENT ACCOUNTABLE

The natural resource curse—which makes countries with rich natural resources more, not less, susceptible to corruption and violent conflict—and extraordinarily high levels of foreign aid[45] have combined to distort the incentives of governance in the DRC. Instead of being forced to improve administrative performance to meet citizens' needs, officials have been able to manipulate donors, contracts, and budgets in an unceasing effort to steal as much of the country's income as possible. Institutions have corroded because there has been no incentive for ministers and managers to make them effective. Breaking these dysfunctional patterns—making government accountable—is a prerequisite to any effort to improve the country's economy, security, and chances for genuine development.

Elections alone will not dramatically improve how government operates—especially elections for leaders in distant cities who have little direct influence on programs that improve individual lives. Indeed, only by helping the local population construct effective "accountability loops"—that is, a system of ballots, increased transparency, and other measures that holds accountable the officials who manage the programs that directly affect citizens—is administrative performance likely to improve.

International donors could do much to create or strengthen such loops and local governance capacity if they focused far more effort on designing and helping implement systems that held officials responsible to their constituents. For instance, they could make their funding of local governments conditional on those governments restructuring themselves into smaller units (such as the 150,000-people "health zones"), each of which would implement key education, social, and infrastructure programs and be held accountable through a system of outside audits and local elections. Citywide administrations would continue to have significant roles in how these programs were implemented, but a portion of their budgets would be allocated to the smaller units. Donors and NGOs could then concentrate on training local-level administrators and managers while improving the mechanisms that hold them answerable to those they served.

No one should be under any illusions that local officials are untainted by the same sort of corruption that riddles the national government in Kinshasa. In fact, because local governments have attracted a lot less international attention than the bureaucracy in Kinshasa, they have been able to operate with far fewer checks on illicit behavior. However, careful design and close monitoring of the system of local accountability loops would reduce the scope of these abuses. Moreover, where officials were chosen by and mandated to service people from their own identity group, populations would have a greater incentive to work with officials to upgrade governance—and be more likely able to exert societal pressure to discipline them than in the current politically fragmented climate.

In order to make this vision a reality, outsiders need to play a far greater role, at least initially, in ensuring that these loops work effectively. For example, IGOs and NGOs would have to play a far greater role in monitoring and even adjudicating electoral processes to prevent them being hijacked by corrupt cliques. External audits of budgets and projects—or even in some cases the installation of independent financial controllers into government organs—and the public release and distribution of all public financial statements would help a population monitor its leaders. Creating public oversight committees and giving them the means to monitor local government bodies would encourage grassroots organizations to actively participate in government.

The international community must also invest more in upgrading what limited local governance capacity there currently exists in the DRC. As noted above, far too little money is spent on augmenting administrative capabilities, and much of this is spent on projects in Kinshasa. Aid agencies direct most of their funding toward international NGOs instead of local governments, and while this may be understandable given the country's current situation, it is unlikely to foster the homegrown managerial skills the government sorely needs, and risks recolonizing the state. The goal should be to strengthen local governance capacity so that the country can wean itself off its chronic dependency on foreign aid and supervision. Numerous steps could be taken toward this end. For instance, when local governments develop a track record of relative efficiency, donors could mandate that NGOs worked through or with local administrators instead of around them, strengthening their position and expertise even further. Although change will be painfully slow at first, and significant and enduring improvements might take decades to achieve, there is really no alternative to this process of strengthening institutions from the bottom up if the DRC is ever to become a functioning state.

CORRECTING A MISDIAGNOSIS

Jan Egeland, the UN Undersecretary General for Aid Coordination, commented in 2006 that the United Nations had "struggled to get resources because Congo . . . was seen as hopeless by many potential donors."[46] But if the international community tried a different approach, it might find that the DRC is not in fact a hopeless case, and that time and money expended on the country can actually yield long-term gains.

At present, however, the DRC remains in a desperate condition, and its new institutional design is highly unlikely to produce a stable and genuinely democratic country. The new constitution's emphasis on top-down administrative structures has, if anything, made the fragile reconciliation between warring factions achieved at peace conferences harder to maintain. By not distributing enough resources and power to regional governments, it turned the national elections into a zero-sum game for state control, giving losers too little stake in an outcome that is dominated by the new president. The deep geographical divisions that the election brought to the fore—and the outbreaks of violence between competing factions that have killed hundreds since—suggest some of the challenges the new national administration faces. The loser in the presidential race and the various groups that boycotted the election will have ample opportunity in the years ahead to harness discontent among those excluded from power.

Meanwhile, without greater attention to improving how local government functions, the country will continue to depend on NGOs for the provision of even basic public services far into the future—and such dependency is highly unlikely to foster the bureaucratic competence, enlightened self-government, and economic expansion necessary to improve the population's meager standard of living.

Fragile states face fundamentally different problems than those found in more advanced countries. Efforts to fix them that emphasize programs unsuited to their circumstances are doomed to fail, no matter how well intentioned. Instead of hoping that better leaders and policies alone might reverse the fate of such territories, the West needs to ask what type of political system might actually foster the homegrown processes that will enable the people of these places to retake control of their lives.

Syria: Countering Sectarianism with Unifying Institutions

Identity conflicts, whether latent or active, haunt almost every Arab state and seriously impede efforts to introduce many political and economic reforms in the Middle East. As the Iraq experience has vividly shown, the region's divided polities face enormous challenges in transitioning to more accountable and open forms of government, especially because their existing regimes, even those that possess formidable security apparatuses, typically have weak, illegitimate formal institutions with little history behind them. As neither more cohesive populations nor more robust governing bodies can be suddenly summoned into existence where they do not exist, Arab countries have been unable (as well as often unwilling) to respond to Western calls to transform their political and economic systems. Yet, might there be an alternative formula for fostering fundamental institutional reform that Arab states *can* employ, a formula, moreover, that does not threaten the kind of upheaval seen in Iraq and other parts of the Arab world that have tried to embrace the Western liberal democratic model?

Syria, a small and poor country of many paradoxes, the historical heartland and in some ways the last bastion of Arab nationalism, offers a microcosm of the challenges facing attempts to modernize and democratize the states of the Middle East. Although it has long been an island of stability in a sea of states riven by religious, ethnic, and even ideological divisions, Syria's complex sociopolitical makeup makes it highly characteristic of its neighborhood—and equally susceptible to the bloody sectarianism that they suffer. Syria's past stability is thus no guarantee of its future stability. Indeed, the intercommunal harmony and political coherence that the country has enjoyed for thirty years have little to do with its people's sense of a common identity and a lot to do with the ability of former president Hafez al-Asad to orchestrate financial incentives and repressive tactics so as to co-opt key groups while suppressing dissent. But Hafez's system may be nearing the end of its useful life, threatened by a weakening economic base, a deteriorating system of social control, and an awakening of communal identities in the aftermath of the U.S. invasion of Iraq. Recent episodes of religious and ethnic discord suggest that the government's time to reform is running short. Even Bashar al-Asad, the son and successor to Hafez, has tinkered with a reform agenda since coming to power in 2000, conscious that underlying economic and social trends threaten his regime's hold on power.

But while everyone seems to agree that Syria's political and economic system needs to change, there is no such agreement on the nature and extent of that change. Although Bashar is first and foremost an authoritarian, as evidenced by his repeated crackdowns on dissidents in recent years, he seems genuinely interested in strengthening his country and believes that some reform is necessary if he is to maintain control over the long term. Bashar's political opposition, based outside the country and historically highly divided, has been able to unify in recent years behind calls for democratic change. For its part, the United States would like to see Syria reform—but not necessarily at the expense of its stability. Although Washington has often ignored Damascus because of more pressing U.S. concerns elsewhere in the Middle East, in recent years U.S. policymakers are showing an increasing awareness of Syria's pivotal role in the region. Damascus has the ability to influence events in Israel, Iraq, Lebanon, Palestine, and indeed throughout the wider Arab world. Furthermore, the United States and its Sunni allies in Saudi Arabia, Egypt, and Jordan are increasingly looking for ways to induce the Bashar government to distance itself from Iran, which is trying to form an arc of radical Shia states stretching from Teheran to Beirut and beyond.

Is it possible to introduce substantial change into Syria without endangering the country's stability? This chapter argues not only that it is, but also that it is impossible to maintain long-term stability *unless* Syria moves toward a more open and accountable system of governance. Effecting any ambitious program of reform, however, demands three things: the patience to introduce change gradually, incrementally, and cautiously, as any transformation that does not threaten stability will only happen in this manner; the flexibility and imagination to re-tailor Western-style democracy and development to fit Syrian conditions; and the readiness to work with, not against, Bashar or some other leading figures within the current regime.

A FRAGMENTED SOCIETY

Syria is a state both young and old, divided by conflicting interpretations of its past. The modern state—an artificial creation that dates only to the Anglo-French partition of the region following World War I—has inherited a unique blend of geographical, ethnic, religious, and ideological heterogeneity that complicates all efforts at constructing a cohesive whole from its disparate parts.

A brief recital of the history of what "Syria" has been illustrates the diversity of the modern state's inheritance. Syria has been the home of historic pan-Arab nationalism,[1] where the first short-lived modern Arab state was based; of Greater Syria, the ancient *bilad al-sham*[2] that encompassed the whole Levant for centuries; of some of the world's oldest cities, with long-standing ties to international trade routes but little connection to nearby rural economies; of peoples conquered and converted by the great monotheistic religions, then abandoned and left to fracture into an ungodly number of sects, each with conflicting loyalties and varying levels of observance; of a complex mosaic of almost two dozen distinct religious and ethnic groups that were traditionally so highly autonomous and self-administering that the area's Ottoman Empire government was limited to simple tax collecting. So rich and varied a history is not an unalloyed blessing. To the contrary, the state's very diversity dominates its political dynamics, limiting policy options, inhibiting risk-taking, and making any government highly defensive. Decades of stability have only partly compensated for the sectarian handicaps that hinder its capacity to develop a lasting identity.

Syria's 19 million people are divided into Sunni Arabs (65 percent), Alawis (12 percent), Christians (10 percent), Kurds (9 percent), Druze (3 percent),[3] and

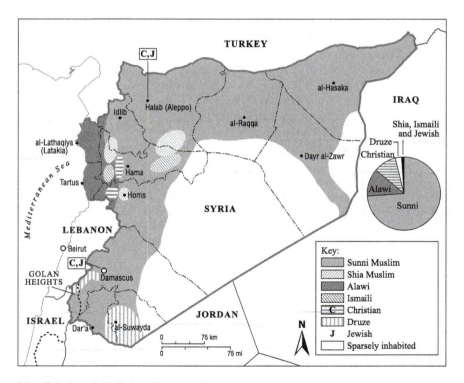

Map 7.1. Syria's Religious Demography
Source: Flynt Leverett, *Inheriting Syria: Bashar's Trial by Fire* (Washington, DC: Brookings Institution, 2005), 3.

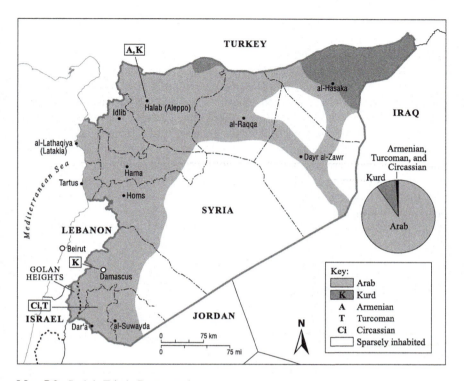

Map 7.2. Syria's Ethnic Demography
Source: Flynt Leverett, *Inheriting Syria: Bashar's Trial by Fire* (Washington, DC: Brookings Institution, 2005), 3.

small numbers of Bedouin, Ismailis, Turcomans, Circassians, and Assyrians (see Maps 7.1 and 7.2). This demographic mosaic is further complicated by divisions within many of these groups. The Christians, for example, are divided into eleven main sects, including the Greek Orthodox, Melkite, Syrian, Maronite, Chaldean, Armenian, and Catholic denominations. The Sunni Arabs range from the highly pious to the very secular and are divided between an urban elite and the rural masses that traditionally have had diverging political loyalties. Like many countries in the post 9/11 era in the Middle East, "the sharpest divide . . . is not so much religious or ethnic as it is ideological and existential, [and it] pits Muslims who want to align politics with religion against those who wish to keep these spheres apart."[4] Of all the groups, the Kurds and the Sunni Islamists are the greatest threats to the Syrian state because their political movements have the cohesion, established agendas, outside support, and sense of grievance to drive them to challenge central authority. The country's dearth of Shiites, however, makes the situation potentially less explosive than that in neighboring Lebanon and Iraq.

Conscious of their country's history as the center of a closely knit region of commanding size and stature, many Syrians have also repeatedly sought an identity in pan-Arabic, Greater Syrian, or Islamic causes, further impeding any attempt to construct a nation-state on Syrian territory. Loyalty to Arab nationalism—which continues to be an article of faith for many Syrians even though it has long since fallen out of favor with Arabs elsewhere—is enshrined in the first article of the country's constitution and explains Syria's generosity to other Arabs whenever a crisis creates a new wave of refugees. Anyone coming from an Arab state may enter the country without a visa and receive the same education and social benefits as Syrians.[5] The desire to reconstitute itself in some version of Greater Syria helps explain the country's preoccupation with Lebanon and historical unwillingness to recognize a number of the borders that separate the state from its neighbors. The weakness of Syria's sense of national identity makes at least some Syrians receptive to the self-confident call of Islamic fundamentalism, and between 1976 and 1982 the country experienced the region's first modern Islamist uprising. Fears over the ability of outsiders to stir domestic religious discontent are part of the reason for the regime's long-standing alliance with Iran, Hezbollah, and Hamas.

The Hafez al-Asad Legacy

Syria struggled mightily after its independence in 1946 to overcome its difficult heritage. It had twenty different cabinets and four separate constitutions during its first ten years. It merged with Egypt in 1958, only to withdraw from that union three and a half years later. It lost the Golan Heights to Israel in the 1967 war. In all, it suffered twenty military-backed coups or coup attempts between 1949 and 1970 and was arguably the most unstable state in the Middle East.[6] All this changed after Hafez al-Asad seized power in 1970.

Although founded on a narrow communal basis (the most sensitive intelligence and military positions were held by members of Hafez's Alawi Qalbiyya tribe),[7] the Asad regime systematically broadened its base of support by judiciously using the powers and spoils of government to co-opt important factions when possible and to crackdown on them when necessary. Hafez's three decades of relatively stable rule testify to the success of his strategy.

One of Hafez's greatest political achievements was the construction of a quasi-corporatist system that aligned the interests of most social groups with his government, effectively buying their loyalty with state employment, education, and various social benefits in a "containment system," as one Damascus analyst puts it.[8] The socialist Ba'th ideology—the party had been in power since 1963 and Hafez was one of its leaders before he took control—was well suited to this program. Its populist economic agenda provided the ideological underpinning for the establishment of a vast patronage network that promoted key non-Alawi constituencies, co-opting them into supporting the regime and making them dependent on it for their well-being. That network has gradually expanded to encompass almost all of Syrian economic life, and today close to 2 million people—whose incomes support perhaps half of the entire Syrian population—receive wages or pensions from the state.[9]

From the outset of his rule, Hafez worked hard to bring many Sunni leaders into his government, and eventually "approximately 60 percent of the cabinet ministers, the members of the People's Assembly and the deputies to the Party Congress"[10] came from the Alawite's main rival for control. He co-opted the powerful Sunni merchant class that had historically dominated the region by offering them business opportunities in partnership with the state, fostering a system of economic dependence and corruption that further cemented his control over key players.

The secular, pan-Arabist ideology espoused by the Ba'th party helped play down communal identities. Sectarian differences blurred to some degree as the socialist system flattened out the disparities and rifts that divided the country, uniformly dispersing social benefits to all groups. Although many Syrians complain of the leadership's corruption, few accuse the government of being dominated by any single group, instead seeing it as a conglomeration of the elites of most, if not all, of Syria's communal groups. Increasing intermarriage over the past generation reinforces these views; two of Hafez's sons, including Bashar, have married Sunnis.

Hafez's economic policies were accompanied by the harsh repression of dissent and the tight control of multiple "overlapping intelligence services, each responsible for tracking different elements of society and, just as important, one another."[11] According to one recent estimate, there is one secret-service member for every 153 Syrians over the age of fifteen.[12] These sticks made the carrots offered by the state's huge patronage network doubly effective. The one major challenge to Hafez's rule, which was posed by the Muslim Brotherhood, was met with brute force, culminating in the 1982 massacre of some twenty thousand and the destruction of most of the old city in Hama, the country's fourth largest urban area.

Although the Hafez model brought stability to the country, provided the population with significant social benefits, and reduced intercommunal tensions, it never fostered the type of accountable institutions and productive economic activity necessary to ensure that the model could sustain itself without outside financial support over the long term. Much like Cuba and some other socialist client states, Syria became reliant on foreign money—Soviet money in the 1970s and 1980s, Arab money at times of war with Israel and during the first Persian Gulf conflict, and Iraqi money in the early 2000s—to fund a significant portion of its national budget. Only the growth of a domestic oil industry in the 1990s gave the country some respite from its financial woes. Today, Syria's gross domestic product per capita is $3,300 a year, measured at purchasing power parity, lower than that of most other states in the region, including Egypt ($4,000), Jordan ($4,300), Morocco ($4,000), and Tunisia ($6,900), and nowhere near that of the major Gulf states.[13]

Bashar's Hesitant Reforms

Bashar al-Asad came to power in 2000—the transition from father to son marking Syria as the first Arab republican hereditary regime—at an especially unpropitious time. Not only was Bashar confronted with an international environment in flux in ways that his father could not have prepared him for, but the domestic patronage system on which his power—and the country's stability— partly depended on was in danger of breaking down.

Although the steep rise in oil prices after 2003 has since given Bashar some economic breathing space (as has the influx of hundreds of thousands of Iraqis with their bank accounts), declining production levels directly threaten the state's already weak fiscal position. The petroleum sector accounted for about one-half of government revenue and two-thirds of export earnings at the end of the 1990s,[14] but output has dropped from a peak of 600,000 barrels a day to about 400,000 barrels a day over the past decade[15] and is expected to cease altogether within the next eight to ten years.[16] Meanwhile Syria's rapidly expanding population (it grows 2.4 percent a year, one of the highest such rates in the world)[17] continues to overtax the ability of the weak private sector and overstaffed public sector to create new jobs, leaving legions of young men unemployed and disaffected. One government agency puts the unemployment rate at 17 percent, and independent estimates run as high as 30 percent.[18]

This financial breakdown is matched by a more serious systemic breakdown typical of multigenerational socialist regimes. As happened in Eastern Europe and the Soviet Union, in Syria the centralized state organs have atrophied as the ideological energy that drove the young regime has dissipated. The "aging of the system," as one Damascus-based commentator puts it, has weakened its tools of control and spread corruption throughout its parts.[19] The Ba'th party, which permeates all state bodies, has become nothing more than "a favored and convenient track to social, economic, and political advancement," with membership skyrocketing to 1.8 million, about 10 percent of the entire population.[20]

Although some significant reform measures have been implemented since Bashar came to power—increases in personal freedom and in the diversity of available goods have brightened the country's previously drab city streets—the overall process of reform has been "slow and piecemeal,"[21] as the *Economist Intelligence Unit* noted. New investment laws, a renewed emphasis on the agricultural sector, and a slew of banking, tax, and currency reforms have attracted an inflow of money from Syrian overseas bank accounts as well as from the Gulf and Iraq. But Bashar's unwillingness—or inability, for fear of the consequences—to break up trade monopolies controlled by leading families or to tackle the institutional weaknesses of the "vast, lethargic bureaucracy"[22] severely stymies a more ambitious agenda. A shortage of competent technocrats, ineffective courts, and widespread corruption continue to limit the country's attractiveness to investors, reducing the chance that the private sector will ever become large enough to act as a safety net for the unemployed and thus enable the regime to feel secure enough to restructure the state sector.

Meanwhile, despite much speculation when he first came to power that he was a closet reformer, the fragility of his power base has made Bashar extremely reluctant to introduce any substantial measure of *political* reform. Although he initially encouraged "constructive criticism, reform, and modernization,"[23] released most of the regime's political prisoners, and allowed the emergence of the country's first opposition groups in decades in what came to be known as the Damascus Spring, Bashar subsequently cracked down on these groups and has repeatedly deferred introducing even those reforms that he has proposed himself. Recent years have seen growing use of intimidation, imprisonment, and exile as tools to squelch some of the same opposition figures he had previously encouraged.

Rising Sectarian Tensions

The fraying of the Asad system, combined with the increase in communal identification spawned by the conflict in Iraq, has brought a noticeable increase in intergroup tensions within Syria, though widespread media coverage of the strife next door has also made the population wary of upsetting the delicate status quo.

The Kurds have long-standing grievances and are potentially the most explosive minority group. Deep resentment regarding the denial by the Syrian state of two to three hundred thousand Kurds of their citizenship for decades, restriction on the use of their language, and widespread bureaucratic discrimination have made the Kurds, now inspired by the freedoms won by their brethren across the border in Iraq, Syria's unhappiest minority. In March 2004, Kurdish demonstrators rioted in many cities, setting fire to cars and battling with the security police.[24] Demonstrators held banners proclaiming "Liberation," "Free Kurdistan," "Kick Out the Arab Settlers," and "Intifada Until the Occupation Ends."[25] Some forty people were killed, including members of the police. Kurdish schools and institutions were burned in retaliation and thousands of Kurds were detained by the security services. Since then, there have been reports of clashes between Christians and Muslims in the fall of 2004 and between Alawites and Ismailis in central Syria in March 2005.[26]

Although not nearly as well organized nationally as the Kurds, the growing number of Islamists—both radicals preaching intolerance and terrorists—also poses a threat to stability. In April 2004, the government foiled an attack on a former United Nations building in Damascus. At the end of the same year, a member of the political secret service was murdered in Homs for trying to clamp down on extremist religious teaching at a mosque.[27] Since mid-2005, a growing number of terrorist cells have been uncovered and broken up by security forces in cities across the country. In one operation, eight people died; in another, an explosives factory was discovered. In June 2006, the security forces fought ten militants behind the state television complex in Damascus, killing four and capturing the rest.[28] As one commentator notes, "These operations undoubtedly indicate that Islamist communities in secular-pan-Arab Syria have started to breed certain fanatical groups."[29]

Adopting a similar strategy to that employed during the Hafez years, Bashar's government has responded to both the Kurdish and Islamist threats with a mixture of compromise, co-option, and force. As well as cracking down on violence and organized activities that might pose a danger to the regime, the government has also reached out to both groups. Bashar has promised to resolve the Kurdish citizenship question. Many of those jailed in 2004 have been released. Officials have said that they will establish a Kurdish council to represent the community's interests in the future.[30] The regime increasingly emphasizes its religious credentials, now calling Islam a unifying force where previously it would have characterized secularism in that fashion. Bashar is shown in the media accompanying Islamic clerics during public functions, even during some meetings with Christian leaders. New mosques are being built throughout the country and some activities that were previously forbidden, such as soldiers praying, are now permitted. The regime's close ties with extremist groups such as Hezbollah and its indirect support for some anti-American forces in Iraq can also be partly explained as an attempt to reduce Islamist opposition to the regime.

AN ARAB GOVERNANCE MODEL

As many within Syria, including Bashar, recognize, the country needs to reform its system of governance. Any transition to a new system, however, will be fraught with dangers for the Syrian people, large numbers of whom depend on the state for their incomes, and all of whom stand to suffer if the process of institutional change spurs the dissolution of the country into competing communal factions.

Although some Western governments and analysts and some opposition figures argue for a rapid transition to a Western-style capitalist and democratic system, Syria's sectarian cleavages underscore the importance of moving gradually to a system more suited to Syria's challenges. Any rapid dismantling of the regime and its welfare and security policies are likely to disturb the carefully constructed mechanisms that hold Syrian society together, unleashing forces that could inundate any compensating measures designed to maintain the peace among competing groups.

Divided polities such as Syria and most other Arab countries face fundamentally different challenges in modernizing than did the nation-states of the West—and therefore need different standards and models to guide their evolution. Preserving security and the unity of the state, rather than promoting Western-style personal freedoms and elections, should be paramount when formulating policies to develop the country. The importance of security and unity in fissiparous polities such as Syria can be easily gleaned from the dismal record of U.S. efforts to introduce Western-style democracy in Iraq; in the absence of security and unity, efforts to introduce even the most basic economic, social, and political reforms are paralyzed. Such a change in priorities would shape how many other problems are addressed. Dismantling army, police, and intelligence units, for example, without providing adequate replacements would lead in Syria, as it has led in Iraq, to chaos. Releasing large numbers of people from government employment in the name of "reform" would create large groups of dissatisfied people who bitterly oppose change. Allowing unrestrained freedom of speech would let some religious and political leaders espouse divisive and extremist causes and encourage violence.

Measures that increase the unity and cohesion of the Syrian state can compensate to some degree for reforms that will undoubtedly open up cleavages in it. Thus, Bashar's work to clarify Syria's borders with Turkey and Jordan, by consolidating the state's sense of itself, will give him greater flexibility with some reforms. The daily tide of satellite television sweeping into Syrian living rooms (the most obvious change to the urban landscape in recent years has been the appearance of a forest of satellite dishes) has also contributed to developing the national consciousness by highlighting the differences between the country and its neighbors, revealing those neighbors' lack of interest in unifying with Syria (something the Syrian media had suggested previously), and depicting the dangers of secessionism as seen in Iraq.

If Syria had a unifying figure—such as a universally accepted monarch—there might be less chance that the country would splinter. Although considered by many in the West to be an anachronism, a royal family with some historical legitimacy to rule is one of the few proven ways of fostering robust institutions in Arab countries. Eight of the twenty-three states in the Arab League, including some of the most stable and economically dynamic, are monarchies. Unifying national figures do not, of course, always have to be kings—the example of Kamal Atatürk in Turkey springs to mind—and Hafez and Bashar have both tried to present themselves as champions of Syrian unity.

Syria, unfortunately, has no one able to play such a role. (The Asads do not command nearly the same level of respect as Atatürk does, and their membership of a minority group—the Alawis—earns them no affection from Syria's Sunni majority.) It does, however, have the opportunity to create an institution to fill much the same role: an institution composed of members accepted by—if not necessarily chosen by—the great majority of its citizens and entrusted with the task of guiding the country's economic and political transition while protecting its stability and unity. Syrians have only to look across their northern border to find an example of just such a body—Turkey's National Security Council (NSC, known within Turkey by its Turkish acronym MGK). Indeed, reformers within Syria have often pointed to the NSC as an exemplar for their own country.[31] According to one Syrian analyst, Zaid Haidar, this "non-liberal democratic model" ("non-liberal" meaning that it prioritizes societal security over personal freedom) could both keep a "tight control on sectarianism" and allow a significant increase in the "freedom of elections and speech."[32] Another analyst believes that this model is the only way to transition to a plural environment without empowering religious radicals who would threaten the unity of the state.[33]

The Turkish Example

The Turkish NSC, originally established after the 1960 coup d'état and later defined within the 1982 constitution as the entity to which the government must always "give priority consideration," was until recently a military-run organ that policed Turkish politics, schools, and the media to ensure that no separatist, overly religious, communist, or "anti-democratic" behavior would undermine national unity or divert Turkey from its secular, modernizing course. The army intervened when democracy was threatened by political violence in the 1960s and 1970s and when Islamists came close to taking power in 1997. Until recently, officers sat on the civilian education and broadcasting boards. In the 2000s, the army and NSC together forced the ruling Justice and Development Party (AK) to shed its Islamic colors and adopt an almost secular agenda. They have also repeatedly taken a strict line on any challenge to the unity of the state, most notably during the 1980s and 1990s, when the army fought and eventually stifled the Kurdish secessionist challenge.

Although many of these activities may be inimical to Westerners steeped in liberal ideas of governance, in immature polities plagued by divided populations, religious extremists, and weak national institutions, a body like Turkey's NSC can play a major role as a protective "umbrella,"[34] shielding the reform process from disruption. (The international community, it may be noted, saw the need for a somewhat similar entity in Bosnia and Herzegovina in the aftermath of the civil war there. Thus, the Office of the High Representative was created and given supervisory power over national institutions, including the power to enact laws.) In such states, the courts, corrupted by money and clannism, are unlikely to be impartial arbiters of political disputes, and local politicians are prone to use inflammatory rhetoric to garner support from their own identity group, even though their behavior weakens an already fragile state. (In the face of such problems in Bosnia, the High Representative has often opted to exercise executive power, imposing legislation and removing officials from their posts in order to ensure implementation of the Dayton accords.)

Syria should follow the Turkish example and establish its own security council, which would function much like an all-powerful judicial body, carefully considering all pertinent issues before deciding what measures are necessary to preserve the unity and secular nature of the state. Membership of this Syrian National Security Council (SNSC) should be determined through a process of extended negotiation and compromise that ensures that each of the country's five major communal groups is represented. Ideally, those representatives would be judges or other people with significant legal experience; in practice, however, the SNSC's membership would probably have to be composed of the most powerful leaders of each community, who alone would have the legitimacy and authority to ensure that the SNSC's decisions were implemented and accepted by all sides. Including the leaders of Syria's military and intelligence units in the SNSC's deliberations and ensuring that these units' leadership is also representative (eventually at least) of the country's diverse population would help to preserve national unity, especially when SNSC-decreed reforms provoked fierce opposition from one or more groups.

Departing from the example of the Turkish NSC, which has never formally offered guidelines as to what it considers acceptable behavior, the SNSC should articulate a clear set of principles regarding the conduct of political parties, the media, schools, and religious bodies. It could, for example, insist that no political party be created on an ethnic or religious basis or openly advocate divisive policies. It could order the arrest of any religious figure who preaches hatred, violence, or even intolerance. It could fine or order the closure of any school that strays from the permitted curriculum and any television station that broadcasts proscribed views. It could make abundantly clear that any behavior that threatened the secular nature of the state would be swiftly halted.

Promoting national unity in this way would not mean denying individual communal groups the freedom to teach in their own language, celebrate holidays in their own style, or pray in their own form. The SNSC could allow groups such as the Kurds and the various Christian denominations far more cultural and educational freedom than the Turkish NSC has allowed minorities. (The Kurds, the only non-Arab group, might also be offered a significant degree of self-government.) Such allowances would help to win widespread acceptance of the SNSC and greater support for—or at least less opposition to—any steps it might take.

As this system became embedded in Syrian society, many previously unimaginable reforms—including, in time, substantial political change—would become more amenable to the elite in Damascus, whose concerns regarding such reforms could be addressed within the structure of the SNSC. The SNSC would actually intervene only occasionally, leaving elected officials to manage almost all the affairs of government (as they do in Turkey, where the Turkish NSC and army interest themselves only in a very narrow range of issues). In fact, once it established itself and gained a reputation for acting forcefully, the mere threat of action by the SNSC would do much to deter any disruptive behavior. As the state became more cohesive (that is, less sectarian) and its institutions more robust, the SNSC would become—like Turkey's NSC—increasingly irrelevant, until eventually it could be dissolved.

The main dangers of this system are that the SNSC would subvert a democratically elected government or become entirely unaccountable and profoundly corrupt. The best way to minimize these possibilities is by establishing and publicizing clear guidelines as to its mandate and to make clear that its members are no less subject to the rule of law than any other government officials. Engaging a larger group of leaders—possibly through a national conference or through the existing parliament—in the formulation of these guidelines would contribute to their wide acceptance.

The existence of the SNSC would remove one of the chief obstacles to introducing a more accountable form of government in Syria—fear that the country will fall victim to the kind of ethnic and religious strife that has plagued countries such as Algeria, Lebanon, Iraq, and Nigeria. With the institutionalization of intergroup cooperation serving as the very bedrock of the state, national leaders could initiate reforms confident that sectarian strife would not endanger the country's stability or widen divisions within society. Growing institutional stability would encourage a more intrepid approach by the authorities, leading to a bolder economic reform agenda and greater impetus for political change. In time, this would lead to free elections at both the local and the national level, a freer press, and greater administrative and judicial reforms as pressure mounts for better governance at all levels. While change might be gradual at first, it would gain momentum as both elites and the general population acquire a greater stake in—and a greater comfort level with—an increasingly open system.

Beyond political reform, any modernization of Syria would also have to include significant restructuring of its decrepit state bureaucracy and state-run companies and the introduction of a slew of reforms designed to animate a potentially vibrant private sector. However, unlike many ex-Communist states in Central and Eastern Europe, which suffered from similar economic ailments but where the unity of the state was never in question, drastic reform measures in Syria could lead to factionalism that threaten its very existence. Hence, popular support for the modernization program would depend upon the state continuing to ensure that all citizens continued to enjoy a decent standard of living. Measures to encourage the equitable distribution of the benefits generated by new investment would help garner wider support for the necessary reforms and limit the scope for intercommunal resentment.

Evolution from Within?

Many Western analysts and opposition figures argue that the kinds of changes proposed here can occur only if the Asad regime is completely overthrown. It is an argument especially likely to receive a favorable hearing in Washington. As *Time* reported in December 2006, "the Bush Administration has been quietly nurturing individuals and parties opposed to the Syrian government in an effort to undermine the regime of President Bashar Assad."[35] The Iraq example, however, shows the dangers of creating a power vacuum in a country as divided as Syria.

Although many people find the idea of cooperating with the regime in Damascus distasteful, Western hopes of seeing Syria reform are more likely to be realized if the West can convince the existing regime or a substantial part of it to undertake that reform itself. If the security forces and a significant proportion of the elite were to support rather than oppose the changes, then the stabilizing elements of the Ba'ath regime—such as its social welfare programs and strong security apparatuses—could be used as a basis of a new, transition-minded government.

How such a transformation takes place will matter almost as much as what kind of transformation it is. The best scenario would see a gradual process whereby the existing, interlocking relationships between the elites of Syria's identity groups evolve through negotiations that generate a broad consensus on how the country can introduce a more pluralistic and accountable system of government. The Asad regime, partly out of weakness, actually has encouraged an environment in which such cooperation and compromise have taken place for many years. If Bashar or a successor regime were to formalize these relationships by bringing them within the framework of an SNSC while avoiding actions likely to promote interelite friction (such as favoring one group over another), many of the troubles experienced by transitioning regimes elsewhere in the region might be avoided. In contrast, the hasty introduction in Syria of a completely open democratic system in which elites jockey through the media for position and compete for a handful of top government jobs—the system that is practiced in Lebanon and, since the U.S. invasion, in Iraq—would only undermine existing relationships and inflame animosities, both among the elites and among the groups they represent.

THE ROLE OF THE WEST

The U.S. experience in Iraq demonstrates the importance of trying to co-opt all or part of an existing regime when promoting change in a fractured Middle Eastern state rather than trying to wipe the slate clean. In the case of Syria, outsiders are more likely to foster constructive change if they encourage either Bashar himself or some other significant element within the regime to introduce democratic changes in ways that do not threaten most of Syria's elite. The SNSC format is ideally suited to this as it offers representatives of the elite a special role during the extended process of transition, thereby reassuring them that they will continue to enjoy at least some measure of power and influence for the foreseeable future.

What, though, are the chances that the current regime will support reform rather than doggedly oppose it? Although Bashar has repeatedly promised to introduce substantial economic and political reforms, he seems to favor an Egyptian model of instituting only limited reforms that leave the economy still shackled by red tape and prey to the government's favorite monopolists and the political system still dominated by the ruling party and the president's cronies, with a toothless opposition in parliament acting purely as window dressing.[36] Therefore, while the West should offer Bashar substantial incentives to launch a serious campaign of reform, it should also proclaim its willingness to offer the same deal to any regime that comes to power in Damascus, irrespective of the new regime's previous level of involvement with the Asad regime.

The West, and especially the United States, has some useful economic, financial, and technical tools at its disposal to convince whatever government rules in Damascus to embrace a comprehensive program of political and economic reform.[37] For example, Washington, in cooperation with the European Union (EU), could offer Syria technical assistance in introducing institutional reforms and access to foreign markets and aid in return for Syria's adherence to a strict timetable of progress. Even Bashar recognized that Syria needs Western carrots to buy off domestic resistance to change, and he sought to use "international economic agreements—particularly an association agreement with the EU—as a lever for impelling greater transparency and spurring policy reform."[38]

In trading assistance for reform, the West should first return to this unapproved (due to worsening relations over Lebanon) association agreement, which offered free trade and help in "defining and starting the implementation of an economic modernization strategy" and "formulating and implementing an institutional modernization strategy and action plan" in return for a specific set of reforms.[39] As soon as these are introduced, the West should ask Damascus to introduce the SNSC and a timeline for some preliminary moves toward a more open political and more effective judicial system, so as to lay a firmer base for the gradual transformation of the state. As certain milestones were reached, the West could also include membership in the World Trade Organization (Syria applied for membership in 2001) as part of a broader package of incentives in return for more reform. Opening up the country economically would force domestic companies to compete internationally, thus encouraging Syrian businessmen to force the pace of administrative and judicial change to improve their own competitiveness. Similarly, Western financial and technical assistance in the formation of more NGOs and a more robust opposition would help push change from below. Including a significant cache of cash in any proposed package of help for the government would help overcome resistance within what will continue to be a very corrupt administration no matter who is in charge. These steps would be but a start on the long path to genuine political reform, but as governing bodies became more accountable and more Syrians gained direct experience with modern systems of governance, outsiders could steadily raise the bar on what they expected of the regime.

FREEDOM VERSUS DEMOCRACY

Western emphasis on freedom—of speech, of assembly, and of expressing one's religious and ethnic identity—can be counterproductive in states lacking the cohesion common in the more developed, prosperous, and stable regimes typically found in the West. In countries such as Syria, Nigeria, and Bolivia that are divided among many ethnic and religious groups and have fragile national institutions, unconstrained freedoms can undermine the modernization process, weakening the unity of the state and causing sectarian frictions or even bloodshed as evidenced by Lebanon's long civil war and by the current conflict in Iraq.[40]

Nurturing a national identity where none exists is essential to any process of democratization and institutional reform. Where groups are more loyal to their subnational—or transnational—communal identities, they are likely to corrupt or emasculate the independence of national governing bodies such as courts and state ministries and to use election campaigns to stir up intercommunal tensions in ways that endanger the unity of the state. The poisonous environment that often results from such competing loyalties hobbles any attempt to upgrade the state's governing bodies, limiting development prospects and threatening to trap the country in a vicious cycle of sectarian competition for control of the state and its resources.

In such countries, enduring democracy can be constructed only in a gradual and piecemeal fashion. Limiting the kinds of freedoms that are introduced at any one time and establishing an NSC to oversee the process of reform may offend the sensibilities of democratic purists, but there may be no other way to foster change—including the embrace of democratic norms—in an environment where institutions are weak and not deeply rooted. The protective umbrella an NSC provides can help preserve enough unity in a deeply divided state to allow the reform process to advance. Other steps that promote cohesion—everything from encouraging patriotic songs and textbooks to building a better highway system to introducing national service—can contribute to this effort to build unity from diversity without threatening traditional subnational group identities and cultures.

Although corrupt and repressive regimes such as the Asad government may be unpleasant to work with, the West needs to accept that working with some part of such an administration may be the only way to foster change without provoking the kind of chaos that has engulfed Iraq and that constantly threatens to erupt in Lebanon. Seeking reform from within the regime may be far more productive than seeking to overthrow it when, as in Syria, the regime is so closely enmeshed within society.

Somaliland: Reconnecting State and Society

The sorry state of Somalia has been regularly in the headlines in recent years, with reports chronicling the rise to power in Mogadishu of Islamic extremists, their subsequent ejection by Ethiopian troops, and the repeated failures of peace conferences to reconcile the country's many factions. As media across the world also reported, the fighting and chaos in late 2006 and early 2007 even prompted U.S. military intervention.

The attention paid to the unfolding drama in the south of Somalia is perfectly understandable, but both the media and the U.S. government are missing an equally important story in the north, where a remarkable political transformation is under way. U.S. inattention to this northern success story is ironic given that Washington has made democratization the centerpiece of its efforts to combat extremism in the Muslim world and promote better governance in developing countries.

The Republic of Somaliland, the secessionist northwestern territory of Somalia, has a far better democratic track record than any of its neighbors on the Horn of Africa and the Arabian Peninsula despite—or, perhaps, because of—a lack of assistance from the international community.[1] Abutting the Gulf of Aden just south of the Red Sea, across the water from Yemen and Saudi Arabia, and bordered by Ethiopia and the rest of Somalia, this strategically important territory is not even recognized by the international community but is arguably the healthiest democracy between Israel and Tanzania. In contrast to the continuing chaos and threat from extremists in much of the rest of Somalia and to the authoritarian governments that surround it elsewhere, Somaliland has held three consecutive elections that met international standards, has a parliament controlled by opposition parties, and has a vibrant economy dominated by the private sector.

Somaliland has achieved these successes by constructing a set of governing bodies rooted in traditional Somali concepts of democracy and governance. In contrast to most postcolonial states in Africa and the Middle East, Somaliland has a chance to administer itself using customary norms, values, and relationships. Far too many poor states are held back by administrative apparatuses and political systems built separately from the societies they are meant to serve, thus rendering those systems illegitimate, ripe for exploitation, and a major hindrance to democratization and development. Although Somaliland's fledgling state institutions are still fragile and have many weaknesses, if properly nourished they can become robust champions of a governance system that is actually reflective of and integrated with the society it is meant to represent—giving the country a far greater chance to develop in the years ahead.

Somaliland's importance to U.S. interests goes beyond its ability to showcase the benefits of democracy and free markets to its neighbors. The Horn of Africa is a crucial front in the "global war on terrorism." The Islamic Courts Union (ICU), which ruled much of Somalia's south until the Ethiopian invasion in December 2006, is widely regarded as a Somali version of the Taliban, led by and linked to a number of known international terrorists.[2] U.S. air strikes in 2007 sought to kill al Qaeda operatives wanted for a plethora of attacks across the region from Kenya to Yemen, including the deadly 1998 bombings on U.S. embassies in Kenya and Tanzania that killed over 250 people. The State Department's *Country Report on Terrorism 2005* claims that terrorist activities in Somalia are "threatening the security of the whole region."

Given all that is at stake throughout the Horn, the United States and its allies have excellent reasons to help consolidate Somaliland's liberal, secular democracy. The rationale for lending a hand is, indeed, even stronger because the nature of Somaliland's democratization process—a societal-led, bottom-up transformation—may be remarkably well suited to many postcolonial societies in the Middle East and Africa. By acting now to bolster Somaliland's security and economic prospects and to rally support among states, both within Africa and beyond, for recognition of Somaliland as an independent sovereign state the West could make Somaliland an exemplar to Muslims throughout the region of the benefits that accountable government can bring.

"THE VERY DEFINITION OF A FAILED STATE"

Somalia represents one of the greatest mismatches between conventional state structures and indigenous institutions among postcolonial countries in Africa. Although a shared ethnicity, culture, language, and religion might seem to be an excellent basis for a cohesive polity, in reality the Somali people are divided by clan affiliations, the single most important component of their identity. Traditional, customary methods of governance are not well suited to the centralized bureaucratic governing structures that colonizers and Westernized elites have repeatedly attempted to impose on the country. Those attempts have brought only chaos and conflict, creating what the Council on Foreign Relations has characterized as "the very definition of a failed state."[3]

The Somali People

Anthropologists typically describe traditional Somali society as stateless, characterized by a wide dispersion of power among clans and subclans. Their long history as pastoral nomads has made the Somali people fiercely independent but also well accustomed to a variety of democratic practices.

The Somali population (some 13 to 14 million people, including those now living in neighboring states) is divided into six major clans—Daarood, Haawiye, Isaaq, Dir, Digil, and Raxanweyn (or Mirifle)—and a number of minority groups (see Map 8.1). Each of the clans consists of subclans that combine or ally with one another in a fluid process of "constant decomposition and recomposition."[4] These "clan-states" typically work through a diffuse and decentralized decision-making process that culminates in a community meeting open to all males—a *shir*—at which major economic, political, and social policies are determined. These societal institutions, and the customary law (*xeer*) that governs behavior within the community, are deeply ingrained within the population's worldview and function independently of modern state structures. Although Islam plays a major role in the lives of a socially conservative people, it is subordinate or complementary to clannism in shaping their outlook.

Starting in the 1880s, European colonialism divided the Somali population among five different political entities: the British Somaliland Protectorate (today's Somaliland), Italian Somalia (the rest of Somalia), French Somaliland (now Djibouti), the Ogaden region of Ethiopia, and Kenya's Northern Frontier District. This launched a process whereby outsiders and Westernized elites attempted to create a new, modern system of government that completely ignored traditional societal norms and relationships. In trying to marginalize long-established patterns, these modernizing efforts ended up permanently disconnecting the state from the society that should have been its foundation.

The new sources of patronage and power generated by the European centralized state structures naturally affected clan behavior. Traditionally, groups had competed *sporadically* for land, water, and grazing rights; a dispute could be settled by informal negotiations, by an arranged marriage, or even by one group opting to migrate over a relatively unpopulated terrain to new pastures elsewhere. Once the centralized government entered the scene, competition became *permanent*, with groups vying not only for land, water, and grazing rights—now controlled by the government—but also for the state's financial and administrative resources. The resulting frictions permanently poisoned interclan relations while debilitating the government's ability to rule effectively.

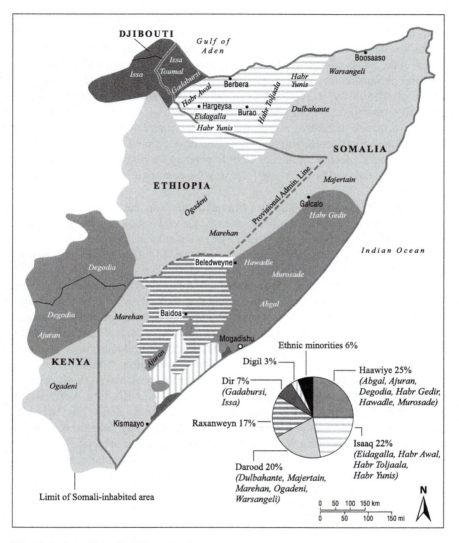

Map 8.1. Somalia's Clan Demography
Source: Central Intelligence Agency.

The Collapse of the Centralized Model

The state of Somalia was formed when the Italian and British colonies united after gaining independence in 1960. Initial euphoria rapidly turned to disillusionment as evidence of state dysfunction mounted. Corruption worsened, electoral politics became increasingly chaotic, and state programs delivered little public benefit. Clannism infected politics and administrative organs as each group sought to maximize its spoils from the system.

This high level of disenchantment led many to welcome Siyad Barre's socialist coup in 1969. However, after introducing some popular reforms in the areas of education, health, and the status of women, Barre's regime suffered a humiliating defeat at the hands of Ethiopia in the Ogaden war in 1977–1978 and encountered growing dissatisfaction with one-party rule. He eventually was forced to depend on the clannish loyalties of members of the Daarood subclans connected to him by birth or marriage; all other groups were pushed out. Barre increasingly used repressive tactics to control a state more or less completely divorced from the surrounding society, eventually depending on development assistance that made up a stunning 57 percent of annual GNP to prop up his highly centralized state.[5] The regime finally collapsed in 1991, leaving the country in the hands of warlords and militias.

In the 1990s, disaffected clans began to carve up the country. The Haari grouping (a subset of the Daarood) in the east created a semi-autonomous region called Puntland; a subset of the Raxanweyn established an autonomous region in the southwest called Jubaland; and the Isaaq clan led efforts in the northeast to build a separate state, Somaliland (see Map 8.2).

Since the fall of Barre, the international community has launched at least fourteen peace initiatives, yet Somalia remains divided, without a functioning central government, the longest-running example of state failure in the postcolonial period. If anything, the authority and cash that outsiders have repeatedly tried to give some central body have distorted traditional relationships—that had maintained a robust society for centuries—and helped entrench the warlords and militias. An initiative launched in 2002 by the Intergovernmental Authority on Development (IGAD is a seven-country regional organization for East Africa based in Djibouti) produced a Transitional Federal Government (TFG). The TFG had never controlled more than one small area around one city near the Ethiopian border before the Ethiopian forces invaded but was nonetheless recognized by the international community as Somalia's legitimate government. Indeed, it gained much of its legitimacy from this international support and the financial aid it received as a result, not from any effort on its own part to gain backing from beyond a narrow clique made up of members of the Daarood and some of its allies.

The ICU, which won control of large areas of southern Somalia in 2006, naturally also had strong clan linkages, with the Hawiye group closely supporting it, partly because the Hawiye saw it as a counterweight to the Daarood-dominated TFG. The ICU was able to expand so rapidly both because of its ability to impose order in a chaotic environment—something much appreciated by a population weary of years of strife—and because it was able to co-opt various subclans with significant stakes in local administration. Even though the regime has dispersed, its Islamist leaders have vowed to fight on with an Iraqi-style guerrilla campaign. Since Ethiopian forces occupied the country, they have been plagued by a series of suicide attacks and cell phone-detonated bombs, making Mogadishu so dangerous as to deter outsiders from sending peacekeepers. Given that the current anarchic

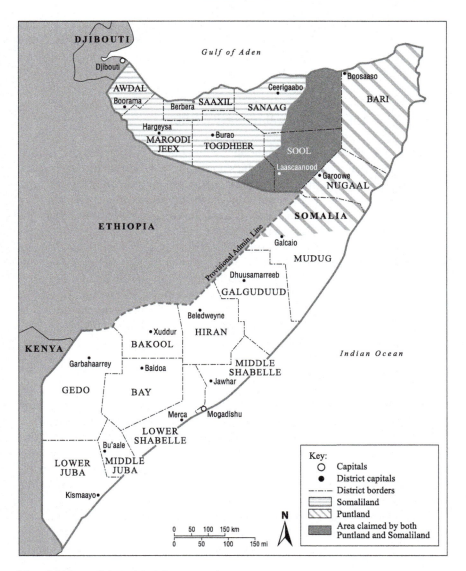

Map 8.2. Somalia's Political Fragmentation
Source: International Crisis Group.

situation is similar to the environment in which the ICU first came to prominence, the prospects for the ICU are by no means bleak.

*   *   *

It is the Somali people who have paid the highest price for these repeated failures at state formation. Somalis are among the poorest and hungriest people in the world;

they have the lowest Human Development Index and the lowest nutrition rates. Average life expectancy is only forty-one to forty-three years, and the mortality rate for children under five exceeds 25 percent. The adult literacy rate may be lower than 20 percent in some parts of the state.[6]

SOMALILAND: THE RISE OF AN ALTERNATIVE MODEL

While the south has been caught up in the cauldron of competing factions, a different model has emerged in Somalia's northeast, in the territory of the original British Somaliland Protectorate. Whereas attempts to build stable state structures in Mogadishu have mostly followed a top-down approach, with outsiders playing a leading role, Somaliland has constructed a functioning government from the bottom up on its own with little outside assistance.

Somaliland was a separate entity under British rule from 1884 to 1960 and a sovereign state for just five days in 1960 before unifying with the former UN Trust Territory of Somalia (administered by Italy) to form Somalia. Thirty-one years later, in 1991, Somaliland declared its independence. The new state consists of six of Somalia's eighteen regions, encompassing slightly more than one-fifth of Somali territory and between one-quarter and one-third of its population.[7]

An Unhappy Marriage

From the formation of Somalia in 1960, northerners were dissatisfied with their lot. Subsumed into the larger, southern-dominated state structures, in which unfamiliar Italian laws and colonial-era elites predominated, they quickly felt like a people apart. When the new administration discriminated against them in its selection of top ministers and army personnel and in its distribution of the state's resources, the northerners' sense of being separate from and mistreated by the south grew and fed upon itself.

Serious challenges to the union began to emerge when the Barre regime lost popular support in the late 1970s. No fewer than ten resistance movements sprang up across the country (each of which was naturally affiliated with its own clan or alliance of subclans), most notably the Somali National Movement (SNM), a group formed in 1981 and closely affiliated with the Isaaq clan that makes up some 70 percent of Somaliland's population.[8] When the SNM attacked the major northern cities in 1988, a full-scale civil war erupted. The government reacted harshly: aircraft taking off from Hargeysa's own airport bombed the city, destroying 90 percent of it. Burao, Somaliland's second largest city, was also reduced to rubble. An estimated 50,000 people were killed and some 1 million made refugees. The brutality of the onslaught convinced northerners that they should find their own solution to the challenge of state building. As one observer has commented, the "sheer brutality of the Mogadishu's attacks during the late 1980s has been burned into the collective memory and has furthered the psychological gulf between north and south."[9]

Nation Building

Somaliland has profited from a unity conferred by its comparatively homogenous population, modest disparities in terms of personal wealth, the existence of a common foe in the south, and a lack of outside interference that might have undermined the accountability that has been forced on its leaders.[10] This cohesiveness—a sharp contrast both with Somalia as a whole and with most other states in Africa—has combined with the enduring strength of traditional institutions of self-governance to mold a unique form of democracy.

From the beginning of Somaliland's independence movement, traditional democratic methods have predominated in efforts to create governing organs. The SNM was notable for its internal democratic practices, holding six or seven elections between 1981 and 1990, changing its leadership through democratic means no fewer than five times in the nine years it fought the Barre regime. A Council of Elders established during this time to resolve disputes and distribute food among the refugees quickly gained substantial legitimacy and, when the war ended, came to play a key role in promoting a process of representative decision making. Within two years of its victory, the SNM turned power over to a civilian administration.

From the time independence was declared, a wide-ranging and inclusive process of national dialogue sought to construct a consensus on the system of political representation that should govern Somaliland. In all, thirty-three "clan peace conferences" took place between 1991 and 1996. Although this consultative process was interrupted twice—by conflicts within the SNM in 1991–1992 and between clans in 1994–1996—continued dialogue eventually yielded a broad consensus and a widely accepted, legitimate government. Stable and increasingly accountable government has delivered security and growing prosperity since 1996.

Of the many clan conferences, all financed domestically by local businesspeople and community leaders, the 1993 Borama *shir beeleed* (Clan Conference) was the most important, producing a Peace Charter—based on the traditional law of social conduct between clans—that established the basis for law and order and a National Charter that defined the political structures of government. The Borama gathering, attended by some five hundred elders, religious leaders, politicians, civil servants, intellectuals, and businesspeople, established the pattern of institutionalizing clans and their elders into formal governing bodies, something that is now referred to as the *beel* (clan or community) system of governance. This "dynamic hybrid of Western form and traditional substance"[11] formalized the role of elders in an upper house of elders (known as the Guurti) responsible for security and managing internal conflicts, and allocated seats in the legislature based on clan numbers. A conference in 1996–1997, after the war, increased the number of seats available to non-Isaaq clans. The 2001 constitution, approved by an overwhelming majority of the population in a national plebiscite, locked in the consensus-oriented decision-making process by limiting the number of political parties to three and requiring them to have significant support in each of Somaliland's six regions. Clans such as the Dulbahante, Warsangeli, and Gadabursi, which have traditionally had good relations with the dominant Isaaq, have supported independence and been involved in the conciliation, state building, and governing process from the beginning, though not the Harti living in Sool and eastern Sanaag near the border with Puntland.

Mohamed Haji Ibrahim Egal, who had been Somalia's prime minister before the 1969 coup and who became Somaliland's president in 1993, provided inspired leadership during the breakaway state's formative years. His government secured access from the local subclan to the revenues of Berbera port, rebuilt government buildings, reopened the central bank with a new currency (the Somaliland shilling), created a new civil service agency, integrated the militia into a national army, and removed roadblocks and informal "taxes" from major roads.

This process of bottom-up state building using traditional forms, now reinforced by three successful democratic elections, has yielded a system with a surprisingly high level of public ownership and fostered a strong national identity and deep sense of pride in the country. It has produced "an unprecedented degree of interconnectedness between the state and society ... in stark contrast to the past when previous regimes received enormous infusions of external assistance without which they could not survive, and as a result became completely divorced from the economic foundations of their own society."[12]

Today, Somaliland has many of the trappings of modern statehood: its own currency, flag, army, vehicle license plates, government ministers, and even airline, Daallo Airlines.

The success of its bottom-up state-building process is evident in the high sense of security felt by its people and the growing buoyancy of its economy. Hundreds of thousands of refugees and internally displaced people have returned home and tens of thousands of landmines have been removed and destroyed. Hargeysa has been completely rebuilt and is now larger than when it was bombed in the late 1980s. Its population has grown from ten thousand to over half a million since independence, and it attracts migrants from Ethiopia and southern Somalia who value its peacefulness and economic vitality. Markets throughout Somaliland are filled with products from around the world; telephone charges are among the cheapest in Africa; and the private sector, not the government, provides electricity, water, education, and health care. Three new universities have been built, privately funded hospitals and schools proliferate, and a number of NGOs are working to improve administrative capacity. Members of the Somali diaspora, more than one hundred thousand of whom live in the United States and Europe, support these efforts through their financial contributions—estimated at $500 million annually[13]—extensive international networks, and knowledge about how a modern society operates.

Successive Elections

Although many of its governing structures are not fully developed and many of its politicians, bureaucrats, and judges are inexperienced, Somaliland has passed a number of democratic milestones that few other states in Africa and the Middle East have reached. Altogether, the country has successfully managed the May 2001 referendum, the December 2002 local elections, the 2003 presidential campaign, and the September 2005 legislative poll. The 2005 House of Representatives elections saw 246 candidates contest 86 seats in an undertaking that involved 982 polling stations, 1,500 ballot boxes, 1.3 million ballot papers, 6,000 party agents, 3,000 police, and 700 domestic observers and 76 foreign observers. The latter "were fairly unanimous in their views that [the elections] were, on the whole, the freest and most transparent democratic exercises ever staged in the Horn of Africa."[14]

Somaliland's democracy has repeatedly surprised outsiders with its robustness. When, in May 2002, President Egal died abroad, power was smoothly passed to Vice President Dahir Rayale Kahin, even though Rayale is from the small Gadabursi clan and had served the Barre regime as a security officer in its fight with the Isaaq. The April 2003 presidential poll was possibly the closest ever fought in Africa, with Rayale winning by only the slimmest of margins—just eighty votes out of almost half a million ballots—and the opposition eventually peacefully accepting the results after all its judicial appeals were struck down.

The country, of course, suffers from many of the maladies common to all poor, underdeveloped states: the rule of law and civil society are both weak; corruption is endemic; nepotism and clannism strongly influence official appointments; the executive branch towers over the other branches of government; the legislature lacks the power to initiate legislation; the judiciary is underfunded and undertrained and is not an effective check on the administration; and a dearth of competent officials makes it almost impossible to expand the mandates of ministries and local administrations. As in many countries—underdeveloped and developed alike— the government has shown itself tempted to sacrifice civil liberties in the name of security. Somaliland's print media is relatively free and criticizes the government, but a weekly magazine that dared to discuss the idea of Somaliland reuniting with Somalia was banned, and the chairman of Haatuf Media Network and two of his journalists were arrested in early 2007 for writing about presidential corruption. The government has at times dealt harshly with anyone advocating unity with the rest of Somalia or a change in the current constitutional arrangement. In the summer of 2007, it jailed three politicians who tried to establish a new, fourth political party.

The *beel* system of government, though responsible for bringing peace and democracy to Somaliland, does bring with it some significant limits on the development of a fully representative and effective democracy. Elders hold a disproportionate amount of power, something modernizers have criticized as reactionary. People with powerful lineages have advantages in applying for government posts, and clannism has hobbled efforts to make the civil service more meritocratic. Compromises intended to ensure that the smaller clans are fully included in the system have given them a disproportionately high number of representatives in the parliament. Although they have the same rights to vote and run as candidates as men, the limited number of women elected to municipal councils and parliament is an outgrowth of their exclusion from traditional governing structures.

Yet, despite these problems, Somaliland has achieved much with very little outside assistance. In fact, the dearth of external involvement has been in many ways a blessing, for it has kept foreign interference to a minimum while spurring self-reliance. The lack of outside interference "has given Somalilanders the opportunity to craft a system of government rooted in the local culture and values that is appropriate to their needs, . . . [which] has increasingly served to forge a separate Somaliland identity, a feeling of self-reliance and a belief that Somaliland is becoming a reality."[15]

THE IMPORTANCE OF INTERNATIONAL RECOGNITION

Notwithstanding Somaliland's success at building a stable, democratic state in a region usually characterized by instability and authoritarianism, the international community continues to refuse to recognize Somaliland as a state. Although this lack of recognition did not significantly hamper Somaliland in its formative years—indeed, as just mentioned, meager external involvement actually served Somaliland well in its early years—its hopes of consolidating and expanding the political and economic gains it has made depend now on winning international acceptance as a sovereign state so as to enjoy the rights and benefits such status confers.

Somaliland's isolation hurts the state in a wide range of areas: governing organs cannot receive bilateral technical assistance from other countries; the World Bank, the International Monetary Fund, the African Development Bank, and bilateral development agencies cannot offer it loans and financial aid; banks and insurance companies will not set up branches within the country; local firms cannot directly import goods because they are unable to open letters of credit without the banks, driving up the costs of products for the whole population; international investors avoid the state because of the lack of insurance and other investment protections, limiting job opportunities for everyone. Many professionals among the diaspora—whose contributions could invigorate Somaliland's legal, accounting, health, and educational systems—are reluctant to return because of the country's uncertain legal status. The threat of continued unrest and even factional fighting or an increase in terrorist activities in the south will continue to hamper Somaliland's development as long as its future is held hostage to events in Somalia.

A STRONG CASE FOR RECOGNITION

The unwillingness of any country to recognize Somaliland has more to do with political self-interest than with a principled abhorrence of secessionism. Other secessionist entities *have* won recognition in recent years, and Somaliland can make a strong case for recognition on a wide variety of grounds: legal, historical, political, and practical.

Its legal and historical case rests on its separate status during the colonial period and its existence, albeit brief, as an independent country in 1960. Except for a short period during World War II, Somaliland was a British territory for over seven decades, unconnected to the rest of what became Somalia. It had clearly demarcated borders that were recognized by the international community—and that could easily be used today (indeed, while Ethiopia and Somalia dispute their common border, Ethiopia and Somaliland have no dispute as to their common boundary). Then, in 1960, Somaliland existed as an independent country for five days, gaining the recognition of thirty-five states, signing a number of bilateral agreements with the United Kingdom, and receiving a congratulatory message from the U.S. Secretary of State.[16] The Somaliland authorities argue today that they are dissolving an unsuccessful marriage rather than seeking secession, and that therefore their case is analogous to the breakup of Sénégambia (Senegal and Gambia) and the United Arab Republic (Syria and Egypt). They also draw parallels with Eritrea, their neighbor to the north, which was originally a colony separate from Ethiopia and which gained its de jure independence in 1993.

The political case rests on widespread dissatisfaction with and even rejection of the union from its inception in 1960, the discrimination northerners faced within the union, the brutality of the Mogadishu government's conduct in the civil war in the 1980s, and the repeated expression by the people of Somaliland of their desire to live independently of Somalia. The May 2001 constitutional referendum was effectively a plebiscite on independence. Although opponents in Sool and eastern Sanaag refused to participate, 97 percent of those who did vote approved the document in a ballot deemed to have been "conducted fairly, freely, and openly . . . and in accordance with internationally accepted standards."[17]

Somaliland actually—and ironically—does a far better job than Somalia of meeting the criteria of the 1933 Montevideo Convention on the Rights and Duties of States, which include having a permanent population, defined territory, a functioning government, and the capacity to enter into relations with other states. Somalia has not come close to having a functioning administration able to assert its control over a significant part of the country's territory since 1991.

Although de jure recognition remains elusive, Somaliland has achieved de facto recognition in a number of ways. In December 2007, the U.S. State Department reported that "the United States continues to engage with the administration in Somaliland on a range of issues, most directly Somaliland's continued progress towards democratization and economic development. In FY 2007, the United States provided a total of $1 million . . . to support training for parliamentarians and other key programs."[18] The European Union has contributed financially and technically to the running of elections for the leadership of the country; the British government has paid for international observers to monitor these. The United

Nations and many international aid agencies operate programs throughout Somaliland's territory and deal with its government. Ethiopia, Egypt, Kenya, Yemen, Italy, France, the United States, and the United Kingdom have all welcomed official delegations from Somaliland and in some cases accorded its leaders the same status as leaders of sovereign territories. Ethiopia, the state that has worked most closely with Somaliland, has a quasi-embassy in Hargeysa with a staff of twelve.[19] Ethiopia and Djibouti accept Somaliland passports. All of this suggests a "creeping informal and pragmatic acceptance of Somaliland as a political reality."[20]

The biggest internal challenge to the state's legitimacy stems from problems it has had gaining the loyalty of two subclans of the Harti grouping that dominates neighboring Puntland, which supports a unified Somalia. Government administration in the districts where these subclans live remains weak or nonexistent. Although this opposition is too small to derail the independence drive (and few new states have no opponents), the Somaliland authorities would probably strengthen their case for recognition by offering a handful of central government positions to the leaders of these groups and making a greater effort to redress whatever inequities they perceive in the social services they receive.

* * *

Given its strong case, why has no country recognized Somaliland? The major argument heard against secession is that it will set a precedent in a region where weakly legitimate states struggle to maintain their unity. Some fear that international recognition of Somaliland will cause the balkanization of Somalia itself. Others mention the possibility that any change in the status quo will derail peace efforts in the south or may ignite conflict between the two states, as has happened in the case of Ethiopia and Eritrea. However, Somaliland's history as a separate state with recognized boundaries gives it a status that few other territories (and no other territories within Somalia) can claim, reducing the chances that others could use its independence as a precedent. Somaliland's refusal to participate in any post-1991 peace conference means that its permanent withdrawal should not affect the dynamics of what has turned into a prolonged and unsuccessful venture. In fact, the rise of the ICU made some security analysts argue before the Ethiopian invasion that only Somaliland's independence could prevent a violent conflict between the two sides.[21]

The African Union (AU) reviewed many of these issues during a fact-finding mission in 2005 and concluded that Somaliland's case was "unique and self-justified in African political history" and that "the case should not be linked to the notion of 'opening a Pandora's box.'" It even admitted that a "plethora of problems confronting Somaliland [are in part] the legacy of a political union with Somalia, which malfunctioned, [and] brought destruction and ruin."[22]

But, despite support for independence from South Africa, Rwanda, Zambia, and several other African states, the AU has been paralyzed because of opposition from Somaliland's neighbors, each of which has a vested interest in the country not gaining recognition. Ethiopia, for example, concerned about the irredentist claims of its own Somali population, has tried to divide and weaken Somalia since winning a bitter war with the Barre regime in 1977, and considers any attempt to strengthen Somaliland—or the TFG for that matter—as inimical to its own interests. Djibouti sees Somaliland as a threat to the port that powers its economy. For their part, Western states have been reluctant to take the lead and consider the matter an internal African one. Arab countries, and Egypt and Saudi Arabia in particular, have vehemently opposed independence to the extent that the latter has sought to sabotage Somaliland's economy by refusing to import any of its livestock since 1997. Many of these neighboring countries prefer to see Somalia remain united because it will act as a strong counterweight to Ethiopia.

A STRONG CASE FOR U.S. SUPPORT

Somaliland offers a unique opportunity to promote good governance and democracy in the Middle East and Africa. Helping the country gain recognition, develop its political institutions, and improve its economy would help to advertise some of the core values espoused by the United States in its drive to undermine Islamic extremism and promote democratization in Muslim countries and throughout the developing world.

Some influential Americans have already acknowledged Somaliland's importance. According to an article in the Washington Post in December 2007, "The escalating conflict in Somalia is generating debate inside the Bush administration over whether the United States should ... shift support to the less volatile region of Somaliland. ... The Pentagon's view is that 'Somaliland should be independent.'"[23] In 2006, the U.S. Combined Joint Task Force—Horn of Africa hosted a meeting in Addis Ababa at which senior military officers from throughout the region argued that an independent Somaliland would be the "first constitutional Muslim democracy in the Horn of Africa (HOA) and [a] proven partner in the GWOT [Global War on Terror]."[24] In the eyes of many, including a number of outspoken former diplomats, such as Dan Simpson, retired U.S. ambassador to Somalia, "It is ... definitely time to recognize the independence of Somaliland."[25]

One of the most effective ways for the United States to support Somaliland's quest for recognition would be to encourage African states and the AU to take the lead on the issue. The United States could, for example, open a small liaison office in Hargeysa to signal its support, as David Shinn, ex-U.S. ambassador to Ethiopia and ex-State Department director of East African Affairs, has repeatedly urged.[26] It could also condition material support for the TFG on its recognition of Somaliland's independence. Its behind-the-scenes influence could help sway South Africa, Nigeria, Kenya, and other leading states on the continent to prod the AU to act. U.S. officials might try to convince Ethiopia that Somaliland's independence would actually achieve Addis Ababa's goal of permanently dividing Somalia.

STRENGTHENING A HOMEGROWN DEMOCRACY

In conjunction with these efforts, the United States could seek to turn Somaliland into a showcase for its neighbors on the Horn of Africa and the Arabian Peninsula by helping the new country build a healthy and vigorous homegrown governing system.

It could, for example, ensure that any assistance it provides to a newly recognized Somaliland is "disciplined enough to avoid undermining [the] internally-driven political and economic processes and overwhelming internally-generated resources,"[27] unlike what has happened in many states across Africa, where aid has distorted the relationship between governments and their peoples, leading to greater authoritarianism and less democracy. Indeed, all outside aid agencies would do well to design their assistance packages to reinforce the "institutions that are rooted in, dependent upon, and accountable to Somali society,"[28] even if this means sacrificing some of the effectiveness of material assistance in the short term.

Foreign aid should be limited to a relatively modest share of the budgets of government at all levels of administration and directed at fortifying existing state-society linkages. Funds could, for example, be given only on a matching basis and where possible in kind or as technical assistance. Self-help schemes originating among community groups could be made a priority over purely government-directed projects. Initiatives that broadened the government's capacity would have multiplier effects on many levels: building revenue-collection capabilities, improving tax and customs systems, and reducing corruption would provide the government with more resources; increasing decentralization, improving local administration, and training ministry officials would enhance the government's ability to connect with its citizens; strengthening the legislature and judiciary and refining the constitution and legal system would bolster the rule of law and the checks that society can impose on executive authority.

HOMEGROWN INSTITUTIONS AND DEMOCRATIZATION

Somaliland highlights the importance of leveraging indigenous institutions in constructing sturdy, accountable governing structures. Catalyzing bottom-up societal processes offers the best chance of overcoming the dysfunction that plagues many postcolonial governments—including all the governments in Mogadishu since independence. Unfortunately, Western governments, international aid agencies, and development banks often urge postcolonial countries to adopt programs that reinforce the overly centralized, utterly discredited structures that seek to ignore or suppress the values and customs that most citizens hold dear.

The standard development paradigm gives "little thought . . . to the possibility that existing state structures might also be the *cause* of instability" in many postcolonial countries, even when "state-like entities such as Somaliland are more viable in terms of their ability to manage their own territory, to provide basic services, and in terms of their internal cohesiveness."[29] Such an approach to state building disregards the enormous and numerous differences between countries and ignores the fact that people want to choose not only their leaders but also their institutions. The international community would do better if it focused on re-tailoring those traditional forms of governance that have evolved to suit local conditions instead of trying to squeeze societies into inappropriate Western state models. Development and democratization work best when a state's institutions are genuine reflections of an organic historical process.

Bolivia: Building Representative Institutions in a Divided Country

Latin America has spent two decades trying to consolidate democracy, but in many countries its foundations remain as shaky as ever. Recent years have seen street protests toppling nearly a dozen elected presidents, a modern caudillo taking charge in Venezuela, and corruption eroding weak institutions almost everywhere. Polls reflect this poor record: only about half the region's population favors democracy over other forms of government and only one-third is satisfied with how democracy works in practice.[1] Dante Caputo, former Argentine foreign minister, has even gone so far as to declare that democracies in Latin America are facing "a slow death. It's dangerous when democracy becomes irrelevant because it does not solve day-to-day problems."[2]

Situated in the heart of South America, atop the Andes, Bolivia (see Map 9.1) embodies many of the problems common across the region. Indeed, nowhere in Latin America are the fault lines between competing visions of the state, of the economy, and of national identity as stark as they are in Bolivia. Divided along ethnic, geographical, and socioeconomic lines, the country has struggled to form a consensus on how to govern itself. Roadblocks and civil unrest toppled two presidents in as many years and the current president, Evo Morales, is the fifth head of state since 2000. Support for democracy fell 15 percent between 1996 and 2005.[3] Morales' landslide victory at the polls in December 2005 reflected this loss of faith: "Evo is the expression of that frustration, that resentment and the search for answers," commented Michael Shifter of the Washington, DC–based Inter-American Dialogue in the final days of the election campaign.[4]

The struggle to build stable democracies in weak Latin American countries mirrors the Herculean task faced by fragile states in many other parts of the globe. Although steadily gaining ground around the world since the end of the Cold War,

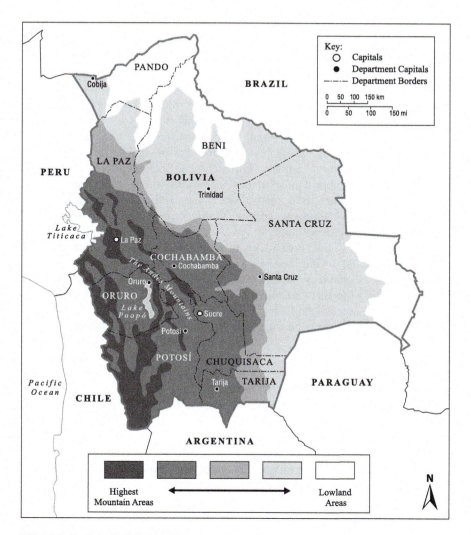

Map 9.1. Bolivia, Political and Topographical Map
Source: Central Intelligence Agency.

representative government has not always ushered in better institutions and faster economic growth, as its advocates have promised. Are these failings caused by some fundamental defect in democracy's DNA or in the formula used to grow democracy in these impoverished lands?

The answer to this question lies in how these states' governing systems have been constructed, what they fail to reflect about the citizens they purport to represent, and their weak institutional roots. Whereas most countries looking to foster democracy within their borders begin by debating the merits of electoral systems, the fairness of balloting, and the appropriateness of presidential or parliamentary systems, polities with divided populations, a dearth of competent officials, and great societal inequities may need to start by considering far more fundamental issues than how to select their leaders—such as how to reconfigure their institutions so that they reflect a genuine national consensus, allow for diverging group aspirations, and take into account a history of weak governance. In many cases, only these more representative, more accountable, and more relevant bodies will offer the chance to construct the kind of state that includes all citizens, fosters growth, and delivers the benefits promised by advocates of democratization.

Devising an institutional framework that better fits Bolivia has importance well beyond that country's borders. Enfranchising Bolivia's diverse population would undercut the appeal of extremist ideologies within the country, which in turn would encourage the spread of democracy and market-based economic policies, promote the investment necessary to lift living standards, discourage drug cultivation, and open a new supply of gas to the region and beyond. If the United States were to help Bolivia construct a governing system more appropriate to its people and situation, it would send a strong message that it wishes to promote the kind of inclusive democracy for which hundreds of millions throughout the region long, and not the elite-centered policies with which it is identified in the minds of the Latin American masses. Much anger would be dissipated, and greater support for U.S. policies, including the war on terrorism, would be forthcoming.

A FRACTURED COUNTRY

Bolivia's past has been so tumultuous that "Bolivianization" at one point became a synonym for political and social decomposition. The country's troubles are the direct result of its demography, geography, history, and long dependence on a few rich natural resources.

Bolivia's population is a unique amalgamation of ethnicities—a remarkable mix of pre- and post-Columbian cultures, institutions, religions, languages, and belief systems. Over 60 percent (the largest such percentage in Latin America) of its 9 million people are members of the indigenous peoples. But this diversity has not generated harmony; to the contrary, the country is polarized by severe divisions and a history of elite exploitation of native groups.

These identity fractures accentuate—and are, in turn, accentuated by—the country's geographic and economic fissures. Whereas roughly two-thirds of the people living in the five highland departments (La Paz, Cochabamba, Chuquisaca, Potosí, and Oruro) identify themselves as Aymara or Quechua, a similar proportion claim no indigenous affiliation in the four lowland areas (Santa Cruz, Pando, Beni, and Tarija).[5] The 2005 election (see Map 9.2) reflected these divisions: Evo's Movement toward Socialism (MAS) polled twice as high (64 percent of the vote) in the highlands than in the lowlands (31 percent).[6]

Steep mountain ranges carve up the country, which explains in part why the three largest cities—La Paz, Cochabamba, and Santa Cruz—lie in three different

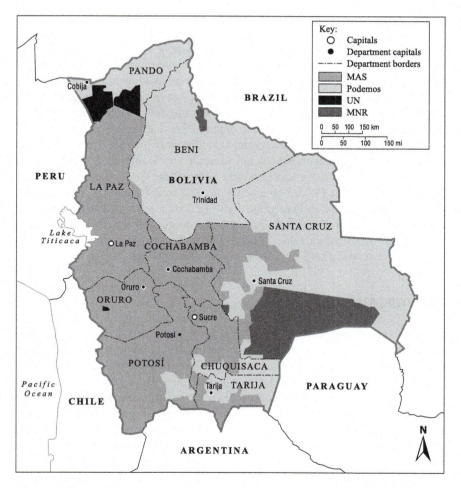

Map 9.2. Bolivia's 2005 Election Results: 2005 Presidential Winner by Municipality
Source: Unidad de Análisis e Investigación del Área de Educación Ciudadana de la Corte Nacional Electoral de Bolivia, *Atlas Electoral Latinoamericano* (La Paz: Corte Nacional Electoral, May 2007), 48.

climatic zones, have economies built on three different foundations, and have populations dominated by three different identity groups (Aymara, Quechua, and mestizo). Most wealth—and the country's hydrocarbon reserves, the spark for the recent political turmoil—is concentrated in the mestizo areas on the lowland plains.

Bolivia's mineral resources—the country was literally founded on the Cerro Rico mines overlooking Potosí (where much of Spain's New World wealth originated)—has fostered unhealthy attitudes toward moneymaking and governance. Its rich deposits of silver, tin, zinc, oil, and gas have generated great wealth for the narrow elite who have traditionally controlled both them and the government, but have provided little incentive for that elite to share its riches or to foster other industries. This situation has spawned a culture in which politicians compete for control of the state's resources instead of seeking to capitalize on the country's natural advantages in such areas as tourism, furniture manufacturing, and jewelry. Consequently, Bolivia has one of most inequitable societies in the world: while the national per capita income is US$870[7] (the lowest figure in South America), some cities average over US$3,000 whereas some villages average less than US$100.[8]

Not surprisingly, these divisions and inequities have produced great instability and ineffectual government. Bolivia has witnessed no fewer than 182 coups since independence. The country scores poorly both on the World Bank's Aggregate Governance Indicator (−0.37 on a scale of −2.5 to 2.5)[9] and on Transparency International's Corruption Perception Index (2.3 on a scale of 1 to 10, on a par with Sudan and Zimbabwe).[10] Bolivia is the hardest country in South America in which to start a business: it takes 187 days on average to get a commercial license, which costs two and a half times the average annual income.[11]

A BREAKING STATE

The surge in unrest since the turn of the century and the election of Evo, Bolivia's first indigenous leader, are in some ways the culmination of a long history of antagonistic intergroup relations and elite domination of the state, brought to a climax by a dispute over how to manage the country's gas reserves and, since Evo's election, over competing visions about how to organize the state.

The profound mistrust between groups complicates any attempt to strengthen government and fix the country's deep-rooted problems. Few of the dynamic mestizo entrepreneurs in Santa Cruz de la Sierra and other lowland areas east of the Cordillera Oriental, on whom the country's economic future depends, trust MAS to act as an effective administrator of the national economy; many even fear that it might seize their property. Meanwhile, indigenous groups on the *altiplano*, such as the Aymara in El Alto, bear a heavy grudge from generations of discrimination at the hands of the state and the elite that controlled it. Many feel that the upper classes have garnered their wealth unfairly and used the government's powers to exploit and disenfranchise the indigenous peoples.

Laws that mandate that a significant share of hydrocarbon royalties must be used within producing departments—already the wealthiest parts of the country—accentuate resentment and inflame passions. Tarija and Santa Cruz, the two richest regions (excluding sparsely populated Pando), received 65 percent of all state royalties in 2004 even though they have only 29 percent of the population. In contrast, the four poorest areas, where 74 percent of Bolivia's extreme poverty cases are to be found, received only 12 percent of hydrocarbon revenue.[12]

This sense of exclusion among the majority of the population prevents the implementation of coherent policy. Recurrent protests that close highways, schools, and even ministries reflect an absence of faith in formal political procedures to effectively arbitrate between disparate interest groups, forcing them to hold society hostage in a bid to secure their demands, with political stability and economic progress as the losers. The same demonstrations also represent a crisis of state legitimacy. As a report issued by the U.S. Agency for International Development (USAID) in February 2005, comments: "Surveys of Bolivian public opinion . . . repeatedly reveal a broad public disdain and contempt for Bolivia's traditional political class, and a perception that the economic system is rigged against all but the minority European-descended traditional elite and foreign interests, particularly large multinational corporations. These sentiments, combined with widespread despair and frustration over the lack of real economic growth and a government seemingly incapable of decisive or effective action, have led to a crisis of basic legitimacy for the Bolivian political and economic system."[13]

Fernando Henrique Cardoso, the former president of Brazil, points to an even more far-reaching and formidable problem: "In varying degrees, the Andean nations face a serious national integration issue. It is not even a problem of democracy. Exclusion is so massive that the majority, composed of indigenous peoples, does not want to be included. It wants to talk about power. The majority says: We are different from those who rule. The very notion of citizenship is not yet present, because there is no agreement about what country one would pledge allegiance to."[14]

UNPOPULAR PARTICIPATION

Bolivia has struggled to establish a stable democracy in large part because its institutions are inappropriate to the country's needs and are not seen as legitimate by a majority of its people. There is little or no national consensus on the overall nature, purpose, and conduct of the state. These problems reflect and are compounded by immense economic inequities, a dearth of competent officials, and the divisive effect of disparate identities.

Until now, attempts to deal with the country's problems have focused on improving government performance, but have ignored identity and regional divisions and the poor investment climate. For example, the most important such reforms launched up to now, the Law of Popular Participation (LPP) and the Law of Decentralization (LOD), enacted in 1994 and 1995, respectively, broke with Bolivia's long history of centralized administration by dividing the territory into 311 municipalities, 187 of them new and covering nearly two-thirds of the entire country.[15] These municipalities were then given 20 percent of national tax revenue to enable them to extend the state's reach into rural areas previously untouched by it. These reforms have made government more relevant to many Bolivians, but they have not gone nearly far enough nor addressed more deep-seated issues.

The LPP's and LOD's most notable successes show how much more could be done to empower the lower classes and improve government performance if more radical steps were taken. Thanks to the two laws, one in four municipalities have elected peasant or indigenous mayors—something inconceivable under the old system that heavily favored the elites that have traditionally controlled the central government. Public oversight committees, newly institutionalized, have encouraged the participation of local, grassroots organizations in many areas, increasing official accountability. A dramatic shift has occurred in patterns of government investment, with funds being transferred from urban to rural areas, and from initiatives to spur economic production to projects in areas such as education, health care, and sanitation designed to foster human capital formation.

But even in rural communities, where the laws have made the most impact, they have fallen short of what might have been achieved because they impose a single, centrally designed structure, ignoring, in effect, the diversity of the country's peoples and their forms of self-government. The LPP and LOD do not even touch upon the deep identity divisions that continue to plague the country. Thus, for instance, many traditional groupings of indigenous people are divided into multiple municipalities, fragmenting their organization and allowing mayors to ignore their representatives and budget requests. Indigenous Municipal Districts, newly established as part of these reforms, have no autonomous powers or independent access to government funds. Most other traditional land-based communal bodies—such as the Aymara Ayllus[16]—remain outside the formal system of law even though they have served as the main self-governing system of these peoples for hundreds of years.[17]

EVO'S MISSED OPPORTUNITY

Although Evo came to power with possibly the strongest electoral mandate in the country's history and far more fiscal flexibility than his predecessors because of higher hydrocarbon royalties and reduced debts from an International Monetary Fund write-off, he has yet to capitalize on these assets to deal with the country's most important challenges. The economy is suffering from a shortage of capital and job-producing growth. A 58 percent decline in investment levels from the late 1990s has caused much hardship in labor-intensive industries, while driving down income levels 19 percent.[18] Meanwhile, Evo's confrontational and centralizing style has weakened Bolivia's institutions and strengthened extremists on both sides of the country's east-west divide, generating rising tension and even violence.[19] Lowland department prefects, newly empowered after being directly elected for the first time in 2005, and backed by their robust business communities, have threatened to hold referenda on autonomy, precipitating a national constitutional crisis—or worse. Meanwhile, instead of using the constituent assembly as a forum within which the two sides can work out their differences, Evo has "ridden roughshod over objections to [his] proposed constitutional reforms" and sought to "impose a new constitution . . . push[ing] national unity to the breaking point."[20]

While a civil war or coup d'état are unlikely given the country's two decades of respectable democratic performance, they cannot be completely ruled out if Evo's administration continues its current approach. Even if these worst-case scenarios are avoided, chronic instability threatens the very existence of the state and will continue to do so until someone (perhaps Evo, perhaps not) displays the visionary leadership necessary to drive the development of a genuine national consensus on how to govern the state among Bolivia's main identity groups (currently represented by Evo's MAS and the party it defeated, Podemos). Such an agreement would enable fundamental institutional reform to be undertaken, which will in turn foster political stability and economic growth.

These problems are not unique to the country. Bolivia's stark historical, sociocultural, and economic divisions are mirrored in several other states in Latin America—such as Ecuador, Guatemala, and Peru—all of which need to negotiate a genuine national consensus on reform. "Fundamental and durable improvements in the region's quality of democracy require that contradictory visions of democracy be reconciled. Traditional elites must accept that indigenous peoples are now permanent players in politics; their needs must be addressed and their cultures respected.... By the same token, indigenous politicians and groups must shift their perspective from that of excluded outsiders to protectors of democratic institutions, laws, and values.... [They] should seek reconciliation, not retribution, and incorporate the best features of Western liberal democracy."[21]

Although Bolivia has never been as socially stratified nor has its discrimination been as systematic as was the case in apartheid South Africa, Bolivia could learn much from how South Africa constructed a sustainable accord between deeply mistrustful groups with sharply diverging agendas. The two countries are among the most inequitable places in the world—put differently, they both have extreme concentrations of wealth and poverty—and many of the same economic trade-offs made in postapartheid South Africa may have to be accepted in Bolivia, too. Any successful reform, for example, must both encourage investment while directing more state largesse toward the traditionally disenfranchised. Bolivia needs to maintain macroeconomic stability, protect private property, and encourage job-creating businesses if the poor are to enjoy a brighter future. Any redistribution of wealth must not be done in ways that undercut commercial contracts and the rule of law; on the contrary, as discussed below, making the country more investment friendly might actually be one of the best ways to spread prosperity. Just as the formerly anticapitalist African National Congress learned how to manage a market economy after it assumed power in South Africa, so MAS must learn a similar lesson if it is not to damage the country's prospects.

REFOUNDING THE BOLIVIAN STATE

"Refounding" the Bolivian state, something Evo has repeatedly called for, requires forming—for the first time—a comprehensive national consensus on how to distribute the country's mineral royalties, energize its economy, and reshape its governing structures.

Redirecting Hydrocarbon Revenues

Any attempt to reshape the country's institutions should start by seeking a more just apportionment of the revenue from exploiting Bolivia's hydrocarbon reserves. Given that poverty is concentrated in areas with limited gas and oil reserves, the current system of allotting a disproportionately large share of royalties to producing departments seems almost deliberately designed to provoke the anger of the disenfranchised. A fairer system would channel far more royalties to impoverished areas in exchange for significantly augmenting departmental autonomy—a major request of Santa Cruz and other lowland departments (see the section on reshaping government).

Nationalizing the industry—as Evo did a few months after taking office—will likely lead to an eventual reduction in the long-term revenue available to Bolivians because of lower efficiencies and levels of investment. The country's hydrocarbon sector has historically grown only when in private hands; previous nationalizations have always led to stagnation in the midterm and falling production levels in the long-term.[22] Indeed, "concerns are growing [within the government] over a lack of new investment... the pace of hydrocarbons output growth has slowed markedly... producing sporadic cuts in... contracts for gas exports to Argentina and Brazil. Domestic supplies... have also been affected."[23] Although Evo has sharply increased royalties by adopting a hard-line negotiating stance with foreign firms, he has also severely reduced the incentives for investment by weakening legal protections on private property, increasing regulatory uncertainty, and forcing the sector to depend on state firms that lack technical expertise. The avoidance of the country by multinational companies in recent years—net investment averaged $900 from 1997 to 2002 but had fallen to –$277 million in 2005[24]—is likely to continue without a reverse of this policy. Gas accounts for a third of all Bolivia's exports and the gas industry has received the lion's share of foreign investment over the past decade, so formulating the right hydrocarbon policy is crucial if Bolivia is ever to lift its people out of poverty. Given the right investment climate, billions more in foreign capital could be forthcoming, increasing annual GDP growth by 1 percent per year.[25]

Furthermore, a significant portion of the additional revenue derived from the oil and gas industry should not be poured into the government's coffers, not least because a considerable amount would fall prey to corruption and wasteful spending. Indeed, "pro-government elements are fighting each other for control of the oil, gas and mining money."[26] Meanwhile, the state's weak implementation capacity has meant that the windfall from increased revenues has not translated into an equivalent rise in public spending. Regional departments invested only 48 percent of their expanded (because of the increase in royalties) budgets. Social investments actually shrunk by 6 percent in 2006.[27] Instead, Evo should distribute a slice of any increase in royalties directly to the Bolivian people, following the model of the Alaska Permanent Fund dividend but giving the poor a proportionately larger share.[28] Citizens over the age of twenty-five, for example, might receive a stipend ranging from $25 to $50 each, depending on their income levels, a significant amount in a country where the poorest earn less than a $100 per year. These stipends would reduce the number of indigent people, boost investment in the production of certain consumer goods (those aimed at the poorer segments of society), and strengthen the government's accountability as the population would take greater interest in how the government managed the hydrocarbon sector and its own expenses. By giving citizens a palpable stake in how the state's mineral resources are exploited, the stipends might also increase support for foreign investment if this could be shown to directly augment individual earnings.

As suggested below, directing more of the total revenue to local governments, as opposed to the departmental and national levels of administration, is also likely to make government action more relevant to solving people's problems, as the LPP and LOD have shown.

Energizing Other Industries

The government also needs to improve the investment climate, which in turn will encourage the growth of the labor-intensive businesses that can provide steady jobs for the hundreds of thousands of underemployed, enlarge the ranks of the middle class, and attenuate Bolivia's deep economic and social divisions.[29] The climate now is so poor that apart from gas and mining, total private investment is a negligible 2–3 percent of GDP.[30]

Despite two decades of macroeconomic reform, Bolivia has actually never enjoyed a genuine market economy because its weak institutions, high levels of poverty, and inadequate education system distort competition and undermine attempts to make everyone equal under the law, greatly favoring a small elite over the majority of citizens. Creating a level playing field will take decades, but Evo could start the process by making the government far more supportive of small firms, especially those launched by members of the lower classes, providing greater opportunities for upward mobility. His administration could, for example, simplify the procedures for starting and running a business, making it far easier and less expensive to manage a company in the formal sector, while providing better support services to the few industries where the country has genuine competitive advantages. Bolivia is a beautiful country that has much, potentially, to offer foreign tourists, but because of poor marketing few have heard of the country's attractions; and because of a weak tourism infrastructure, those who do visit Bolivia find many of the facilities not up to international standards. A handful of clothing, jewelry, and furniture-making companies together export $150 million of goods each year and employ one hundred thousand Bolivians; the number of such companies would be greatly increased if the country had permanent trade deals with target markets—especially with the United States—and enhanced export-promotion capacities.[31] As USAID's Bolivia Country Strategic Plan explains, "the only practical way to achieve real growth is by accessing other markets."[32]

The greater political stability garnered through the forging of a new national consensus should also enable the government to clamp down on the various protests that interrupt legitimate business activity. Repeated road blockades that disrupt tourists, business trips, and delivery schedules discourage investors and visitors from even considering Bolivia in their plans.

Reshaping Government

Bolivia urgently needs to reshape its governing institutions so that they are better able to deal with the realities of its fragmentation and weak administrative capacity. Instead of unrealistically expecting the evolution of an efficient central-ized regime that determines policy to the satisfaction of all its citizens, Bolivia should learn from its experiences in implementing the LPP and LOD reforms, and heed the advantages of directing far more funding and responsibility to regional and local governments. The country should also learn from the experiences of other states divided by language, history, and identity, and follow their lead by transforming itself into a more decentralized, identity-based federation of entities that are obliged to compromise at the national level. A "bottom heavy, top light" structure is probably the only way to overcome the long history of administrative dysfunction and intergroup acrimony, making institutions far more representative, relevant, and responsive in the process.

In contrast to the past, when the state sought to centralize all decision-making while imposing a single, elite-defined, homogenous mestizo identity on the whole population, this new, federated Bolivia would treasure diversity and would seek to accommodate diverging visions of the country within one sovereign territory. To some degree, identity would be regionally based, giving indigenous groups authority in areas they have long sought while permitting the more capitalist-oriented lowland areas a greater say in how they manage their economies. Such an arrangement, however, would have to include a permanent redistribution of the revenue from hydrocarbon taxes from the wealthier lowland areas to the poorer highland areas (as discussed above) to create an equitable division of the state's assets.

This system would emulate some of the features that other divided polities—such as Switzerland, Belgium, Spain, and Canada—have used to cope with their own diversity. A significantly greater portion of government funding would be spent locally and regionally (just 30 percent is spent there now), as authority over cultural, educational, and some economic and legal matters were decentralized. Indigenous regions would be able, for example, to redesign education systems to better take account of local needs, discarding curricula that ignored their traditions, emphasizing bilingualism, and redesigning schedules to maximize student attendance. Historical land tenure arrangements could be recognized. Traditional law—representing widely accepted informal norms and institutions—could be documented and formalized as a legal means to adjudicate disputes.[33] Lowland areas, in contrast, could continue to use existing Westernized structures. They could also adopt a more market-oriented economic system than those elsewhere might prefer. The federal government would shift from being a rigid, self-important, highly unresponsive body to a more limited organ forced to facilitate locally inspired initiatives in areas such as education, health, and culture; it would play a major role in training the newly empowered.

In order to ensure that compromise—not confrontation—was the norm at the national level, something mature federations like Switzerland find second nature but that Bolivia might find difficult, the country might also consider adopting some form of departmental supermajority voting for important issues. Any decision regarding the allocation of the national budget, the appointment of judges to national courts, the management of mineral assets, or other potentially controversial issues would require the support of two-thirds or three-quarters of all departments. This structure would force disparate groups to work together by forcing a permanent coalition of regions onto the national stage.

Unfortunately, Evo has often acted as if he plans to duplicate Hugo Chávez's "democratic authoritarianism" in Bolivia, deeply polarizing the country in the process. He has subverted rival centers of power by forcing out independent voices in the judiciary, central bank, and military—undermining the country's already weak institutions. A bill that would have allowed the central government to scrutinize governors' accounts and allow the MAS-led congress to impeach them led six departments—including two that are dominated by indigenous groups—to symbolically break relations with the central government in November 2006. Conflict over the issue of regional autonomy led to violence between supporters of the central government and local police in Cochabamba, resulting in three deaths and over one hundred casualties in February 2007. In November 2007, Evo convened the constituent assembly—in military barracks, without the opposition present, and with police noisily battling protesters outside—to ram the new constitutional framework through under dubious legal circumstances (the need for a two-thirds majority was ignored). Three more died and hundreds were injured in the protests. Some fear that "gradual disintegration [of the country] is a real risk."[34]

Legitimizing Government

Beyond these changes, programs that increase government transparency and accountability by augmenting citizen participation in the deliberative and decision-making functions of government offer perhaps the best chance to legitimize and improve the performance of a highly discredited and ineffectual system. On the local level, citizen participation could be spurred in numerous ways: by making some decisions dependent on referenda; by providing more resources for the oversight committees formed during the 1990s reforms; by giving local NGOs a greater role in evaluating how well government functions; by publishing detailed financial records; and (as discussed above) by designing government bodies to better overlap with informal structures. Greater citizen participation in decision making has "the potential to transform the nature of state-society relations . . . [by] empowering sectors of society that previously had a limited voice in politics."[35] As shown in Mexico, Guatemala, Brazil, and elsewhere in the region, "participatory and deliberate approaches to governance have helped create new institutional channels that link leaders with citizens and give a measure of credibility to the political system, as well as to leaders who run them."[36] Basing these practices "on traditional indigenous self-governing practices that emphasize consensus-seeking, community participation, leadership rotation, and reciprocity—norms and institutions that constitute valuable social capital"—could go a long way toward integrating within the state groups that have historically been excluded.[37]

Changes should also be made to the symbols of power and identity in Bolivia. For instance, redesigning national emblems to better represent the country's diversity would signify to all Bolivians that a new order was in place, one that welcomes and values all citizens. Far too many statues, street names, and buildings represent only one version of the state's past, one that excludes a majority of its inhabitants. Integrating the Andean flag, the Wiphala, sacred to indigenous peoples, into the national one would be a good start. Elevating indigenous languages to the same status as Spanish in highland areas could both improve literacy and enable many more poor people to participate in the economy and political system. (Evo's attempt to institutionalize these languages statewide, however, has predictably caused a divisive backlash.)

A DELICATE ROLE FOR OUTSIDERS

Bolivia's heavy dependence on foreign investment and aid give outsiders a special—if highly delicate—role to play in the years ahead. Although the United States has historically been the most influential external actor, Brazil, the region's most powerful country and Bolivia's most important foreign investor, will have a far easier time shaping negotiations between disparate groups because its actions will not automatically be viewed suspiciously by most Bolivians.

Bolivia has one of the highest per capita aid dependencies in the hemisphere, with as much as one-tenth of GDP coming from donor assistance.[38] Eighteen multilateral and bilateral donors provide $500 million annually in concessional loans and donations; the United States supplied some $655 million between 2000 and 2004.[39] USAID is the largest bilateral donor in Bolivia and the country would be eligible for $598 million from the Millennium Challenge Account—if it met certain U.S. conditions on governance.

Whatever Evo may say to please his more extremist supporters—he often shouted, "Long live coca! Death to the gringos!" at campaign rallies, and shortly after the elections he denounced President George W. Bush as "a terrorist"—his actions suggest that he is well aware of Bolivia's heavy dependence on American aid and markets. Although he has repeatedly showed that he is not a moderate at heart since winning the election, he has at least declared that he would consider a trade pact with the United States and with other Andean countries if it could be shown to benefit the poor;[40] has insisted that his pro-coca stance does not mean he favors the manufacture and sale of cocaine; and has met business leaders and stressed his support for private investment. He has also had a number of positive meetings with U.S. diplomats and has spoken with President Bush by phone.

The importance of foreign investment to any effort by Evo to improve the lives of the people who voted for him will continue to restrain his more radical tendencies in the short term—and could lead to a partial reversal in the medium term. As USAID has noted, "Foreign investment represented about 48% of total investment in the period 1995–2003, due to extreme shortages of domestic investment capital.... This dependence on foreign investment is also a dependence on foreign investors' favorable perceptions of Bolivia as an investment destination, which greatly magnifies the negative economic impact of high levels of social and political unrest."[41] In early 2007, the Economist Intelligence Unit reported that "the government has quietly given assurances that whatever it may say in public it will not act against companies operating legally."[42]

Brazil has significant leverage in Bolivia both because of its role as the country's major business partner and because its president, Luiz Inácio Lula da Silva, has significant credibility with Evo. Petroleo Brasileiro SA, Brazil's state-owned gas company, has invested $1.6 billion in Bolivia and is responsible for as much as 20 percent of the country's GDP.[43] Brazil is also Bolivia's main overseas market, taking in 40 percent of Bolivian exports.[44] Lula's background is remarkably similar to that of Evo: each man was born into a poor family, spent many years as a union leader, and rode a tide of Leftist sentiment to become his country's first lower-class leader. But Lula has used his power responsibly, emphasizing fiscal restraint, public-sector reform, economic expansion, and export promotion; he offers a very different blueprint of reform to that of Venezuela's anti-American firebrand, President Hugo Chávez. Lula could play a critical role in encouraging Evo to "talk on the left, but have his policies located closer to the center," as Carlos Toranzo, a La Paz based political analyst, has put it.[45]

Despite its role as the major provider of aid, the U.S. government is strongly disliked by many Bolivians because of the widespread perception that its policies sustain elite domination at the expense of the majority. As a result, Washington will be able to influence events most effectively by exerting its influence indirectly and invisibly, through Brazil, through diplomatic channels, and through subtle manipulations of its aid and trade policies. Instead of threatening to abruptly cut the flow of money and reduce business ties because Bolivia's new administration engages with coca farmers, meets with Venezuelan and Cuban leaders, and issues anticapitalist statements, the United States should recognize that these largely symbolic activities pose little threat to American interests. It should focus instead on actions by Evo that are likely to have a more tangible consequence, such as whether his policies actually encourage or discourage cocaine exports and strengthen or undermine democracy. The United States might also gain from publicly—but delicately—supporting any effort by Evo designed to create far more representative institutions based on a genuine new national consensus. Bush took a step in this direction by declaring during his phone call with Evo that the United States is committed to "helping the Bolivian people realize their aspirations for a better life."[46] American diplomats have adopted a cooperative tone and pragmatic approach since Evo's election. Future U.S. support for reforms that appropriately addressed the country's divisions and inequities would be a pleasant surprise for many Bolivians and would help in rehabilitating America's political reputation within the region.

REPRESENTATIVE INSTITUTIONS AND DEMOCRACY

Bolivia exemplifies a phenomenon far too common across Latin America and much of the developing world. Even though the country has spent two decades following the international community's standard economic and political reform agenda, regularly holding elections, practicing responsible fiscal management, and liberalizing markets, its government, society, and economy do not meet the needs of most of its people. Bolivia's implementation of these supposed remedies have succeeded only in generating widespread and deep resentment against the elite that seems to benefit from these policies—and against their chief proponent, the United States.

Outsiders far too often equate free elections and free markets with representative government and equal competition. While formulas for development that emphasize free elections and free markets may work in countries with cohesive populations and robust institutions, they rarely achieve much in states plagued by deep social and ethnic divisions and weak governments. The world is littered with fragile states that have followed the developed world's prescriptions but have seen few of the promised benefits.

Dysfunctional countries of this type call out for the creation of a new strategy, one that recognizes that identity divisions, social inequities, and weak national bureaucracies are permanent features of the local landscape that cannot be wished away and must instead be worked around. Institutions must be redesigned to better meet the needs of splintered populations, and to enhance the ability of local and regional, as well as national, government to spur economic and political development. In the absence of such a redesign, the state risks becoming irrelevant, with democracy and capitalism becoming discredited, even despised, and the poor and the disenfranchised being won over by demagogues and extremists.

As the leading advocate of the benefits of democratization and liberalization, the United States faces the greatest backlash when these supposed panaceas are seen to fail. It also risks appearing enormously hypocritical when it champions these two causes while simultaneously adopting policies that undermine them, such as urging fragile states to hold elections and open markets without supporting programs that would enable more people to participate as equals in both. By overemphasizing policies that have often enriched and empowered a select few at the expense of the many in highly unequal societies, the democratizing and liberalizing message is being grossly mistranslated, with dire consequences in some cases. Growing Latin American disillusionment with democracy is hurting American efforts to discredit extremists, stamp out terrorism, spread the rule of law, open up trade opportunities, and diversify its oil and gas suppliers. The United States needs to focus far more effort on promoting representative institutions if its calls for representative government are to be effective.

*　　*　　*

Time is running short for Evo and his opponents to reconcile their differences and transform Bolivia through nonviolent means. Although Evo has failed to use the mandate he gained from having won a landslide victory to bring the country together to forge a consensus on how Bolivia can find peace and prosperity for all its citizens, the growing polarization and violence might just offer a second opportunity—or at least a forced course correction—for him to set forth on a more conciliatory path. If the two sides can replicate South Africa's achievements in a society wracked by similar problems, they would both help their country overcome a troubled legacy and set a powerful example for countries throughout the region. The United States and its allies in the region can and should support any effort that is designed to deepen and broaden the roles of democracy and capitalism in Bolivia.

Pakistan: Redirecting a Country's Trajectory

Terrorism has many sources, but if it can be said to have a center, it lies in Pakistan, where the Taliban and al Qaeda hide today, and from where jihadis have spread out across the globe. Hosting hundreds of armed extremists, possessing the world's eighth largest nuclear arsenal, and dominated by a military that has spent decades fine-tuning the use of Islamists to extend its foreign and domestic interests, Pakistan poses a unique foreign policy challenge to the West. Although an "absolutely essential ally" in the fight against terrorism, as U.S. officials have repeatedly emphasized,[1] the country actually endangers international security through its fragile and dysfunctional governing system.[2] Meanwhile, Washington has consistently pursued a strategy built on false assumptions about Pakistan's condition that has only made the country more unstable and more dangerous.

Few countries have as much potential to cause trouble, regionally and worldwide, as this state of 165 million people.[3] The source of militants fighting NATO in Afghanistan and India in Kashmir and of fanatics organizing terrorist acts from New Delhi to London, Pakistan itself has gradually fallen victim to a spreading insurgency; in 2007, the country was hit by sixty suicide bombings (up from six the year before) and was roiled by the assassination of former prime minister Benazir Bhutto. Pakistan's combination of violent sectarian divides, pitifully weak governing institutions, and abysmal education, health, and employment conditions make it a textbook example of a fragile state. Its self-serving military has repeatedly undermined attempts to introduce genuine democracy and has entrenched itself institutionally and economically deep within the entrails of government and society. By emasculating the rule of law, overcentralizing authority, and allying with various religious parties, military governments have exacerbated the fractiousness that challenges Pakistan's cohesiveness. Even though the February 2008 elections restored civilian rule to Islamabad, the country's elites have a long record of using their dominance of the state for their own benefit, suggesting that dramatic institutional change is unlikely in the near term.

The United States has not helped matters. To the contrary, it has contributed to Pakistan's gradual deterioration over many years by repeatedly prioritizing short-term objectives over long-term concerns. This state, possibly "the most dangerous place in the world,"[4] according to Stephen Cohen, one of America's most prominent analysts of the country, "represents everything . . . in the forefront of U.S. concerns: religious fundamentalism, terrorism, weapons of mass destruction in possession of a failing state, a military dictatorship masquerading behind a pale democratic façade."[5] Yet, Pakistan's complex society and interconnected ailments remain little understood in Washington.[6] Since the country's founding in 1947, U.S. policymakers have sometimes simply ignored the country; more often, they have focused on its role in their larger strategic calculations, while ignoring the need to tackle its deep-seated problems. Today, Washington is in danger of using its considerable leverage over Pakistan's government in ways that simply worsen the state's internal problems.

Given the nature and extent of Pakistan's troubles, only a long-term campaign—lasting decades—aimed at improving weak institutions, separating the military from the state, and improving social conditions can hope to give the government the capacity to develop the country and eliminate the societal ills that have caused the growth in terrorism. The many commonalities Pakistan shares with its democratic and rapidly developing neighbor India offer some grounds for hope that a program aimed at redirecting the state's trajectory by leveraging its latent capacities might succeed—but only if Pakistan is willing to follow India's example in focusing more on developing itself economically and politically, and not, as historically been the case, on its geopolitical insecurities and internal divisions. Foreign, especially U.S., pressure on Pakistan can help to nudge it in that direction but, ultimately, success will depend on the formation of an alliance between civilian and military leaders and the creation within the country of a strong reformist bloc favoring change. Even then, change will come only slowly, with progress being marked by a series of imperfect solutions to one or another of Pakistan's numerous problems.

A FRACTURED COUNTRY

Situated at the confluence of three civilizations and divided religiously, ethnically, and ideologically between opposing concepts of the state, Pakistan has struggled to form a cohesive identity and build stable institutions since its birth in 1947. Even the country's original shape testified to its incoherence, with Pakistan consisting of two distinct parts, one lying to the east and one to the west of India. The West Pakistani elite used its control over the army and bureaucracy to dominate the young state even though East Pakistan had a majority (55 percent) of the population.[7] When, in 1970, the country's first—and until now only—genuinely free elections gave a Bengali autonomist party, the Awami League, control over the legislature, the West Pakistani elite resisted relinquishing its power and, after tense negotiations failed, launched a brutal campaign against the people of East Pakistan. That campaign was counterproductive, however, for after India intervened on the side of East Pakistan in 1971, Pakistan's armed forces were forced to withdraw and East Pakistan established itself as the new sovereign state of Bangladesh.

Pakistan as it has existed since then consists of five main ethnolinguistic groups—Punjabi, Sindhi, Mohajir, Pashtun, and Baluch—that constantly jockey for influence over the state's governing institutions, money, and natural resources (see Map 10.1). Islamabad's close involvement with Afghanistan's internal affairs is a consequence in part of the role Pashtuns play in that country as its largest ethnic group, and in part of Pakistan's concerns over possible irredentist activity across the two countries' common border, which Afghanistan has never recognized.[8] The Pakistan-India border remains even more unsettled; it has been the scene of three wars since the Partition of the British Raj and is today the perch from which many Pakistanis—especially those in the military—still look longingly at Kashmir, the only majority Muslim province within India. Pakistan also has seven self-governing tribal agencies (known as the Federally Administered Tribal Areas, or the FATA), all located on its border with Afghanistan and controlled only nominally by the state (tribal customs trump Pakistani law there).

The Punjabis are the most numerous (accounting for 58 percent of population) and most powerful group in the country, dominating the economic, political, and especially military elites. Seventy-five percent of the army comes from three Punjabi districts and two adjacent North-West Frontier Province (NWFP) districts that contain only 9 percent of the country's population.[9] Not without reason, some people refer to Pakistan as "Punjabistan." Baluchistan, by contrast, is sparsely populated, with only 5 percent of the country's population located in 44 percent of its landmass; it has the richest natural resources of any province yet has little representation within the establishment. The central government's efforts to develop the province, accompanied as they have been by an influx of educated Punjabis, have stirred Baluch animosities toward the state. Although the country has made immense strides in integrating the great majority of its diverse ethnic groups, institutional overcentralization has fanned sectarian tensions throughout the country.

Although Pakistan was founded as an Islamic state and continues to pay tribute to the idea that its diverse people are united by their common faith, religious divisions are rapidly growing and have been until recently the leading cause of domestic terrorism. Relations between the country's Shiites, who make up 15 percent of the population, and Sunnis, who account for the remaining 85 percent, have grown increasingly antagonistic since the Iranian revolution and the Soviet invasion of Afghanistan in 1979 prompted a resurgence of religious sentiment. The state's inability to meet the public's demand for education in many impoverished

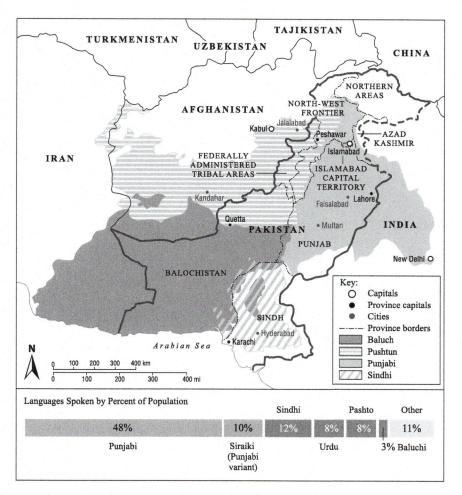

Map 10.1. Pakistan's Ethnic Demography
Sources: Central Intelligence Agency and the *New York Times*.

areas provided the opportunity for various religious organizations to step in, each espousing a different strain of Islam. Today, there are more than ten thousand madrasas, run by as many as 245 different religious groups; more than a few of these schools promote fundamentalist causes and justify the use of violence, and they are the main source of the country's growing militant and jihadist problems.[10]

Although the growing importance of Islam since 1979 has made the country seem increasingly Middle Eastern in orientation, fundamentally Pakistan remains a South Asian state, one that is dominated by a plateau region—consisting of its two most populous provinces—that shares a cultural and institutional legacy with the northwest region of its democratic neighbor, India (see Map 10.2). Indeed,

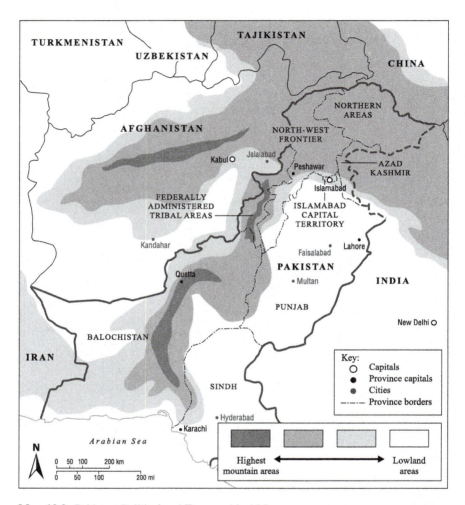

Map 10.2. Pakistan, Political and Topographical Map
Source: Central Intelligence Agency.

Pakistan has never embraced the blatant authoritarianism practiced in the Middle East and Central Asia, and instead has sought to maintain at least a façade of democratic propriety: competitive (albeit manipulated) elections, a critical (albeit self-censoring) media, and constitutional (albeit sometimes dubiously so) government.

Pakistan, however, has been unable to follow India in building an inclusive polity, a robust democracy, and a dynamic economy. At the country's outset, a variety of factors conspired to shape the trajectory of the state's development, setting its institutional structure on a self-reinforcing course—"path dependent" is the technical term—ever since. The country's difficult birth, lopsided ethnic make-up, geographical divisions, the early demise of its founder, and its persistent and sometimes very violent conflict with India have all encouraged the antidemocratic tendencies latent within its elite. Great social inequities—exacerbated by gaping cultural divides between classes—have yielded a narrow establishment that is a state within the state, dominant over all levers of economic and political power, and more interested in advancing its own interests than in promoting the development of the country.[11] Although industrialization, urbanization, improved communications, and an inflow of remittances have all combined to significantly enlarge the middle class, genuine democracy "has an improbable future in Pakistan."[12]

AN OVERBEARING MILITARY

The domination exercised over Pakistan by its military, the most powerful institution in a state of weak institutions, and the generals' tendency to impose a top-down governing structure on this diversity has consistently undermined the democratization of the country's society and politics, while exacerbating ethnic and religious tensions and weakening the state and the rule of law. Pakistan's army—which is the only arm of the military that really matters within the country—has played an outsized role in the country's affairs since independence and is now so entrenched in power that even the onset of civilian rule is unlikely to cause the army to cede significant influence over major parts of Pakistan's decision-making apparatus.[13] Fear of India has made Pakistan's political leaders all too eager to empower military officials. Fear of Soviet expansionism and, more recently, of Islamist terrorists has made Western states all too eager to build up Pakistan's army without any regard for how this might affect the state. And fear of the masses has made Pakistan's elite all too ready to partner with—and even submit to—the military.

The army's ascendancy goes far deeper than its periodic overthrow of civilian leaders. Its three coups—in 1958, 1977, and 1999—and long spells in office (from 1958 to 1971, from 1977 to 1988, and from 1999 to 2008) have been complemented by a masterful manipulation of the political stage, especially during the last civilian interregnum, when the military and intelligence agencies played a major hand in rigging polls, underwriting political parties, and dismissing prime ministers.[14] In sharp contrast to India, which has suffered only one eighteen-month interruption of its electoral process since Partition, Pakistan's political system has been directly or indirectly controlled by its military since 1977. (This ascendancy was clearly evident in Musharraf's strong reluctance to shed his uniform despite intense criticism over many years—he rightly saw that the top military post was more powerful than that of the presidency.)

As the military has became more and more embedded in the entrails of the state, it has extended its preeminence both institutionally and economically so that today it is hard to judge at times whether Pakistan's government works for the country as a whole or just for the military (or at least the military-elite partnership). The Musharraf regime has cemented the army's institutional and economic positions in a number of ways. The establishment in 2004 of a military-controlled National Security Council has formalized the military's stranglehold over future governments. Musharraf's strengthening of the powers of the presidency in 2002 has made it easier for the military to manipulate future civilian governments. Musharraf also installed hundreds of serving and retired military personnel in public positions.[15]

The military also plays a considerable role in business. Using a "very unfair, unequal, unlevel playing field to its advantage,"[16] the military has taken control of enterprises in everything from cereals to banks to agriculture to construction, making it the largest commercial player in the country, responsible for 4 percent of GDP. It also now owns 12 percent of state land. These assets—worth well over $100 billion and enriching senior officers in numerous ways—give the military such a large stake in how the government operates that its financial interests alone act as a disincentive to withdraw from the political scene.[17]

The Military: Exacerbating Ethnic Tensions

Although civilians have played their part in overcentralizing the Pakistani state, it is the country's military that has led the way in empowering Islamabad at the expense of provincial administrations, creating a top-down system of government that better fits its own concept of bureaucratic discipline. As Musharraf explained in 2002, when he sought to reform the constitution to give himself more power, "Unless there is unity of command, unless there is only one man in charge on top, it [the system] will never function."[18]

Pakistan has attempted to introduce a federal system of government several times in its history—each of the country's three constitutions instituted such a system, with the last, the 1973 document, being the most accommodating to the regions—but each step forward has subsequently been reversed by the military in Islamabad. The center has undermined the provincial assemblies, prevented the enactment of constitutional provisions to create institutions to promote dialogue and compromise between the center and the provinces, exercised powers not assigned to it, and monopolized the state's authority to collect taxes.

Such actions have strengthened the identification of the center with Punjabi interests and have provoked fierce opposition from every other major group: Bengalis from the 1960s to 1970, Sindhis from the 1950s through to the 1990s, Mohajirs in 1985–2003, Pashtuns in 1947–1958 and 1973–77, and Baluchis in 1947, 1958, 1963, and 1973–77.[19] In Pakistan's earlier days, when the idea of Pakistan was less rooted in the minds of its inhabitants, regional protests were often bound up with struggles for independence and liable to degenerate into armed rebellion; today, regional unrest is more likely to be driven by demands for pride, status, money, natural resources, water, jobs, and social equality and only in extreme cases to produce great acts of violence.

Interethnic tensions declined during Pakistan's democratic interlude that lasted from 1988 to 1999, but increased under the Musharraf regime.[20] Since 2003, the state has been embroiled in serious problems in the NWFP, Sindh, and the FATA. Baluchistan, where half of the population is impoverished and the provincial government has deep financial woes despite producing most of the country's natural gas, is engaged in an increasingly violent revolt that has killed over four hundred soldiers.[21] Musharraf's heavy handling of the situation and his government's insistence on pushing ahead with a number of large development projects without any regard for local concerns significantly intensified local hostility toward the state. Meanwhile, Pashtun extremists in the tribal areas have been openly fighting the army and dispatching suicide bombers into major cities.

The Military: Exacerbating Religious Tensions

The repeated exploitation of religion by Pakistan's leaders, most egregiously when the military and intelligence agencies have funded and armed extremists to fight their battles in Afghanistan and India, has helped spawn competing sectarian movements that have weakened Pakistanis' sense of a common Islamic identity and unleashed radical militias into a society unable to control them. Governments, even military governments, have great difficultly standing up to organizations and individuals claiming to act in the name of Islam, even if they espouse sectarian or extremist causes. In 2007, for instance, the Musharraf regime waited a very long time before confronting student militants in the Red Mosque complex in Islamabad, despite repeated and flagrant provocations by the students' leaders.

The military's use of religious parties to strengthen its hold on government has led the state to play an expanded role in sectarian disputes, including arguments over such issues as who qualifies as a Muslim (the Ahmadi sect was declared non-Muslim in a 1974 constitutional amendment) and what form of Islamic ideology the country should promote. Official patronage of religious affairs has intensified competition between various Sunni and Shiite Islam clerics and their sects and subsects, encouraging a divisive and destabilizing fractionalization of religion. Since the Islamic revolution in Iran in 1979, the government has taken an increasingly anti-Shiite line, causing deep resentment. Some four thousand people, mostly Shiites, have been killed and thousands more have been injured in clashes between zealots.[22]

The military's use of the more extreme of these religious groups, such as the Taliban, to help fight its battles in Afghanistan and India has, over time, created a potential fifth column within the country. The barely accessible mountainous landscape of the FATA, the deep ambivalence tribesmen there feel toward the Pakistani state, and the cultivation of overseas fund-raising networks have allowed some of these groups to outgrow the military's ability to control them. Fighting in 2006 and 2007 between the army and Taliban fighters cost hundreds of lives and repeatedly exposed the weaknesses of the army, the police, and the government's paramilitary forces. Over the longer term, these extremist groups could leverage the deep resentment against the central state that exists in some of the most under-developed parts of Pakistan, generating a broad, ethnically based fundamentalist challenge to the national government that would be more dangerous than anything it has dealt with up to now. In January 2008, Aftab Khan Sherpao, a former interior minister, warned that in the Northwest Frontier Province there is "a risk of 'total Talibanization.'"[23]

The Military: Weakening the Political System

Pakistan's democratic interludes have strengthened state cohesion by creating something akin to a national two-party system and by co-opting ethnolinguistic movements into the state's political framework. By contrast, the country's military rulers have traditionally sought to vitiate mainstream political forces by weakening those forces and allying instead with religious groups that (because they have relatively small bases of support) pose less of a challenge to the military's power.

Pakistani democracy, it should be made clear, has a poor track record of delivering good governance, with the country's two major parties—the Pakistan People's Party (PPP) and the Pakistan Muslim League (PML)—performing dis-mally when in power. (The excitement that greeted their return to government in 2008 will likely dissapate in few short years.) Even so, their competition for votes has focused on winning the political middle ground rather than the extremist margins, and they have distributed government patronage widely throughout the country. As the lower classes have enjoyed more access to power through the ballot box, so the elite's grip on the state has weakened.

In previous decades, democratic rule also allowed for better representation of ethnic interests at the provincial level and greater negotiation between the center and the provinces, giving the government more legitimacy and reducing both resentment toward the state and sectarian conflict. In contrast to military rule, which has presided over the disasters of the civil war in East Pakistan, the breeding of Islamic militancy, and repeated regional uprisings, the democratic years brought relative quiet, with the only major unrest occurring in the 1970s in Baluchistan.

Musharraf, like the other generals who have sat in the president's office, worked closely for most of his rule with religious groups while weakening the mainstream parties that are the greatest challenge to his control. He kept the country's two most popular politicians—Nawaz Sharif (leader of the PML) and Benazir Bhutto (head of the PPL)—in exile until 2007 and changed the eligibility criteria for holding elected office in such a way as to disqualify many politicians from the two main parties. Meanwhile, he gave groups that some analysts have accused of "direct involvement with terror networks"[24] a greater role in Pakistan's government than at any time in the country's history. The Muttahida Majlis-e-Amal (MMA), an alliance of six Islamic parties created and aided by the military, won 11 percent of the popular vote and 20 percent of the parliamentary seats in the 2002 poll, a far better showing than those parties had achieved before. The MMA also captured control of the NWFP and joined a coalition government in Balochistan, marking the first time that Islamic parties have had a hand in government in any part of the country. (The freer 2008 election ejected the MMA from power in favor of secular parties.) Meanwhile, Musharraf's myopic focus on retaining power led to government neglect of the rising threat from extremists in 2006 and 2007, despite a report from his own Interior Ministry that "the Taliban were spreading so fast that 'swift and decisive action,' was needed to prevent the insurgency from engulfing the rest of the country."[25]

The Military: Weakening the State

The military's stranglehold on the state's budgetary resources, together with the elite's obvious lack of interest in fostering social development among the general population, has seriously inhibited the extension of the state to all parts of Pakistan, leaving a significant number of people and places underserved by the government and encouraging the growth of organizations—typically, religious organizations—that are willing and able to provide needed services. The military's heavy-handedness in dealing with these underserved local populations—especially since 9/11—has encouraged some of these groups to turn increasingly toward active opposition to the state.

The country's elite has repeatedly shown an unwillingness to invest in the social advancement of the Pakistani masses, seeing them both as a threat to its hold on power and as an underclass undeserving of a better life. "Pakistan's public education system has failed because it is not valued enough by the politically important components of the state's leadership."[26] The same could be said about other important public services, such as health services and the courts. The elite has always been satisfied with a half-democracy led by "a paternalistic government that meant well and shared power only when required to do so."[27] The praetorian democracy established by the military met the elite's basic requirements and ensured that its members would never be threatened by the empowerment of the masses.

The military domination of the political scene since the late 1970s has corresponded with a precipitous decline in the quality of life for most Pakistanis. (Not all of this was the army's fault, for the "economy has been under the tutelage of the international lending agencies, the IMF and the World Bank," which have emphasized budget cutting over social development.)[28] Development expenditures plunged from 9.3 percent of GDP in 1980–1981 to a mere 2.1 percent in 2000–2001.[29] This drop hit Pakistan's poorest classes the hardest: the country ranked one hundred and twentieth on the United Nations Development Programme's Human Development Index in 1991, ahead of both India and Bangladesh; by 2003 it had fallen to one hundred and forty-fourth, behind both countries and the lowest-ranking state outside of Africa except for Nepal.[30] While the percentage of the population in poverty in India fell from 45 percent in 1983 to 26 percent in 2001, in Pakistan the comparable figure rose from 17 percent in 1987 to 33 percent in 2001. Almost three-quarters of all Pakistani women cannot read. Almost one-half of the population does not have access to health services. There are nine soldiers for every one doctor and three soldiers for every two teachers in Pakistan.[31]

This poor record has encouraged the growth of extremist groups, especially in the seven tribal agencies, Pakistan's main source of international terrorism. The remnants of al Qaeda, including Osama bin Laden, fled to the FATA when defeated in Afghanistan, and are most likely still finding sanctuary there. Taliban-inspired militias control parts of the area, and some attacks against NATO and U.S. troops in neighboring Afghanistan have been launched from the FATA. Yet the Pakistani military, which has used religious groups to strengthen its hold on power and implement its foreign policies, has traditionally been reluctant to impose its will on the FATA and uninterested in extending state services into those territories. From 2006 to 2007, for instance, Musharraf opted not to send troops into the FATA to confront terrorists directly. (In contrast, the secular political party that triumphed in the NWFP in 2008 elections seeks to develop the tribal areas and being them into the mainstream of Pakistani political life.)

The FATA continue to be treated as pseudo-colonies six decades after in-dependence even though a majority of their inhabitants would prefer the FATA to be fully incorporated within Pakistan and FATA's residents to be given the same rights and services as full citizens.[32] FATA residents are "probably the most neglected Pakistanis," which helps explain their susceptibleness to the promises and threats made by Islamist radicals. Waziristan, where militant activity has been most noticeable, has a literacy rate of around 10 percent and only one hospital bed for every six thousand inhabitants. Eighty percent of boys attend madrasas, while girls get no education at all.[33]

The Military: Weakening the Rule of Law

The military's repeated manipulation of laws, courts, and judges (something of which many members of the civilian elite have been equally guilty) has weak-ened institutions and contributed to the widespread lawlessness within Pakistani society. After each of the three military interventions in the country's political affairs, the military has abrogated or suspended the constitution before securing a fake legitimacy by manhandling the courts into endorsing military rule. The Musharraf regime, for instance, purged the courts of judges that might challenge the president's position (in 2000, to cite the most notorious example, all judges were required to take an oath to abide by his Provisional Constitutional Order—an act that would violate their oaths to uphold the constitution), filled key posts with allies, and manipulated the flow of cases to the disadvantage of litigants challenging government actions. Despite the role judges played in restoring democracy to the country in 2008, and despite the rhetoric of Pakistan's new civilian government regarding the restorration of their powers, history suggests that the new regime will also seek to manipulate the judiciary when it serves the regime's interests.

*   *   *

The record of the Musharraf regime was not entirely bad. Most notably, it presided over the reinvigoration of Pakistan's economy—a rejuvenation spurred in part by the enormous infusion of U.S. cash since 9/11. His administration continued and extended economic reforms launched under the previous regime, and the results helped transform the country's macroeconomic and fiscal environments. Large increases in aid, debt forgiveness, and remittances increased investment rates and led to sharp rises in equity (up over 1,000 percent from 1999 to 2006) and land prices. Growth reached over 8 percent in 2005, private consumption doubled from 2003 to 2005, and foreign reserves increased from $1.7 billion in 1999 to $13 billion in 2006.[34] The regime also deserves credit for its management of Pakistan's relations with India, which improved significantly; for shutting down the network run by A. Q. Khan (the founder of Pakistan's nuclear program) to sell nuclear technology; and for its response to the devastating 2005 earthquake in Kashmir.

These accomplishments, however, cannot compensate for the grievous harm the regime inflicted on the country. The military's—and to a certain degree the elite's—actions steadily increased sectarianism, religious extremism, and violence within the country while severely damaging the country's institutions. As the *Economist* explained in July 2006, "perhaps the most damning criticism of General Musharraf is that he continues to do grave damage to the long-term political health of Pakistan. In his seven long years in office, he has insinuated the army into every nook and cranny of Pakistani public life, weakening institutions that were feeble already, emasculating its political parties and reducing parliament to a squabbling irrelevance."[35] Given elite co-option with much of what the militory has forged, the system of praetorian rule he helped to entrench will not be easily dislodged.

WHAT HOPE FOR REFORM?

Reasons for Pessimism

Pakistan offers an immense challenge to anyone willing to tackle its many problems. The country needs dramatic changes in the nature and structure of its institutions and the conduct of its elite, yet such changes are highly unlikely to be introduced by those who benefit from the current system. Those changes are also unlikely to be vigorously pressed by outsiders. Washington, which has the greatest influence over Islamabad, showed how reluctant it is to disrupt the status quo when it refused to seriously challenge the Musharraf government; that reluctance is only strengthened when U.S. policymakers see how entrenched the military's power has become and how little enthusiasm there is for genuine reform of the state's governance system among many in the establishment. U.S. dependence on the army to conduct counterterrorist operations within Pakistan's borders just reinforces these tendencies. Such a passive approach, however, ensures only that Pakistan's internal situation will continue to deteriorate and that the dangers it poses for the rest of the world will continue to grow.

The United States' best option is to adopt a dual strategy that encourages whatever reform is possible without disrupting the establishment in the short term, while gradually improving the competence and independence of the state's institutions over the long term. Unfortunately, past U.S. policy in Pakistan does not encourage much optimism about Washington's appetite for long-term perspectives. Washington has repeatedly emphasized its own immediate regional objectives at the expense of Pakistan's long-term development in its dealings with the state, often ignoring or unintentionally encouraging events within the country that have been detrimental to U.S. as well as to Pakistani interests. It has established three separate alliances with Pakistan: the first to confront the Soviet Union in the 1950s; the second to oppose the Soviet-installed regime in Afghanistan after 1979; and the third to combat terrorism after 9/11. In each case, Washington has pumped in aid and security assistance in exchange for Pakistan accepting an American diktat over one or more parts of its foreign policy. Islamabad, however, seems always to have insisted that Washington not directly interfere in events within the country's borders. This approach was especially evident during the 1980s, when the United States ignored the military-controlled regime's nuclear program, close involvement with various extremist (and even virulently anti-American) groups, corrupt misuse of U.S. financial aid, and dismemberment of democratic institutions. At other times, when the United States has not felt the need to purchase control of some part of Pakistan's foreign policy, it has simply relegated Pakistan to an almost trivial status—as occurred during the 1990s and early 2000s, when Washington ignored the rising militancy within Pakistan's borders and in neighboring Afghanistan that would eventually produce the 9/11 attacks. Many of the country's worst problems today are the blowback from this long history of poor U.S. policy toward Pakistan.

This same pattern has been evident since 9/11. The United States has reengaged Pakistan after a period of censure (prompted by Pakistan's nuclear test in 1998 and military coup in 1999) because an immediate regional foreign policy objective (ousting the Taliban and al Qaeda from Afghanistan) came to the fore. Although Washington has placed more emphasis in recent years than in the past on Pakistan's social and economic development, Washington is once again ignoring much of Pakistan's domestic scene, even though conditions and government policies there promise to aggravate the regional threats to U.S. national security. Most U.S. financial aid, for example, is concentrated on military assistance and general fiscal support, with very little funneled toward improving how institutions work or extending state services into impoverished areas. Until recently, less than 1 percent of U.S. aid was being spent on education even though education should be a centerpiece of any strategy to reform the country and reduce extremism within its borders.[36] Almost no money was invested in democracy programs until 2006, and the amounts expended thereafter were paltry and went chiefly to a body controlled by Musharraf.[37] Where Washington has made its presence most felt domestically—in its manipulation of the political system to suit its own short-term interests—its actions have stirred much public resentment without necessarily ameliorating Pakistan's myriad problems.

With the U.S. political system—as always—promoting short-term perspectives, Washington is behaving as though it sees little or no connection between, on the one hand, Pakistan's political, social, sectarian, and institutional afflictions and, on the other hand, the vigor of terrorist movements in the region. Washington continues to give almost unconditional support to the state (except for urging it to do more to root out terrorism in the tribal areas) even though its large infusions of aid (over $10 billion through the end of 2006, not including several large debt write-offs),[38] supplies of important military equipment (including F-16 fighter aircraft), and influence among Pakistan's most important donors and lenders provide Washington with considerable leverage over the country, especially if used in ways that do not directly threaten the ruling class.

Reasons for Optimism

Pakistan is in a parlous condition, but it is not a hopeless case. Despite decades of misrule, it still possesses assets that could be invaluable were Washington to make a long-term commitment to helping Pakistanis refashion their state. Unlike most Muslim countries in the Greater Middle East, Pakistan has significant experience with competitive elections, a court system and legal profession that prize their independence (as evidenced by the 2007 protests over Musharraf's attempts to fire the chief justice), a reasonably free and critical media, and a strong political opposition. In contrast to places such as Palestine, Egypt, and Jordan, where elections have rewarded militants, free elections in Pakistan have consistently strengthened moderates. Pakistan's people have a sufficiently strong sense of a common identity that, given the right governing institutions, they could create a reasonably cohesive state-nation, much as the citizens of India have done. Unlike most fragile states, Pakistan is not afflicted by an incoherent geography, a lack of economic potential, a citizenry that is utterly divided, or governing bodies that are incurably brittle. On the contrary, many of its troubles are self-inflicted (albeit reinforced by how outsiders have dealt with it). Given different circumstances, it could have developed differently; given different policies now, it could yet transform itself into a vigorous state similar to India, with which it shares much common history.

Malaysia is also a good model for Pakistan to emulate. The country is economically dynamic, more or less democratic (though ruled by one party for decades), Muslim, and has successfully navigated the complexities of its ethnically diverse population. It is also a part of the East Asia economic area, which should inspire Pakistan to focus more on engineering an economic takeoff (such as India has enjoyed in recent years). Musharraf himself seemed to consider Malaysia an excellent model of economic and political development; the West would be wise to portray its reform agenda as helping Pakistan to follow in Malaysia's footsteps.[39]

Malaysia has probably gained more from globalization than any other Muslim state, consistently garnering large inflows of investment into its manufacturing sector from companies such as Intel, Dell, and Samsung, leading to sustained annual growth of over 7 percent between 1970 and 1997. Following the East Asian model pioneered by Japan and the four Asian tigers, Malaysia transformed itself from an unstable, ethnically divided, highly inequitable, and poor country into a dynamic, manufacturing export-led, highly literate, far more inclusive and equitable middle-income country in two generations. Merchandise exports grew from $1.7 billion in 1970 to $160.6 billion in 2006, making the relatively small country the nineteenth largest exporter in the world.[40] Meanwhile, the percentage of the population in poverty fell from 49.3 percent in 1970 to 5.5 percent in 2000.[41]

Reform and the Role of the United States

To effect significant change in the way that Pakistan is governed, Washington needs to adopt a multitiered strategy. Instead of simply trying to engineer a government amenable to its interests, Washington should be seeking to engage Pakistan on a much broader front in order to foster the processes within the country necessary to produce political, economic, and social development. Some areas can be tackled now, but many of the most important problems require a sustained campaign—lasting at least a generation—if significant headway is to be made.

In addition to urging Pakistan to follow Malaysia's example, the United States should make a point of pushing for reforms that the country's elite sees as in its own interests. For example, the restructuring of Pakistan's economy, the most obvious success Musharraf could claim from his time in power, could be expanded to encourage more investment, more competition, and more jobs, all of which would do much to improve growth prospects, while spreading its benefits among the general population (far too many of the reforms pressed by the U.S. government and international financial institutions tend to enrich only the well-educated classes). A greater emphasis could be placed, for example, on fostering the growth of small businesses and improving the administrative climate for investment by reducing the unfair bureaucratic and legal advantages that the military and the elite currently enjoy.

Washington should also concern itself with the condition of Pakistan's society—from which so many terrorists spring and within which so many other terrorists hide. Diverting just a small amount of the tens of billions of dollars that the United States spends annually to try and protect itself against terrorism and using that money instead to fund infrastructure, education, and health projects in areas underserved by the state would have significant long-term—and highly cost-effective—benefits for the United States and its allies. Public education in particular needs to be improved and expanded, with the madrasa networks being integrated into the state system (and extremism purged from the classroom) and the curricula changed to teach Pakistan's masses the skills they need to compete in the global economy. The $750 million, five-year plan for social spending in the tribal areas announced by the Bush administration in 2007 is a step in the right direction, but it is too little to make a substantial impact on what is a statewide problem.

In the longer term, the United States needs to adopt a policy that encourages the gradual restructuring of governing bodies, making them far more representative, legitimate, inclusive, and effective, thus strengthening the capacity of the state to deal with the roots of the country's sectarian divisions, deep inequities, and growing extremism. These initiatives would concomitantly diminish the role of the military and the civilian establishment.

Empowering Pakistan's diverse communities at the provincial and local level is essential if the state's political economy and system of governance are ever to be adequately reformed. Decentralizing the state as articulated in the 1973 constitution, including giving each province more direct control over its own revenues and natural resources, is essential if Baluchistan and other areas are to be pacified, fully integrated with the state, and developed. Incorporating tribal areas into the country (and thus dissolving the FATA), giving their citizens the same rights as citizens enjoy elsewhere in Pakistan, and extending government services into these areas would give the authorities far greater capacity to reduce the extremism that the current arrangement encourages. If the government distributed its largesse—its funds for schools, health care, transportation, and so forth—equally throughout its territory, much of the anger now directed at the authorities would be reduced. Allocating important national jobs—including those within the military—equally among the country's disparate groups would make the state seem far more representative of all its people than it is now.

Measures that strengthen the rule of law and reduce the ability of the country's elite to manipulate the state for its own ends—such as reducing the executive's authority over the judiciary—are essential if the government is ever to be seen by the great majority of Pakistan's population as their legitimate agent. Strengthening the capacity and independence of state organs at all levels of government—through training, salary increases, greater transparency, better-managed elections, and the empowerment of political parties and NGOs—is essential if the state is to extend its reach, improve the range and quality of its services, and reduce inequities in their delivery. Fortifying institutions such as the Supreme Court, electoral commission, national and provincial legislatures, anticorruption bodies, and independent budget offices will force Pakistan's rulers to do a better job of serving the people. Strengthening the independence of the media is especially important in a country where it is probably one of the few institutions able to hold the military and elite accountable for their actions. U.S. engagement with a broader spectrum of Pakistani society—including moderate Islamists—will make it seem less self-serving, weakening support for extremists.

Leveraging the experiences and capacities of states with similar social and cultural backgrounds, such as Malaysia, would probably be far more effective than simply hiring Western consultants with little experience in an environment like Pakistan's. Similarly, encouraging the military to work with Turkey's armed forces might spread some of the latter's ethos—and its commitment to a democratizing, secularizing, Westernized state—to Pakistan.

Although the United States can use its considerable leverage over Pakistan to launch many of these reforms, only by co-opting a significant segment of the elite—including some part of the military establishment—can Washington ensure that the reforms are actually implemented. To this end, the United States should devote much greater effort to educating the top echelons within Pakistan's society and military of the danger to their own positions posed by a continuation of the state's current course toward greater extremism. Ultimately, however, the United States needs to draw the military and civilian elite into a bear hug that protects and rewards them, while forcing them to adopt the kinds of reforms outlined above. Holding free and fair elections on a regular basis will help to foster the processes that can drive Pakistan onto a more positive trajectory. Ensuring that the military stays sufficiently supportive of reform and counterterrorist operations while its influence over the state is gradually reduced will require far greater diplomacy and a more judicious use of carrots and sticks than Washington has shown up to now.

LEARNING FROM THE PAST

Every country has many possible paths along which it might evolve given its fixed set of sociocultural, geographical, and historical legacies. Although Pakistan is often grouped with other Muslim countries in the greater Middle East, Islam is only one of many factors influencing Pakistan's internal development—and, until 1979, it could even have been considered a secondary factor. While fundamentalist religious ideas have strengthened their sway over Pakistan's people in recent years, especially with the war in Iraq and growing access to satellite television, many of the factors that have shaped India's successful postcolonial evolution from a potentially fragile state to an economic and political powerhouse are still present within Pakistan; they may be dormant at present but they could be activated if circumstances within the country were different.

If Pakistan were to adopt the right institutional framework, it could follow India (and Malaysia, another former British possession) on the path toward prosperity and stability. But for this to happen, Pakistani leaders and U.S. policymakers must first learn the great lesson of Pakistan's postcolonial history: actions geared toward gaining a short-term advantage can have disastrous long-term consequences, especially if those actions are taken without any attempt to assess their broader implications.

Azerbaijan: Pressing Reform on an Autocracy

On July 13, 2006, world leaders congregated on the Turkish coast to celebrate the inauguration of the first pipeline bringing oil from the Caspian Sea to the Mediterranean. The oil flowed all the way from Azerbaijan through the Baku-Tbilisi-Ceyhan (BTC) pipeline, which cost $4 billion to construct but which will eventually deliver 1 million barrels of oil a day to the Turkish coastline. This oil, newly emerging onto world markets, signaled the rise of Azerbaijan from a backwater state to a significant energy supplier to the West and a strategic partner of the United States. The extension of an existing gas pipeline as far as Greece and Italy, slated for completion in 2012, promises to solidify this position and increase the country's importance to the European Union.[1] These developments are a particularly significant accomplishment for U.S. foreign policy, which has led an energetic Western diplomatic effort for more than a decade to create oil and gas pipelines from Azerbaijan that would pass through neither Russian nor Iranian territory.

Azerbaijan has reserves of at least 7 billion barrels of recoverable oil, the second-most among Caspian Sea states, and at least 30 trillion cubic feet of natural gas.[2] Its oil wealth alone is expected to be worth at least $160 billion over the next twenty years, making it one of the world's most important new suppliers.[3] As President George W. Bush declared in April 2006, Azerbaijan has "a very important role to play" in guaranteeing energy security around the world.[4] Its geopolitical importance as Iran's northern neighbor and at the potential center of Washington's Central Asian energy strategy (which seeks to deny Russia and Iran any control over the region's oil) has made the state a priority of the Pentagon.[5] U.S. military assistance has increased, including, according to some reports, investments in "cooperative security locations" (unmanned facilities with prepositioned equipment and logistical arrangements), maritime surveillance radars to help interdict illicit weapons of mass destruction,[6] and listening stations along the Iranian border.[7]

Thus, there was good reason to uncork the champagne in Washington and other Western capitals when Caspian oil was finally pumped on to a tanker in the Mediterranean. Yet, while this triumph deserves acclaim, other aspects of Western policy toward Azerbaijan are less laudable. Indeed, they are so shortsighted, cynical, and contradictory that they risk undermining efforts to turn Azerbaijan into a stable, prosperous, and reliable ally.

At the heart of the problem is an all-too-common clash between short-term and long-term objectives, between, on the one hand, a readiness to do whatever is necessary—including turning a blind eye to authoritarianism—to secure a geostrategically important country as an ally and, on the other hand, an awareness that only by promoting accountable government in that country will it acquire enduring stability as a state, an energy supplier, and a military partner.[8]

Both the United States and the European Union invited Azerbaijan's president, Ilham H. Aliyev, to visit just a few months after they had criticized his government's handling of parliamentary elections as marred by "major irregularities and fraud."[9] Washington and, albeit to a lesser extent, Brussels have provided diplomatic and military support for the regime in Baku in recent years despite numerous international surveys rating the country as one of the least free and most corrupt.

Meanwhile, Azerbaijan has seen a slow but steady rise in its number of observant Muslims, not least because of growing dissatisfaction with the highly inequitable distribution of wealth and with government maladministration and repression. As in neighboring Iran, in Azerbaijan Shiism is the dominant religion, and the danger exists that the Azeri population will be radicalized in the same—anti-Western—fashion as their coreligionists in many other parts of Central Asia and the Middle East. The thwarting in October 2007 of a major terrorist attack on Western targets in Baku, the country's capital, and the subsequent arrest of dozens of extremists highlight the danger of this radicalization.[10]

Azerbaijan's stability—and, indeed, the stability of the entire Caucasus—is further imperiled by the continuation of the country's festering ethnic conflict with Armenia, which won a war between the two states in the early 1990s. Resentment among Azeris, especially the hundreds of thousands displaced by the war, runs high, and hopes of exacting revenge on the Armenians are fueled by thought of the arms that Azerbaijan can buy with its new oil wealth. Aliyev's government, which has been amplifying its belligerent rhetoric as the oil windfall approaches, is in the process of boosting its military spending from $135 million in 2003 to $1 billion in 2009.

The long-term future for Azerbaijan and for Western access to Caspian Sea oil and gas reserves depends upon the U.S. government working with its European allies to fashion a less contradictory and more nuanced strategy to help Azerbaijan resolve its two main problems—bad governance and the conflict with Armenia. If Washington and Brussels stop tolerating authoritarianism and saber rattling in Baku, and start replacing empty rhetoric about peace and democracy with a set of policies tailored to Azerbaijan's sociocultural and political circumstances, the chances of Azerbaijan enjoying a stable and prosperous future will improve substantially.

AT THE CROSSROADS OF ASIA AND EUROPE

Azerbaijan lies on the southeastern edge of the Caucasus, at the crossroads of diverse civilizations. Wave after wave of immigration and conquest from the earliest recorded times have left a distinctive and complex legacy among the peoples that live in the region's three states: Azerbaijan, Georgia, and Armenia (see Map 11.1). Azerbaijan's multilayered and multifaceted national identity— and the current challenges it faces as a state—reflects this geography, history, and legacy.

Turkic speaking, but historically part of the Persian Empire,[11] Azeris have a much thinner history as an independent and unified group than do their Caucasus neighbors—a fact that helps explain their incomplete transition to nationhood and relatively weak cohesion. Historically, the inhabitants of today's Azerbaijan were ruled by a dozen or more sultanates and khanates—regional petty princedoms— that retained varying degrees of autonomy until the beginning of tsarist rule in the nineteenth century and that have bequeathed a legacy of allegiance to local, rather than national, authority. Azerbaijan today is characterized by great ethnic diversity—the country contains not only Azeris but also substantial minorities of Russians, Armenians (until 1988 at least), and smaller Caucasian nationalities such as Talysh and Lezgins—and by sharp social, geographical, and income differences, which separate cosmopolitan Baku from some of the most deprived towns and villages in the Caucasus.[12]

The most obvious outside legacies today are from the two centuries of Russian mastery: a majority of people in Baku understand Russian; hundreds of dead factories and ugly, Soviet-era apartment blocks scar industrial centers such as Sumgayit; and the country's administrative, political, and business cultures manifest some of the worst aftereffects of the Communist period. A corrosive kleptocracy overwhelms government organs: Azerbaijan ranked as one of the seven most corrupt countries in the world in an October 2004 survey carried out by Transparency International.[13] It scored just below Russia on the 2006 Index of Economic Freedom, placed one hundred and twenty-third out of one hundred and fifty-seven countries, far behind its Caucasus neighbors.[14]

Two factors largely explain why the country has not become as authoritarian as its Central Asian neighbors across the Caspian Sea. The first of these is the residual effect of the wave of European ideas about democracy and civil rights that splashed onto Azerbaijan's shores a century ago. From 1881 to 1918, when the oil industry first effectively fell under Bolshevik control, Azerbaijan dominated international markets, supplying as much as half of the world's petroleum. Foreign investors and workers from across Europe flooded into the area seeking opportunity

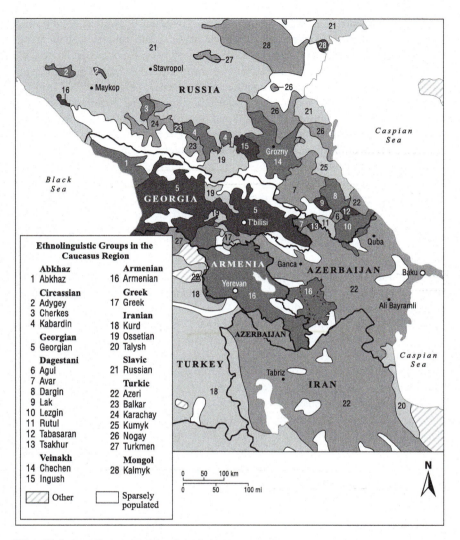

Map 11.1. The Caucasus' Ethnolinguistic Demography
Source: Central Intelligence Agency.

and bringing the latest and most progressive ideas with them. The boom left an important heritage on the Caspian: not just a small constellation of European-style architectural gems in Baku, but a longing among its intelligentsia to be accepted into the European family of nations. Azeri officials, scholars, businesspeople, and students all seek acceptance by Western countries, organizations, and academic bodies; few even bother visiting their eastern or southern neighbors, never mind seeking to emulate them. The second factor guarding against authoritarianism is the strong influence that Western ideas about governance exert in neighboring states such as Turkey, Azerbaijan's strongest ally and the country to which it is closest culturally and linguistically (the two countries share a common language).

A new wave of Western investment is revitalizing Azerbaijan's oil industry today. The $10 billion so-called contract of the century, signed in 1994 by the Azerbaijan government and a consortium of oil companies, has led to a flood of foreign investment in oil exploration and development. Additional money has poured into gas exploration. Western-organized efforts to construct oil and gas pipelines that skirt Russia and Iran have attracted yet more investment.

The growth of the hydrocarbon sector, however, has led to the type of unbalanced development commonly found in mineral-rich states, with a small clique acquiring enormous wealth and power while the majority of the population is economically marginalized and politically disenfranchised. At the same time, government maladministration and the rising prices that have accompanied the inflow of new money threaten to keep much of the population impoverished. The collapse of the planned economy in the early 1990s and the subsequent inflationary spiral fueled by the growing energy sector have combined to wipe out almost every other manufacturing sector. The oil sector today accounts for two-thirds of industrial production and more than 90 percent of the value of the country's exports.[15] But it contributes little to employment.[16] Despite having one of the highest rates of GDP per capita among the former Soviet republics due to its oil wealth, Azerbaijan has the second-highest proportion of undernourished people.[17] The personal incomes of 49 percent of the population fall below the poverty line.[18] Many observers attribute the inexorable rise in the number of devout Muslims, as evidenced by the thousands who come to pray on Fridays at the Abu Bakr mosque in Baku and by growing pockets of adherents elsewhere, to a widespread sense of helplessness in the face of the dislocations caused by an economic and political tumult that seems to benefit only a privileged few.[19] The number of local Salafis—fundamentalist Muslims—has rapidly increased, reaching as high as ten thousand, according to one estimate.[20]

A DEMOCRATIC FAÇADE

Aliyev's Increasing Authoritarianism

Azerbaijan's weak sense of statehood and feeble formal institutions have made attempts to improve governance difficult to sustain, despite strong prodemocratic sentiments among many of its people. From 1918 to 1920, the first time the country was genuinely united, Azerbaijan was—to quote a phrase often heard in the country—the "first Muslim democratic republic in the world," complete with laws that provided for the equal suffrage of women before many Western states did.[21] Although these democratic impulses did not at the time extend far beyond the educated elite in Baku, the experience left a deep imprint on Azeris of all classes, which helps explain Azerbaijan's robust, if brief, embrace of democracy immediately after the fall of the Soviet Union in 1992. Even the authoritarian government that came to power in the wake of a bloodless coup in 1993, prompted in large part by the country's failings in its war with Armenia, has felt a far greater obligation to observe at least the rudiments of democracy in its rhetoric and political processes than have authoritarian states to its north, south, and east.

Recent years, however, have seen a ruling elite dominate the levers of power and display diminishing interest in building upon that modest democratic legacy, preferring instead to use the country's growing hydrocarbon wealth to more firmly entrench itself in power. Heydar Aliyev, the current president's father and the country's ruler from 1993 to 2003 (when terminal illness forced him to hand power to his son), was no champion of unfettered democracy and always rigged national elections to ensure he maintained power. Heydar did, however, feel strong enough politically to permit a relatively open environment in which opposition parties were allowed to campaign in competitive elections, independent media were allowed to criticize political leaders, and NGOs were allowed to organize antigovernment demonstrations. In contrast, his son, Ilham, has felt less politically secure and has displayed a clumsier and heavier political hand, more or less openly repressing any opposition. He has overseen two badly flawed elections, the first of which, in 2003, was followed by a violent police crackdown on dissent that involved the arrest of more than six hundred opponents of his regime. Noncompliant editors are regularly harassed and even jailed, and the independent media now engages in considerable self-censorship.[22] Ilham's administration has also promoted a Central Asian-style personality cult, as evidenced by the thousands of pictures of father and son that now dot the country, and the monuments, streets, and squares erected and named in honor of Heydar. Both father and son have depended on the support of the so-called Nakhichevan Clan, made up of people from their home turf in the Nakhichevan enclave (located between Armenia and Turkey, see Map 11.2), which has alienated other clans, regions, and ethnic groups and has weakened the nation-building process that started after independence.

The completion of the BTC pipeline and the rising price of oil have only reinforced the leadership's belief that Western calls for political reform can be safely dismissed. Ilham's visit to the White House in April 2006 and to Brussels in November 2006, so soon after the second discredited ballot, further strengthened these views. Indeed, in Brussels, the leader of the European Commission publicly expressed support for Ilham, and declared that Azerbaijan's imperfect democracy should be seen within the context of "the situation in a country that is in a very peculiar region."[23]

This deterioration in political freedom can be seen in independent evaluations of Azerbaijan's democratic practice. Freedom House downgraded the country from "Partly Free" to "Not Free" in 2003, precisely at the time of the transition. In June 2006, Azerbaijan's "democracy rating" was 5.93 on a scale of 1 (a consolidated democracy) to 7 (a consolidated authoritarian regime), even worse than Russia's 5.75.[24]

The Organization for Security and Cooperation in Europe (OSCE) flatly stated that the November 2005 elections did not meet international standards because of the "interference of local authorities, disproportionate use of force to thwart rallies, arbitrary detentions, [and] restrictive interpretations of campaign provisions."[25] A U.S. State Department spokesman concurred, declaring that "there were major irregularities and fraud [during the election] that are of serious concern."[26]

The Western Response: A Mismatch between Rhetoric and Action

The Western response to this deteriorating record of respect for democracy has been marked by pious but empty declarations of support for Azerbaijani democracy; an overly narrow attitude toward democratization and how outsiders might encourage it; and, especially in Washington, a cookie-cutter approach to the use of aid that actually limits the West's ability to improve standards of governance in Azerbaijan. The cumulative effect on the Aliyev government has been minimal.

Both Washington and Brussels have repeatedly stressed the importance of democracy, only to subsequently ignore their own proclamations in seeking closer ties with the regime in Baku. In the fall of 2005, for instance, President Bush dispatched a letter and a senior envoy to Aliyev promising to "elevate our countries' relations to a new strategic level" if an honest vote was held.[27] Senior administration officials in Washington suggested that an invitation for Azerbaijan's president to visit the White House would be contingent on Ilham holding fair and free elections.[28] In the event, however, geopolitical concerns seemingly caused the administration to quietly discard these conditions when, in April 2006, it decided to host Aliyev despite the shoddy conduct of the election. (In contrast, the White House shunned the administration of resource-poor Ukraine when President Kuchma's actions did not meet Western standards of governance, even seeking to marginalize him at international gatherings.)[29] Understandably, the *New York Times* commented that the invitation raised "fresh questions about the degree to which American standards are malleable."[30]

The European Union has behaved in much the same way. Despite assertions by the EU external relations commissioner in the run-up to the November 2005 elections that the conduct of those elections would be a "litmus test" for closer relations with the European Union and "that Azerbaijan's democratic record will also weigh heavily on an eventual EU decision on whether to give the country a neighborhood 'action plan' at all,"[31] the European Union later signed just such a partnership action plan in November 2006. Critics understandably complained that "the union is prepared to compromise its own standards in exchange for access to Azerbaijan's vast energy reserves."[32]

Such actions raise important questions about whether either the United States or the European Union actually has a coherent and sustainable long-term strategy toward Azerbaijan. Inviting Aliyev to Western capitals and encouraging Azerbaijan to join Western organizations (such as the Council of Europe, which it joined in 2001) fosters not only a façade of respectability that helps the current regime retain power but also feeds resentment against the West. Many local analysts, indeed, have noted a slow rise in such sentiment over the last decade,[33] a sharp contrast with neighboring Georgia, where strong U.S. support for democratization has done much to boost the public image of the United States in that country.

What Western policymakers need to do, of course, is to not let their short-term geopolitical interests in strategically important states undermine those countries' long-term stability and development. But to do this they need to tone down their muscular rhetoric about democracy and to tone up their underdeveloped appreciation of what accountable government entails and of the need to adjust their policies to better foster this given the local circumstances and local restraints. Embracing a broader and more nuanced conception of how a population might hold its leaders accountable and what is entailed in effective state building, in which free and fair elections are only one of many indicators of progress toward a more robust polity and economy, will make U.S. and European rhetoric about democracy seem less hypocritical and their efforts to foster change more successful. By overemphasizing the conduct of elections in its rhetoric, in its allocation of aid, and in its use of diplomatic carrots and sticks, the West has undercut its ability to effect the significant reforms in governance that would make leaders more responsible to their people. Instead of trying to force a regime over which it has limited leverage to conduct free and fair elections, the United States and Europe might deploy their influence in more productive ways to make budgets more transparent, judges more honest, and local governments more accountable to citizens.

A FESTERING CONFLICT

A Frozen War

The second major issue threatening Azerbaijan's stable development is its frozen war with Armenia over Nagorno-Karabakh and the possibility that it might again erupt into armed conflict. Although the current stalemate has held since 1994, simmering tensions combined with the changing balance of power caused by Azerbaijan's rapidly rising petrochemical revenues threaten to reignite the violence. Even if a renewal of fighting can be avoided, the current state of affairs holds back economic and political progress throughout the Caucasus, preventing the area from weaning itself from Russian influence and developing in ways that would bring the Caucasus states more securely into the Western fold. Meanwhile, the continuing Azeri belief that Nagorno-Karabakh is part of Azerbaijan's historical patrimony despite its overwhelmingly Armenian population and history of Armenian self-rule[34] severely limits Azerbaijan's ability to seek a resolution that might actually help consolidate the state (for, by example, physically linking its two parts)[35] and improve the lives of the country's citizens.

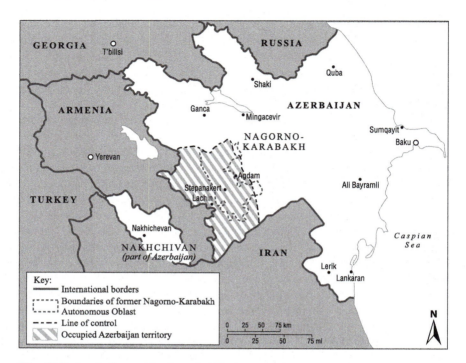

Map 11.2. Azerbaijan and Its Occupied Territory
Source: International Crisis Group.

Karabakh, a beautiful and mountainous area of Azerbaijan, which, even before the war, had a predominantly ethnic Armenian population, was the scene of the bloodiest war to arise in the wake of the Soviet Union's collapse, killing more than thirty thousand people and displacing more than one million in the early 1990s. Armenian-backed forces won the conflict and continue to occupy the area and seven surrounding districts (more than 13 percent of Azerbaijan's territory; see Map 11.2).[36] Still scarred with bombed-out buildings and abandoned villages, Karabakh remains a source of violence: sniper fire and landmine incidents claim dozens of lives a year.[37] Commercial and social contacts between the two peoples, who had lived as neighbors for centuries and who continue to work alongside one another in markets, retail stores, and restaurants in Georgia and Russia, are almost nonexistent across their common border.

Although some outsiders have occasionally seen a glimmer of hope in negotiations held in recent years, few within the region expect any breakthrough in the near future. In fact, many analysts see ominous signs, especially with the opening of the BTC pipeline and the wealth it is bringing to Baku. Sabine Freizer of the International Crisis Group (ICG), the author of one of the most comprehensive reports on the conflict, sees Azerbaijan's position hardening as oil revenues begin to flow and as frustrations with the stalemate grow. "There is a level of belligerence that is just incredible, because they think they can ultimately win," she says.[38] Aliyev declared in June 2005 that "the enemy should know that the Azerbaijani army can liberate its land at any moment, and when necessary we will mobilize all our force to achieve that."[39] The situation is expected to become increasingly dangerous as 2012 approaches because Azerbaijan's oil money is projected to peak around that date.[40]

An Inadequate International Approach

Although both the United States and Europe have been engaged in the peacemaking process through the so-called Minsk Group—a body of mediators cochaired by the United States, France, and Russia and working under the OSCE to resolve the conflict—neither Washington nor Brussels has demonstrated a sense of urgency in its efforts to break the impasse and does not seem worried that the conflict might endanger its growing interests in the region.[41] Rather than developing a comprehensive strategy that will resolve the intractable conflict and lay the foundations for the antagonists' long-term development, the United States and the European Union have engaged in a fundamentally passive diplomatic process that defers potentially difficult decisions while avoiding actions that might harm their own short-term interests in the region.

The Minsk Group has facilitated negotiations between the two sides since 1994, but has not achieved anything of substance for two reasons:[42] First, the process has offered neither incentives for the parties to make the compromises necessary to reach a peace agreement nor threatened repercussions for failing to do so.[43] Instead, external aid to and investment in both countries continues unabated, providing indirect support for both sides to stick to their rigid positions. Second, the talks facilitated by the Minsk Group have involved only the two countries' presidents and top diplomats; no effort has been made to widen the discussions to include current and former residents of Karabakh or to prepare either society for the inevitably difficult compromises that must accompany any agreement.[44]

EXPANDING THE AGENDA

Azerbaijan has the potential to follow in the footsteps of Turkey, its close cultural and economic partner, in gradually evolving into the type of democratic state that the West has repeatedly called upon it to become. But given Azerbaijan's current authoritarian makeup and substantial natural resource reserves, Western efforts aimed at encouraging the country's democratic evolution depend for their success upon adopting a far more nuanced strategy on the twin issues of Azerbaijan's continuing conflict over Nagorno-Karabakh and its increasing level of political repression.

Improving Governance

The West will achieve more productive change in Azerbaijan if it focuses on the broader goal of improving governance rather than the narrow agenda of democratization (especially when it tends to define the latter in terms of balloting alone). Instead of using inflated rhetoric to encourage electoral reform, it should seek to raise the quality of the government's performance and the level of its accountability. Such improvements will not transform Azerbaijan overnight into a fully democratic state, nor will they ensure that the next elections are entirely free and fair, but they will nourish a more democratic society and governance system that, *over time*, will lay the foundations for a genuinely democratic country. Although the West's ability to influence how Azerbaijan conducts its elections is limited (not least because the regime depends upon its manipulation of elections to remain in power), the U.S. and European governments do have many tools available to them that could be used to improve how government functions in the country. Western leverage would also be significantly enhanced if Washington and Brussels were to join forces to create a coherent, broad-based policy for Azerbaijan's development.

To begin with, the West can barter items that the Azeri elite badly wants—such as prestigious visits to foreign capitals (Aliyev's trips to Washington and Brussels are cases in point), meetings with international leaders, promotional opportunities for major Azeri companies, and membership in Western organizations such as the European Union, the Organization for Security and Co-operation in Europe (OSCE), and the North Atlantic Treaty Organisation (NATO)—in exchange for concrete steps to improve governance. It can also exploit Azerbaijan's relationship with Turkey, using Turkey's exceptional progress in recent years in improving the quality and accountability of its institutions as an example of what the Azeri elite should strive to achieve.

Second, it can improve governance in Azerbaijan by supporting a number of measures that, in combination, might transform the country's state-society relationship and inspire its rulers to work much harder to improve the quality of Azerbaijanis' lives. Supporting overseas educational programs for Azeri judges, ministers, government officials, and future leaders, for example, would in time encourage a change in the kleptocratic culture that currently dominates formal state bodies at all levels. At present, such programs cater to just a few dozen Azeris annually; they should be expanded to allow hundreds each year to experience directly how governments in more developed states work. EU members along the Baltic and in central Europe that suffered from the same kind of postcommunist ailments that still bedevil Azerbaijan could play an important role in these training programs by sharing their experiences and advice. Turkey, however, by virtue of its linguistic and cultural ties to Azerbaijan, is ideally suited to play the central role in transferring knowledge and standards of behavior.

Another useful step toward better governance in Azerbaijan would be to improve the transparency of budgeting. This can be encouraged by a variety of means: parliamentary oversight of all government-related finances, the publishing of detailed reports on proposed and actual expenditures, audits by independent third parties, and monitoring of government performance by civil society organizations. External pressure can also help in this regard. Azerbaijan's creation of a State Oil Fund (SOFAZ) in 1999 and its participation since 2003 in the Extractive Industries Transparency Initiative (EITI) were both spurred by pressure from a combination of Western governments and local NGOs. Strengthening compliance with the EITI and with the International Monetary Fund's Code of Good Practices on Fiscal Transparency should be high priorities going forward.[45] Increasing the number and effectiveness of nongovernmental bodies that have the capacity to review and critique government operations and spending at both national and local levels will greatly increase society's ability to exercise some check on official behavior.

Additional measures that improve bureaucratic efficiency, bolster the rule of law and the judicial system, protect property rights, control corruption, improve the quality of regulation, strengthen enforcement mechanisms, and enhance the public's access to information and the independence of the media would similarly help to gradually transform the state-society relationship—and eventually foster a more accountable government that genuinely seeks to serve its population.[46]

Efforts focused on improving the functioning and relevance of state organs, if complemented by programs that improve the investment climate, will expand employment opportunities beyond the petrochemical sector and spread wealth more widely (thereby enhancing both social cohesion and the public's stake in the state building process). The best two programs to improve Azerbaijan's business environment are the European Union's Neighborhood Policy (ENP)—a program that offers EU neighbors a privileged relationship with the organization in return for an agreement to undertake political and economic reforms[47]—and the series of steps necessary to qualify for membership of the World Trade Organization (WTO). The former, the implementation of which was laid out in an agreement between Azerbaijan and the European Union signed in 2006, promises to inspire a large number of legal, administrative, and institutional changes in Azerbaijan's governance. While the European Union works with Azerbaijan in this fashion, the United States should encourage Azerbaijan to join the WTO, as Georgia and Armenia have both done. Enacting the reforms necessary to qualify for WTO membership will improve Azerbaijan's trading climate and reduce the number of government-sponsored monopolies that plague the economy.

Rebuilding Societal Ties across Borders

If the West is to help Azerbaijan settle its conflict with Armenia over Nagorno-Karabakh, three things must happen. First, Washington must make resolving the conflict as high a priority as it has made the development of the pipelines to transport the Caspian Sea's oil to Western markets (indeed, inattention to settling the conflict may well destroy all Washington has achieved in developing the pipelines), and, together with Brussels, it must push leaders on both sides to work harder to settle their differences.

Second, the United States and European Union need to provide a framework within which to address the animosities that fester at the societal level on both sides. Without more support for concessions among the Azeri and Armenian populations, their leaders are unlikely to make the compromises necessary to break the stalemate. To foster such support the United States and the European Union should fund or help organize a series of programs to break down the walls of misunderstanding and hatred that divide the two societies. Different initiatives could target different groups (for example, government officials, the media, civil society, and community leaders), but all programs would share the objective of generating greater sensitivity, tolerance, and understanding of the other side and greater cross border engagement at all levels.

Third, at the same time as they work with Baku and Yerevan to resolve the conflict, the United States and the European Union should develop mechanisms to bring together Azerbaijan and Armenia in the context of pan-Caucasus and multinational economic and military cooperation, thereby reducing border tensions, while building interdependence between the two states. A portion of ENP aid, for instance, could target regional integration schemes (as well as confidence-building activities). Encouraging Azerbaijan to join the WTO and increasing business ties across the closed borders should also feature prominently in this strategy. Another important element should be to enlarge the role of both the European Union and NATO in the region. While EU membership is not on the cards for any country in the Caucasus over the next few years, closer economic and political ties with Brussels would help bring the belligerents together. NATO membership is probably the most tempting carrot the West has to offer, and the West should offer Azerbaijan and Armenia the prospect of full NATO membership in the long term and closer ties with the organization in the short term if they can reach a peace settlement. (Georgia is already eagerly seeking NATO membership and has just been offered "Intensified Dialogue" status by the alliance.) Azerbaijan has been one of the most enthusiastic members of NATO's Partnership for Peace initiative and has long expressed a strong desire to join the organization.[48] Armenia has increased its ties with NATO in recent years and would probably not want to be excluded from any new NATO program that Azerbaijan joined.

THE BEACHHEAD TO CENTRAL ASIA

The West faces the same policy conundrum in the case of Azerbaijan that it does in respect of other countries that possess both geostrategic importance and autocratic regimes, namely, how to secure Western interests while promoting political and economic reforms that will make Azerbaijan's government more accountable to its people. With greater accountability will come greater legitimacy, greater stability, and greater prosperity—both within Azerbaijan itself and within the Caucasus as a whole. Unfortunately, the American and European governments have failed to formulate a policy for Azerbaijan that effectively balances these dual objectives (as Washington has failed to do in places such as Egypt, Saudi Arabia, and Pakistan). Unless the West develops a coherent strategy that overcomes the contradictions inherent within its current policies, it risks alienating Azeris, as U.S. actions have alienated people throughout the Middle East, by its continued support of a repressive and kleptocratic regime.

The international community's approach to the conflict over Karabakh is similarly flawed. By failing to press both sides to make peace or even to help lay the groundwork for an eventual settlement, Washington and Brussels are virtually guaranteeing that the conflict will, in fact, erupt again sooner or later— and probably sooner, given the oil wealth about to pour into the coffers of a regime that has publicly declared its intention to retake Nagorno-Karabakh by force. The West would serve its—and Azerbaijan's—long-term interests better if it took a more active role, and sought a formula that helped both sides promote nation building and state consolidation without wounding either side's national pride.

Azerbaijan should not be regarded by Western governments as another geostrategically important but inconveniently undemocratic ally, as another excuse for empty rhetoric and shortsighted policies. Instead, the United States and the European Union should see Azerbaijan as a beachhead for change throughout Central Asia—and even in parts of the Middle East. Its oil, corrupt institutions, and repressive rulers pose many of the same problems that bedevil its neighbors to the east and south, but its Western orientation and history of collaboration with Western powers make it far more open to Western assistance in the task of improving its governance. A comprehensive strategy that fully acknowledges Azerbaijan's sociocultural and political circumstances could, over time, help the country to become a full-fledged member of the West and an example for other Central Asian and Middle Eastern states to emulate.

Notes

Introduction: Chapter 1

1. The White House, *The National Security Strategy of the United States* (Washington, DC: White House, September 2002), 4.

2. U.S. Agency for International Development (USAID), *Fragile States Strategy* (Washington, DC: USAID, January 2005), 1.

3. Karen DeYoung, "World Bank Lists Failing Nations That Can Breed Global Terrorism," *Washington Post*, September 15, 2006, A13.

4. U.K. Prime Minister's Strategy Unit, *Investing in Prevention: An International Strategy to Manage Risks of Instability and Improve Crisis Response* (London, UK: Prime Minister's Strategy Unit, February 2005), 7 and 10.

5. World Bank, *Fragile States: The Low-Income Countries Under Stress (LICUS) Initiative* (Washington, DC: World Bank, 2005).

6. Stewart Patrick, "Weak States and Global Threats: Fact or Fiction?" *Washington Quarterly* 29(2) (Spring 2006): 31.

7. U.K. Department for International Development (DFID), *Why We Need to Work More Effectively in Fragile States* (London, UK: DFID, January 2005), 27–28.

8. World Bank Independent Evaluation Group, *Engaging with Fragile States: An IEG Review of World Bank Support to Low-Income Countries Under Stress* (Washington, DC: World Bank, 2006).

9. Carnegie Endowment for International Peace, "The Failed States Index," *Foreign Policy* (July–August 2005): 56–65.

10. Jeremy M. Weinstein and Milan Vaishnav, "A Mismatch with Consequences: U.S. Foreign Policy and the Security-Development Nexus," in *Short of the Goal: U.S. Policy and Poorly Performing States*, ed. Nancy Birdsall, Milan Viashnav, and Robert L. Ayres (Washington, DC: Center for Global Development, 2006), 10–13. The Millennium Challenge Account restricts aid to countries that meet a set of rigorous performance criteria.

11. Patrick, "Weak States and Global Threats," 29.

12. U.K. Department for International Development, *Why We Need to Work More Effectively in Fragile States*, 8. DFID, however, has gone furthest in integrating sociopolitical analysis into its development programs. See Chapter 4.

13. Organization for Economic Co-operation and Development (OECD), *Principles for Good International Engagement in Fragile States Preamble* (Paris, France: OECD, April 7, 2005), 2.

14. Stewart Patrick, "The World Bank Report on Fragile States: 5 Takeaways," *Global Development: Views from the Center* (an Internet blog run by the Center for Global Development), September 15, 2006. See http://blogs.cgdev.org/globaldevelopment/2006/09/the_world_bank_report_on_fragi.php.

15. World Bank Independent Evaluation Group, *Engaging with Fragile States: An IEG Review of World Bank Support to Low-Income Countries Under Stress* (Washington, DC: World Bank, 2006), ix.

16. Robert I. Rotberg, "Failed States in a World of Terror," *Foreign Affairs* 81(4) (July–August 2002): 127–140.

17. James Mayall, "The Legacy of Colonialism," in *Making States Work: State Failure and the Crisis of Governance*, ed. Simon Chesterman, Michael Ignatieff, and Ramesh Thakur (New York: United Nations University Press, 2005), 57.

18. His more famous work is *Institutions, Institutional Change and Economic Performance* (Cambridge, UK: Cambridge University Press, 1990).

19. See, for example, Mancur Olson's *The Rise and Decline of Nations* (1982); Hernando de Soto's *The Other Path* (1989) and *The Mystery of Capital* (2000); Ernest Gellner's *Nations and Nationalism* (1983); David Landes' *The Wealth and Poverty of Nations* (1998); and Lawrence Harrison and Samuel Huntington's edited volume, *Culture Matters* (2000).

20. Michael Woolcock and Deepa Narayan, "Social Capital: Implications for Development Theory, Research, and Policy," *World Bank Research Observer* 15(2) (August 2000): 225.

21. RAND, Terrorism and Development: Using Social and Economic Development to Inhibit a Resurgence of Terrorism (Santa Monica, CA: RAND, 2003), 34–35.

Chapter 2

1. Institute of Development Studies (IDS), *Signposts to More Effective States: Responding to Governance Challenges in Developing Countries* (Brighton, UK: IDS, 2005), 1.

2. Amos Sawyer, *Beyond Plunder: Toward Democratic Governance in Liberia* (Boulder, CO: Lynne Rienner Publishers), xii.

3. John R. Nelson, *Liberty and Property: Political Economy and Policy-Making in the New Nation, 1789–1812* (Baltimore, MD: Johns Hopkins Press, 1987), 1.

4. James Dobbins, Seth G. Jones, Keith Crane, and Beth Cole Degrasse, *The Beginner's Guide to Nation-Building* (Santa Monica, CA: RAND Corporation, 2007).

5. Nassrine Azimi, "Do Not Neglect Culture," *International Herald Tribune*, May 8, 2007.

6. James Mayall, "The Legacy of Colonialism," in *Making States Work: State Failure and the Crisis of Governance*, ed. Simon Chesterman, Michael Ignatieff, and Ramesh Thakur (New York: United Nations University Press, 2005), 57.

7. "High productivity, as Adam Smith insisted so much, requires a complex and refined division of labour. Perpetually growing productivity requires that this division be not merely complex, but also perpetually, and often rapidly, changing." Ernest Gellner, *Nations and Nationalism* (Ithaca, NY: Cornell University Press, 1983), 24.

8. Quoted in Alberto Alesina and Enrico Spolaore, *The Size of Nations* (Cambridge, MA: MIT Press, 2003), 179.

9. Douglass North, *Institutions, Institutional Change and Economic Performance* (Cambridge, UK: Cambridge University Press, 1990), 61.

10. Gretchen Helmke and Steven Levitsky, "Informal Institutions and Comparative Politics: A Research Agenda," *Perspectives on Politics* 2(4) (December 2004): 727.

11. Douglass C. North, "Institutions," *Journal of Economic Perspectives* 5(1) (Winter 1991): 97.

12. Overseas Development Institute (ODI), *Governance, Development, and Aid Effectiveness: A Quick Guide to Complex Relationships*, ODI Briefing Paper (London, UK: ODI, 2006), 1.

13. Department for International Development (DFID), *Making Governance Work for the Poor: Eliminating World Poverty*, White Paper on International Development (London, UK: DFID, July 2006), 20.

14. ODI, *Governance, Development, and Aid Effectiveness*, 1–2.

15. United Nations Development Programme (UNDP), *Human Development Report 2002* (New York: UNDP, 2002), 51.

16. As the United States Agency for International Development (USAID) puts it: "Without good governance, it is impossible to foster development. No amount of resources transferred or infrastructure built can compensate for—or survive—bad governance." See http://www.usaid.gov/fani/overview/overview_governance.htm.

17. Ha-Joon Chang, "Institutional Development in Developing Countries in a Historical Perspective: Lessons from Developed Countries in Earlier Times," Paper presented at the European Association of Evolutionary Political Economy Annual Meeting, November 8–11, 2001, Sienna, Italy, 1–2.

18. IDS, *Signposts to More Effective States*, 44.

19. Johannes Jütting, *Institutions and Development: A Critical Review*, Working Paper No. 210, OECD Development Centre (Paris, France: OECD, July 2003), 11.

20. Helmke and Levitsky, "Informal Institutions and Comparative Politics," 725–726.

21. Donatella Della Porta and Alberto Vannucci, *Corrupt Exchanges: Actors, Resources, and Mechanisms of Political Corruption* (New York: Aldine de Gruyter, 1999), 15.

22. Helmke and Levitsky, "Informal Institutions and Comparative Politics," 725.

23. North, *Institutions, Institutional Change and Economic Performance*, 91.

24. Helmke and Levitsky, "Informal Institutions and Comparative Politics," 729.

25. North, Foreword in Jean-Philippe Platteau, *Institutions, Social Norms, and Economic Development* (Amsterdam, the Netherlands: Harwood Academic Publishers, 2000), xi–xii.

26. UN Office of the High Representative for the Least Developed Countries, Landlocked Developing Countries and the Small Island Developing States and United Nations Development Programme, *Governance for the Future: Democracy and Development in the Least Developed Countries* (New York: UN-OHRLLS and UNDP, 2006), 51.

27. Benedict Anderson, *Imagined Communities: Reflections on the Origins and Spread of Nationalism* (London, UK: Verso, 1983).

28. "Social capital . . . bolsters the performance of the polity and the economy, rather than the reverse: Strong society, strong economy; strong society, strong state." Robert Putnam, *Making Democracy Work: Civic Traditions in Modern Italy* (Princeton, NJ: Princeton University Press, 1993), 176.

29. "A country's social cohesion is essential for generating the confidence and patience needed to implement reforms: citizens have to trust the government that the short-term losses inevitably arising from reform will be more than offset by long-term gains . . . countries strongly divided along class and ethnic lines will place severe constraints on the attempts . . . to bring about policy reform." William Easterly, Jozef Ritzan, and Michael Woolcock, *Social Cohesion, Institutions, and Growth*, Working Paper No. 94 (Washington, DC: Center for Global Development, August 2006), 1–2.

30. Simon Chesterman, Michael Ignatieff, and Ramesh Thakur, "Conclusion: The Future of State-Building," in *Making States Work: State Failure and the Crisis of Governance*, ed. Chesterman, Ignatieff, and Thakur (Tokyo, Japan: United Nations University Press, 2005), 360.

31. See, for example, Pierre Englebert, *State Legitimacy and Development in Africa* (Boulder, CO: Lynne Rienner, 2000).

32. IDS, *Signposts to More Effective States*, 45.

33. Chang, "Institutional Development in Developing Countries in a Historical Perspective."

34. IDS, *Signposts to More Effective States*, 45.

35. Ibid., 44.

36. Ibid., 4.

37. Of course, not every developed state fits this model perfectly, but almost all come close. The Swiss may be linguistically and religiously heterogeneous, but they have a long history as a unified people and a set of widely accepted and unique governing institutions. Spain and Canada are indeed weak nation-states, with each encompassing at least two distinct identity groups. But one group dominated for centuries during each country's formative years and a significant majority of each minority group has accepted the national identity and institutional compact, at least until now. Belgium is perhaps the exception to the rule, with its short history and weak national ties. However, Belgium, like Switzerland, Spain, and Canada, has prospered at least in part because it has developed federated structures that take into account its diversity and because its good neighborhood has bolstered the institutional strength of its system of governance.

38. "Social cohesion determines the quality of institutions, which in turn has important impacts on whether and how pro-growth policies are devised and implemented . . . key development outcomes (the most widely available being "economic growth") should be more likely to be associated with countries governed by effective public institutions, and that those institutions, in turn, should be more likely to be found in socially cohesive societies." Easterly, Ritzan, and Woolcock, *Social Cohesion, Institutions, and Growth*, 1–2.

39. It is, not coincidentally, one of the few non-Western states never to have been colonized. Mayall, "The Legacy of Colonialism," 46.

40. Bernard Lewis, *The Multiple Identities of the Middle East* (New York: Schocken Books, 1998), 19–20.

41. Jeffrey Herbst, *State and Power in Africa: Comparative Lessons in Authority and Control* (Princeton, NJ: Princeton University Press, 2000), 154.

42. The other three states are Somalia, Lesotho, and Swaziland. Somalis use clans to identify themselves rather than ethnicity and therefore the latter cannot be the basis of

a stable political order. The latter two are small monarchies with roots dating back to the precolonial order. Paul Nugent, *Africa since Independence* (New York: Palgrave Macmillan, 2004), 79.

43. Ibid., 426–427.

44. Edwin Williamson, *The Penguin History of Latin America* (London, UK: Penguin Books, 1992), 256.

45. Ibid., 486.

46. Victor Bulmer-Thomas, *The Economic History of Latin America since Independence* (Cambridge, UK: Cambridge University Press, 1994), 45.

47. Williamson, *The Penguin History of Latin America*, 247.

48. Abelardo Morales-Gamboa and Stephen Baranyi, "State-Building, National Leadership and 'Relative Success' in Costa Rica," in *Making States Work: State Failure and the Crisis of Governance*, ed. Simon Chesterman, Michael Ignatieff, and Ramesh Thakur (Tokyo, Japan: United Nations University Press, 2005), 235–236.

49. Robert Pringle, *Democratization in Mali: Putting History to Work*, Peaceworks no. 58 (Washington, DC: United States Institute of Peace, October, 2006), 2, 7, 13, 53, and 54.

50. Ibid., 66.

51. Ricardo French-Davis, Oscar Muñoz, and José Gabriel Palma, "The Latin American Economies, 1950–1990," in *Latin America: Politics and Society since 1930*, ed. Leslie Bethell (Cambridge, UK: Cambridge University Press, 1998), 172.

52. Juan J. Linz and Alfred Stepan use the term "state nation" elsewhere with a somewhat similar meaning, though there are some differences. See, for example, Juan J. Linz, Alfred Stepan, and Yogendra Yadav, *"Nation State" or "State Nation"? Conceptual Reflections and Spanish, Belgian and Indian Data*, Background Paper for *Human Development Report 2004* (New York: UNDP, 2004).

53. He adds that these forces were reinforced by certain "intelligible, common cultural forms . . . a civilizational bond, that in fact extended beyond the territorial borders of contemporary India." Sunil Khilnani, *The Idea of India* (New York: Farrar, Straus, and Giroux, 1997), 154–155.

54. Ibid., 172–173.

55. Ibid., 194.

56. See chapter 3 of Herbst, *State and Power in Africa*. The quotations are on pp. 64, 67, and 79.

57. "Until roughly the 1920s the mass of the population—poor whites, mixed-bloods, Indians and blacks—were excluded from the political system." Williamson, *The Penguin History of Latin America*, 374–375.

58. Andrew Meier, *Black Earth: A Journey through Russia after the Fall* (New York: W.W. Norton, 2003), 76.

59. Shawn Donnan, "Dili Dilemma: How Blunders in Building a Nation Are Being Brutally Laid Bare," *Financial Times*, June 12, 2006, 13.

60. Göran Hydén, *No Shortcuts to Progress: African Development Management in Perspective* (London, UK: Heinemann, 1983), 7.

61. Hippolyt A. S. Pul, "Belonging and Citizenship in Africa," *Democracy at Large* 1(3) (2005): 10.

62. Mirsolav Hroch, "From National Movement to the Fully-Formed Nation: The Nation-Building Process in Europe," in *Mapping the Nation*, ed. Gopal Balakrishnan (New York: Verso, 1996), 78–97.

63. Louis Kriesberg, "Identity Issues," in *Beyond Intractability*, ed. Guy Burgess and Heidi Burgess (Boulder, CO: Conflict Research Consortium, University of Colorado, July 2003).

64. Lewis, *The Multiple Identities of the Middle East*, 9 and 15.

65. Khilnani, *The Idea of India*, 153.

66. Kwesi Kwaa Prah, *African Wars and Ethnic Conflicts: Rebuilding Failed States*, Background Paper for *Human Development Report 2004* (New York: UNDP, 2004), 8–9.

67. Williamson, *The Penguin History of Latin America*, 512 and 566.

68. Barnett R. Rubin, *Central Asia Wars and Ethnic Conflict: Rebuilding Failed States*, Background Paper for *Human Development Report 2004* (New York: UNDP, 2004). 6.

69. Kriesberg, "Identity Issues."

70. Joel Kotkin, *Tribes: How Race, Religion, and Identity Determine Success in the New Global Economy* (New York: Random House, 1992), 17.

71. Ibid., 4–5.

72. Putnam as quoted in John Lloyd, "Harvard Study Paints Bleak Picture of Ethnic Diversity," *Financial Times*, October 8, 2006.

73. Eduardo Porter, "The Divisions That Tighten the Purse Strings," *New York Times*, April 29, 2007.

74. "Divided Over Disease," *Foreign Policy* (January–February 2008): 32.

75. Kriesberg, "Identity Issues."

76. Michael Slackman, "Where Outsiders, and Fear, Loom Over Daily Life," *New York Times*, July 11, 2007.

Chapter 3

1. Obviously, not all of these precolonial societies were equipped with an institutional structure that could be adapted to the modern world.

2. Such "states brought together groups that until then were following different historical trajectories and building alternative political institutions. . . . This is not merely a matter of weak states facing strong societies. The crux of the problem is that there were competing institutional claims to sovereignty within the state." Pierre Englebert, *State Legitimacy and Development in Africa* (Boulder, CO: Lynne Rienner Publishers, 2000), 91.

3. James Mayall, "The Legacy of Colonialism," *Making States Work: State Failure and the Crisis of Governance*, ed. Simon Chesterman, Michael Ignatieff, and Ramesh Thakur (New York: United Nations University Press, 2005), 37.

4. Carolyn Logan, *Overcoming the State-Society Disconnect in the Former Somalia: Putting Somali Political and Economic Resources at the Root of Reconstruction*, United States Agency for International Development, Regional Economic Development Services Office for East and Southern Africa (September 2000), 7.

5. Virginia Luling, "Come Back Somalia? Questioning a Collapsed State," *Third World Quarterly* 18(2) (1997): 288–289.

6. Adolphus Slade as cited in Mahmud Kemal Inal, *Osmanli Devrinde Son Sadri-azamlar* (Istanbul, Turkey, 1940–1953), 1982.

7. "External public funding has resulted in a growing role for the donor agencies in day-to-day decision-making and the increasing marginalization of central state decision-making bodies to the benefit of ad hoc, donor-funded, parallel institutions." Nicolas van de Walle, *African Economies and the Politics of Permanent Crisis, 1979–1999* (Cambridge, UK: Cambridge University Press, 2001), 59 and 61.

8. Mayall, "The Legacy of Colonialism," 47.

9. Logan, *Overcoming the State-Society Disconnect in the Former Somalia*, 8.

10. Institute of Development Studies (IDS), *Signposts to More Effective States: Responding to Governance Challenges in Developing Countries* (Brighton, UK: IDS, 2005), 45.

11. "Differences in legitimacy among African states 'explain' from one-third to one-half of the variance in their developmental fortunes. The direct effects of legitimacy on the quality of governance are even stronger." Englebert, *State Legitimacy and Development in Africa*, 9.

12. David Easton, *A Systems Analysis of Political Life* (New York: Wiley, 1965), 278.

13. Simon Chesterman, Michael Ignatieff, and Ramesh Thakur, "Conclusion: The Future of State-Building," in *Making States Work: State Failure and the Crisis of Governance*, ed. Chesterman, Ignatieff, and Thakur (New York: United Nations University Press, 2005), 363.

14. Michael Hudson, *Arab Politics: The Search for Legitimacy* (New Haven, CT: Yale University Press, 1977), 389–390.

15. Ibid., 4.

16. William Easterly, *Can Institutions Resolve Ethnic Conflict?* Policy Research Working Paper Series 2482, The World Bank, February 2000, 12.

17. Simon Chesterman, Michael Ignatieff, and Ramesh Thakur, "Introduction: Making States Work," in *Making States Work: State Failure and the Crisis of Governance*, ed. Chesterman, Ignatieff, and Thakur (New York: United Nations University Press, 2005), 2–3.

18. William Easterly, Jozef Ritzan, and Michael Woolcock, *Social Cohesion, Institutions, and Growth*, Working Paper No. 94 (Washington, DC: Center for Global Development, August 2006), 14.

19. Putnam quoted in Shanker Vedantam, "One Thing We Can't Build Alone in Iraq," *Washington Post*, October 29, 2007, A3.

20. Robert Putnam, *Making Democracy Work: Civic Traditions in Modern Italy* (Princeton, NJ: Princeton University Press, 1993), 177.

21. Ibid.

22. Douglass North, *Institutions, Institutional Change and Economic Performance* (Cambridge, UK: Cambridge University Press, 1990), 99.

23. Johannes Jütting, *Institutions and Development: A Critical Review*, Working Paper No. 210, OECD Development Centre (Paris, France: OECD, July 2003), 30.

24. William Easterly and Ross Levine, "Africa's Growth Tragedy: Policies and Ethnic Divisions," *Quarterly Journal of Economics* 112(4) (November 1997): 1203–1250.

25. Putnam, *Making Democracy Work*, 170.

26. Ibid., 171–172.

27. Kenneth J. Arrow, "Gifts and Exchanges," *Philosophy and Public Affairs* 1 (Summer 1972): 357.

28. Putnam, *Making Democracy Work*, 182–183.

29. Michael Woolcock and Deepa Narayan, "Social Capital: Implications for Development Theory, Research, and Policy," *World Bank Research Observer* 15(2) (August 2000): 237.

30. North, *Institutions, Institutional Change and Economic Performance*, 63 and 67.

31. Paul Collier, *The Political Economy of Ethnicity*, Paper prepared for Annual World Bank Conference on Development Economics (Washington, DC, April 20–21, 1998), 17–18.

32. Mayall, "The Legacy of Colonialism," 47.

33. "Cote d'Ivoire: What's in a Name? A Fight for Identity," *IRIN* (Integrated Regional Information Networks, part of the United Nations Office for the Coordination of Humanitarian Affairs), November 1, 2005.

34. World Bank, International Finance Corporation and Oxford University Press, *Doing Business in 2005* (Washington, DC: World Bank, 2005), 120.

35. Hudson, *Arab Politics*, 2.

36. Illegitimacy in effect "raises the relative returns, for the elites, of neopatrimonialism over developmental statehood . . . neopatrimonialism is not an African cultural feature but rather the equilibrium outcome of a set of historical conditions." Englebert, *State Legitimacy and Development in Africa*, 5–6.

37. Hudson, *Arab Politics*, 395.

Chapter 4

1. As Liberia's ex-president Amos Sawyer has explained, "People start from the assumption that there must be a centralized authority, there must be this, there must be that, and then they try to manipulate things to make them fit into that mould. Very often the results of such manipulation have been disastrous and counterproductive." Louise Andersen, *Democratic Governance in Post-Conflict Liberia: An Interview with Dr. Amos Sawyer*, DIIS Working Paper No. 2007/20 (Copenhagen, Denmark: Danish Institute for International Studies, 2007), 11.

2. Kwesi Kwaa Prah, *African Wars and Ethnic Conflicts: Rebuilding Failed States*, Background Paper for *Human Development Report 2004* (New York: UNDP, 2004), 16.

3. Johannes Jütting, *Institutions and Development: A Critical Review*, Working Paper No. 210, OECD Development Centre (Paris, France: OECD, July 2003), 36.

4. Robert Pringle, *Democratization in Mali: Putting History to Work*, Peaceworks No. 58 (Washington, DC: United States Institute of Peace, October 2006), 60–61.

5. Institute of Development Studies (IDS), *Signposts to More Effective States: Responding to Governance Challenges in Developing Countries* (Brighton, UK: IDS, 2005), 46–47.

6. "States which can raise a substantial proportion of their revenues from the international community are less accountable to their citizens and under less pressure to maintain popular legitimacy. They are therefore less likely to have the incentives to cultivate and invest in effective public institutions." Todd Moss, Gunilla Pettersson, and Nicolas van de Walle, *An Aid-Institutions Paradox? A Review Essay on Aid Dependency and State Building in Sub-Saharan Africa*, Working Paper No. 74 (Washington, DC: Center for Global Development, January 2006), 1.

7. "Several studies [found] that tax revenues and level of foreign aid have had a significant negative correlation." Nicolas van de Walle, *African Economies and the Politics of Permanent Crisis, 1979–1999* (Cambridge, UK: Cambridge University Press, 2001), 73.

8. "In some countries where governance is weak and deteriorating, no aid should be provided at all . . . in some countries with the most recalcitrant governments . . . the bulk of assistance should be directed through NGOs." Steven Radelet, "Strengthening U.S. Development Assistance," in *Security by Other Means: Foreign Assistance, Global Poverty,*

and American Leadership, ed. Lael Brainard (Washington, DC: Brookings Institution, 2007), 109.

9. van de Walle, *African Economies*, 208 and 228.

10. See http://www.odi.org.uk/whats_next_portals/fragile_states/index.html.

11. Martin Kramer, "Democracy Promotion: Plan B," http://www.martinkramer.org, December 4, 2006, http://www.geocities.com/martinkramerorg/2006_12_06.htm.

12. Juan Linz, Alfred Stepan, and Yogendra Yadav, *"Nation-State" or "State-Nation"? Conceptual Reflections and Spanish, Belgian and Indian Data*, Background Paper for *Human Development Report 2004* (New York: UNDP, 2004), 7.

13. Ibid., 9.

14. Such actions do not necessarily lead to ethnic cleansing as critics of this approach claim; on the contrary, more secure identity groups—secure in their empowerment and control of state bodies—often tend to be more liberal in dealing with minorities in their midst than do identity groups who feel oppressed and victimized.

15. Note that "total budgetary resources allocated to local governments [in Africa] were typically miniscule, while only 2 percent of public employees did not work for the central government, a quarter of the levels prevailing in Asia and half of those in Latin America." van de Walle, *African Economies*, 125.

16. Not coincidentally, precolonial government in Africa, faced with enormous difficulties in broadcasting power, creating infrastructure, constructing loyalties, and controlling large amounts of land, typically consisted of a central authority and a series of concentric circles radiating out from the core, with central authority diminishing the farther out one went, a system far removed from the imported European territorial-based system. See Jeffrey Herbst, *State and Power in Africa: Comparative Lessons in Authority and Control* (Princeton, NJ: Princeton University Press, 2000), 35–57.

17. IDS, *Signposts to More Effective States*, 6.

18. See, among others, Andres Oppenheimer, "Lack of Integration Hurts Central America," *Miami Herald*, June 10, 2007, and "Central American Integration: Together Again, After All These Years?" *Economist*, May 14, 2005, 41.

19. Michel Cahen, "Success in Mozambique?" in *Making States Work: State Failure and the Crisis of Governance*, ed. Simon Chesterman, Michael Ignatieff, and Ramesh Thakur (Tokyo, Japan: United Nations University Press, 2005), 230–231.

20. Paul Collier, "Editorial: Rethinking Assistance for Africa," *Economic Affairs* (London, UK) 26(4) (December 2006): 2–4.

21. Nick Grono, "Fragile States: Searching for Effective Approaches and the Right Mix of Instruments," Presentation to the Danish Ministry of Foreign Affairs, Copenhagen, January 29, 2007.

22. Simon Chesterman, Michael Ignatieff, and Ramesh Thakur, "Conclusion: The Future of State-Building," in *Making States Work: State Failure and the Crisis of Governance*, ed. Chesterman, Ignatieff, and Thakur (New York: United Nations University Press, 2005), 370.

23. "The private sector merits only two very narrow mentions in the Millennium Development goals." Lael Brainard and Vinca LaFleur, "The Private Sector in the Fight against Global Poverty," in *Transforming the Development Landscape: The Role of the Private Sector*, ed. Lael Brainard (Washington, DC: Brookings Institution Press, 2006), 2.

24. "The private sector accounts for 90 percent of jobs in developing countries, and poor people rate self-employment and jobs as the two most promising ways to improve

their situation." Warrick Smith, "Unleashing Entrepreneurship," in *Transforming the Development Landscape: The Role of the Private Sector*, ed. Lael Brainard (Washington, DC: Brookings Institution Press, 2006), 31.

25. "In some countries poor infrastructure, burdensome regulation, contract enforcement difficulties, crime, and corruption can amount to more than 25 percent of sales—or more than three times what firms typically pay in taxes." Ibid., 34.

26. Developing countries received $255 billion in foreign direct investment in 2004 according to the United Nations Conference on Trade and Development, "World FDI Flows Grew an Estimated 6% in 2004, Ending Downturn," Press Release (Geneva, January 1, 2005). They received only $52 billion in aid (amount actually disbursed, net of debt service) according to Development Assistance Committee (DAC), *Development Cooperation Report* (Paris: France, OECD, 2003) as quoted in UNECA, *Economic Report on Africa 2004*, 35.

27. Howard Wolpe and Steve McDonald, "Burundi's Transition: Training Leaders for Peace," *Journal of Democracy* 17(1) (January 2006): 137.

28. See Thomas Carothers, "The 'Sequencing' Fallacy," *Journal of Democracy* 18(1) (January 2007): 12–27.

29. Including strengthening compliance with the EITI (where appropriate), with the International Monetary Fund's Code of Good Practices on Fiscal Transparency, and with Transparency International's many anticorruption prescriptions.

30. Diana Cammack, Dinah McLeod, Alina Rocha Menocal, and Karin Christiansen, *Donors and the 'Fragile States' Agenda: A Survey of Current Thinking and Practice* (London, UK: Overseas Development Institute, March 2006), 47. However, as one review of a DFID strategy document complained, "the radical implications of this message are not pursued.... No coherent explanation emerges of why governance is bad in so many developing countries, or how more effective and accountable public institutions might be expected to evolve." Mick Moore and Sue Unsworth, "Britain's New White Paper: Making Governance Work for the Poor," Book Review article, *Development Policy Review* 24(6) (2006): 709.

31. See, for instance, David Rohde, "Army Enlists Anthropology in War Zones," *New York Times*, October 5, 2007, A1.

32. Greg Jaffe, "Midlevel Officers Show Enterprise in Iraq," *Wall Street Journal*, December 29, 2007.

Chapter 5

1. Douglas Farah and Richard Shultz, "Al Qaeda's Growing Sanctuary," *Washington Post*, July 14, 2004.

2. UK Department for International Development (DFID), *Why We Need to Work More Effectively in Fragile States* (London, UK: DFID, January 2005), 27–28.

3. Nancy Alexander, *Judge and Jury: The World Bank's Scorecard for Borrowing Governments* (Washington, DC: Citizens' Network on Essential Services, April 2004).

4. As measured by the Human Development Index in United Nations Development Programme (UNDP), *Human Development Report 2003* (New York: Oxford University Press, 2003), 237–241.

5. World Bank, *Memorandum of the President of the International Development Association to the Executive Directors on a Regional Integration Assistance Strategy for West Africa* (Washington, DC: World Bank, July 11, 2001), 3.

6. Ibid., 58–60, and UNDP, *Human Development Report 2003*, 278–281 and 291–294.

7. Nancy Birdsall, "New Issues in Development Assistance," Paper prepared for the Conference on Emerging Global Economic Order and Developing Countries, Bangladesh Economic Association, Dhaka, July 2004, 13.

8. See http://www.forbes.com/business/2005/08/31/ivory-coast-civil-war-cx_0831 oxan-ivorycoast.html.

9. UNDP, *Human Development Report 2003*, 278–281.

10. World Bank, *Memorandum*, 2.

11. World Bank International Finance Corporation and Oxford University Press, *Doing Business in 2005* (Washington, DC: World Bank, 2005), 120.

12. United Nations Economic Commission for Africa (UNECA) and World Bank, *Africa Transport Technical Note: Improving Management and Financing of Roads in Sub-Saharan Africa* for the Sub-Saharan Africa Transport Policy Program (SSATP), December 1999. See the SSATP Web site, http://webhttp://web.worldbank.org/WBSITE/ EXTERNAL/COUNTRIES/AFRICAEXT/EXTAFRREGTOPTRA/EXTAFRSUBSAHT RA/0,,menuPK:1513942~pagePK:64168427~piPK:64168435~theSitePK:1513930,00. html; UNECA, *Economic Report on Africa 2004: Unlocking Africa's Trade Potential* (Addis Ababa, Ethiopia: Economic Commission for Africa, 2004), 163.

13. Commission for Africa, *Our Common Interest: Report of the Commission for Africa* (London, UK: Commission for Africa, 2005), Box 8.3, 258.

14. These figures exclude Nigeria, however, where offshore oil resources have attracted more investment than aid. World Bank, *World Development Indicators* (Washington, DC: World Bank, 2004), 334–337; UNDP, *Human Development Report 2003*, 291–294.

15. UNECA, *Assessing Regional Integration for Africa* (Addis Ababa, Ethiopia: Economic Commission for Africa, 2004), 251–252.

16. World Bank, *Memorandum*, 18.

17. Ibid., 17.

18. Ibid., 31.

19. See http://web.worldbank.org/WBSITE/EXTERNAL/EXTOED/EXTREGPRO PART/0,,contentMDK:21174399~pagePK:64168427~piPK:64168435~theSitePK: 3300628,00.html and executive summary (available at this Web site), xviii.

20. Congressional Research Service Issue Brief, *Africa: U.S. Foreign Assistance Issues* (Washington, DC: Congressional Research Service, January 4, 2005); United States Agency for International Development, *West African Regional Program* (Washington, DC: USAID, 2004).

21. Nancy Birdsall, *Underfunded Regionalism in the Developing World* (Washington, DC: Center for Global Development, November 2004).

22. UNECA, *Assessing Regional Integration for Africa*, 99.

23. Developing countries received $255 billion in foreign direct investment in 2004 according to the United Nations Conference on Trade and Development, "World FDI Flows Grew an Estimated 6% in 2004, Ending Downturn," Press Release (Geneva, January 1, 2005). They received only $52 billion in aid (amount actually disbursed, net of debt service) according to Development Assistance Committee (DAC), *Development Cooperation Report* (Paris, France: OECD, 2003) as quoted in UNECA, *Economic Report on Africa 2004*, 35.

24. Sheila Page and Sanoussi Bilal, *Regional Integration in Western Africa*, Report prepared for the Ministry of Foreign Affairs of The Netherlands (London, UK: Overseas Development Institute, September 2001), 16–17.

25. Page and Bilal, *Regional Integration in Western Africa*, 8.

26. World Bank, *Memorandum*, 4.

27. Joyce Mulama, "Slowly Does It," Inter Press Service (Johannesburg, South Africa), July 4, 2007.

28. Anatole Ayissi, *Cooperating for Peace in West Africa: An Agenda for the 21st Century* (Geneva, Switzerland: United Nations Institute for Disarmament Research, 2001), viii.

29. UNECA, *Assessing Regional Integration for Africa*, 24.

30. Ernest Harsch, "Making African Integration a Reality," *Africa Recovery* 16(2–3) (September 2002): 10.

31. Paul Masson and Catherine Pattillo, *Monetary Union in West Africa: An Agency of Restraint for Fiscal Policies?* (Washington, DC: International Monetary Fund, December 21, 2001), 12.

32. For a description of the importance of these to development, see World Bank, International Finance Corporation and Oxford University Press, *Doing Business in 2005*.

33. Economic Community of West African States, *Annual Report 2002* of the Executive Secretary (Abuja, Nigeria: ECOWAS, December 2002), 76–78.

34. Victoria K. Holt, *Making Conflict Resolution and Prevention in Africa a "Top Priority": G8-Africa Action Plan and Considerations for Sea Island*, Commissioned by the G8-Africa Partnership Project of the Council on Foreign Relations, March 31, 2004, 4.

35. See http://www.whitehouse.gov/news/releases/2005/07/20050708=3.html.

36. See http://www.defensenews.com/story.php?F=1680073&C=europe.

37. See http://thomas.loc.gov/cgi-bin/cpquery/?&item=&&sid=cp109TtjuH&&refer=&&r_n=sr277.109&&dbname=cp109&&sid=cp109TtjuH&&sel=TOC_375957&.

38. See West Africa and European Community, *Regional Cooperation Strategy Paper and Regional Indicative Programme for the Period 2002–2007* (Brussels, Belgium: European Commission, 2002); PricewaterhouseCoopers, *Sustainability Impact Assessment (SIA) of the EU-ACP Economic Partnership Agreements: West African ACP Countries* (Paris, France: PWC, January 30, 2004).

39. European Commission, *Free Trade Areas: An Appraisal*, SEC (95) 322 (Brussels, Belgium: Communication from the Commission, March 8, 1995); Sanoussi Bilal, "Can the EU Be a Model and a Driving Force for Regional Integration in Developing Countries?" Paper presented at the Euro-Latin Study Network on Integration and Trade, Florence, Italy, October 29–30, 2004, 13–16.

40. ECOWAS, *Annual Report 2002*; Union Economique et Monetaire Ouest Africaine, *Report annuel de la Commission sur le Fonctionnement et l'Evolution de l'Union 2003*, Annual Report of the Commission on the Functioning and Evolution of the Union, Niamey, Niger: UEMOA, January 10, 2004; West Africa and European Community, *Regional Cooperation Strategy Paper*.

41. DAC, *Development Cooperation Report* as quoted in UNECA, *Economic Report on Africa 2004*, 35.

Chapter 6

1. Ross Mountain, UN Humanitarian Coordinator in Congo, quoted in "Congo Remains World's Deadliest Catastrophe—UN," Reuters, May 14, 2006.

2. This figure comes from a survey conducted by the International Rescue Committee. See Stephanie McCrummen, "Groups Sign Deal to End Long Fight in E. Congo," *Washington Post*, January 24, 2008, A13.

3. See http://counterterrorismblog.org/2006/08/the_drc_and_uranium_for_iran.php# trackbacks.

4. Jeffrey Gluckman, "Despite the Rain and Tension, Millions Vote in Congo," *New York Times*, October 30, 2006, A8.

5. Estimates range from 3 million to 10 million. The highest number is cited by Adam Hochschild in *King Leopold's Ghost* (Boston, MA: Houghton, Mifflin, 1998).

6. Crawford Young, "Contextualizing Congo Conflicts: Order and Disorder in Postcolonial Africa," in *The African Stakes of the Congo War*, ed. John F. Clark (New York: Palgrave Macmillan, 2002), 17; and Georges Nzongola-Ntalaja, *The Congo: From Leopold to Kabila* (London, UK: Zed Books, 2002), 66; Robert B. Edgerton, *The Troubled Heart of Africa: A History of the Congo* (New York: St. Martin's Press, 2002), 180.

7. Edgerton, *The Troubled Heart of Africa*, 176.

8. Ibid., 154.

9. Kevin C. Dunn, *Imagining the Congo: The International Relations of Identity* (New York: Palgrave Macmillan, 2003), 140.

10. Ibid.

11. William Reno, *Warlord Politics and African States* (Boulder, CO: Lynne Rienner Publishers, 1998), 154.

12. Dunn, *Imagining the Congo*, 140.

13. Reno, *Warlord Politics and African States Africa*, 154.

14. Young, "Contextualizing Congo Conflicts," 24.

15. USAID/DRC, *USAID/DRC Integrated Strategic Plan FY 2004–2008* (Washington: USAID, March 2, 2004), 6.

16. Rene Lemarchand, "The Democratic Republic of the Congo: From Failure to Potential Reconstruction," in *State Failure and State Weakness in a Time of Terror*, ed. Robert I. Rotberg (Cambridge, MA: World Peace Foundation, 2003), 29.

17. Mungbalemwe Koyame and John F. Clark, "The Economic Impact of the Congo War," in *The African Stakes of the Congo War*, ed. John F. Clark (New York: Palgrave Macmillan, 2002), 208.

18. Lydia Polgreen, "Congo's Death Rate Remains Unchanged since War Ended in 2003, Survey Shows," *New York Times*, January 23, 2008, A8.

19. The World Bank calculates a country's level of governance by averaging six indicators: voice and accountability; political stability; government effectiveness; regulatory quality; rule of law; and control of corruption. See http://www.worldbank.org/wbi/governance/govdata/.

20. The human development index is "a composite index measuring average achievement in three basic dimensions of human development—a long and healthy life, knowledge, and a decent standard of living." United Nations Development Programme, *Human Development Report 2005* (New York: Oxford University Press, 2005). See http://hdr.undp.org/statistics/data/countries.cfm?c=COD.

21. See http://www.cyberwonders.com/law/index.php/intl/2005/12/21/dr_congo_new_constitution.

22. USAID/DRC, *USAID/DRC Integrated Strategic Plan*, 6.

23. United Nations Development Programme, *Human Development Report 2003* (New York: Oxford University Press, 2003), 277.

24. Jeffrey Herbst, *State and Power in Africa: Comparative Lessons in Authority and Control* (Princeton, NJ: Princeton University Press, 2000), 151.

25. Ibid., 147.

26. Edgerton, *The Troubled Heart of Africa*, 183–184.

27. See UNICEF, *Enquete nationale sur la situation des enfants et des femmes*, MICS2/2001 (Kinshasa, DRC: UNICEF, July 2002), 31, 43, and 69.

28. International Crisis Group (ICG), *Congo: Consolidating the Peace*, Africa Report No. 128 (Kinshasa, DRC, and Brussels, Belgium: ICG, July 5, 2007), i.

29. For a summary of the constitution's main features, see http://www.cyberwonders.com/law/index.php/intl/2005/12/21/dr_congo_new_constitution. For a discussion on the constitution's demerits, see http://headheeb.blogmosis.com/archives/031007.html.

30. International Committee in support of the Transition (CIAT) members have "promoted their economic interests, allegedly helping companies obtain mining contracts and lucrative state tenders directly from the presidency." ICG, *Congo: Consolidating the Peace*, 3.

31. World Bank, *Transitional Support Strategy for the Democratic Republic of the Congo* (Washington, DC: World Bank, January 26, 2004), 27 and 29.

32. Ibid., 41–42.

33. See http://www.usaid.gov/locations/sub-saharan_africa/countries/drcongo/. The data here was culled from the agency's "data sheets" for programs during the 2005–2006 fiscal year. A USAID employee who worked in the DRC for two and a half years explained in a September 2007 interview that the agency allocated little money to improving government institutions in 2005–2006 because it was assumed that staff would turn over after the elections. However, the employee also noted that USAID and other aid agencies had indeed often underfunded programs to build up state capacities in countries such as the DRC.

34. ICG, *A Congo Action Plan*, Africa Briefing No. 34 (Nairobi, Kenya, and Brussels, Belgium: ICG, October 19, 2005), 5.

35. World Bank, *Transitional Support Strategy for the Democratic Republic of the Congo*, 20.

36. David Lewis, "UN Deaths are Price of Congo Peacekeeping Offensive," Reuters, January 24, 2006.

37. ICG, *Congo: Consolidating the Peace*, I, 12–15, and 26.

38. David Lewis, "Sitting on Gold but Living off Nothing in Congo," Reuters, January 30, 2006.

39. Some peacekeepers have been caught "aid[ing] and abett[ing]" groups smuggling gold out of the country, having a "very friendly and cozy relationship" with militias they were supposed to be fighting, and conducting "widespread sexual abuse." Colum Lynch, "Pakistani Forces in Congo Aided Gold Smugglers, the U.N. Finds," *Washington Post*, July 23, 2007, A12.

40. ICG, Congo: *Consolidating the Peace*, 26.

41. Dorina Bekoe and Christina Parajon, *Developing and Managing Congo's Natural Resources*, USIPeace Briefing (Washington, DC: United States Institute of Peace, July 2007).

42. "Who Benefits from the Minerals?" *Economist*, September 22, 2007; William Wallis and Rebecca Bream, "Alarm Over China's Congo Deal," *Financial Times*, September 19, 2007.

43. See http://europa.eu.int/comm/echo/field/drc/background_en.htm.

44. During the elections in 2006, the UN Mission in the Democratic Republic of the Congo (MONUC) was tasked with distributing ballot boxes and registration cards to "its 21 major cities"; ICG, *A Congo Action Plan*, 2.

45. See, for example, Todd Moss, Gunilla Pettersson, and Nicolas van de Walle, *An Aid-Institutions Paradox? A Review Essay on Aid Dependency and State Building in Sub-Saharan Africa*, Working Paper No. 74 (Washington, DC: Center for Global Development, January, 2006), where the authors conclude "that states which can raise a substantial proportion of their revenues from the international community are less accountable to their citizens and under less pressure to maintain popular legitimacy. They are therefore less likely to have the incentives to cultivate and invest in effective public institutions."

46. Reuters, "U.N. Pleads for Aid to Save Lives in Congo," *New York Times*, February 13, 2006, A3.

Chapter 7

1. Damascus holds this special role in Arab mythology because it was the center of the greatest Arab empire, the Umayyad dynasty. The Umayyad mosque in Damascus's old city is still considered to have a special significance in Islam, ranking fourth among religious sites after those in Arabia and Jerusalem.

2. "The land of the left hand," is the Arabic name for the land north of the Hejaz (it was leftward as one looked east), and traditionally encompassed what is today Syria, Lebanon, Jordan, and Israel. The term can also refer to the area dominated by Damascus, and the word *al-sham* in Arabic standing alone can refer to the city itself.

3. See http://www.state.gov/r/pa/ei/bgn/3580.htm.

4. Daniel Brumberg, "Islam Is Not the Solution (or the Problem)," *Washington Quarterly* 29(1) (Winter 2005–2006): 104.

5. The country started requiring visas of some Iraqi refugees in September 2007.

6. Flynt Leverett, *Inheriting Syria: Bashar's Trail by Fire* (Washington, DC: Brookings Institution, 2005), 23.

7. See International Crisis Group (ICG), *Syria Under Bashar (II): Domestic Policy Challenges*, Middle East Report No. 24 (Brussels, Belgium: ICG, February 11, 2004), 2; and Eyal Zisser, "Appearance and Reality: Syria's Decision-Making Structure," *Middle East Review of International Affairs* 2(2) (May 1998): 29–41.

8. Interview with Samir Altaqi in Damascus, January 10, 2007.

9. Nimrod Raphaeli, *The Syrian Economy Under Bashar al-Assad*, Inquiry and Analysis Series, no. 259 (Washington, DC: Middle East Media Research Institute, January 13, 2006).

10. Zisser, "Appearance and Reality," 36.

11. Rachel Bronson, "Syria: Hanging Together or Hanging Separately," *Washington Quarterly* 23(4) (Autumn 2000): 95.

12. Carsten Wieland, *Syria: Ballots or Bullets? Democracy, Islamism, and Secularism in the Levant* (Seattle, WA: Cune Press, 2006), 38.

13. Central Intelligence Agency, *The World Factbook, 2004* (Washington, DC: Central Intelligence Agency, 2004); available at https://www.cia.gov/cia/publications/factbook/index.html.

14. Leverett, *Inheriting Syria*, 34.

15. "Syria's Economy Is Becoming a Little Bit More Open," *Economist Intelligence Unit*, January 31, 2007.

16. "Syria: He Doesn't Know Where to Go," *Economist*, February 11, 2006, 44.

17. "Is Syria a Reforming Character?" *Economist Intelligence Unit*, January 2, 2007.

18. Wieland, *Syria: Ballots or Bullets?* 63.

19. Interview with Altaqi.

20. Eyal Zisser, "What Does the Future Hold for Syria?" *Middle East Review of International Affairs* (Herzliya, Israel) 10(2) (June 2006): 16.

21. "Is Syria a Reforming Character?" *Economist Intelligence Unit.*

22. ICG, *Syria Under Bashar (II): Domestic Policy Challenges*, 6.

23. Joshua Landis and Joe Pace, "The Syrian Opposition," *Washington Quarterly* 30(1) (Winter 2006–2007): 45.

24. Wieland, *Syria: Ballots or Bullets?* 53.

25. Ibrahim Hamidi, "Syria's Stability May Well Be in Kurdish Hands," *Daily Star* (Beirut, Lebanon), May 6, 2005.

26. Interview with Ibrahim Hamidi in Damascus, January 10, 2007.

27. Wieland, *Syria: Ballots or Bullets?* 86. Some analysts believe that the Syrian government staged these attacks to burnish its anti-Islamist credentials in Western capitals, but considering a similar rise in such incidents in all Arab states bordering Iraq since 2003, it would be surprising if none occurred.

28. Ibid., 193.

29. Ibrahim Hamidi, "Islamist Streams on the March in Syria: The Authorities Launch 'Pre-emptive Strikes' against Takfiri Dens," *Al-Hayat* (London-based Arabic newspaper), January 4, 2006.

30. Hamidi, "Syria's Stability May Well Be in Kurdish Hands."

31. Damascus-based analysts such as Samir Altaqi, Ziad Haidar, and Samir Seifan all suggested this would be the best future scenario for Syria, though they differed over how likely the current regime would want to or be able to bring it about.

32. Interview with Ziad Haidar, January 17, 2007.

33. Interview with Samir Seifan, January 18, 2007.

34. A metaphor used by Altaqi during his interview with the author.

35. Adam Zagorin, "Syria in Bush's Cross Hairs," *Time*, December 19, 2006.

36. This is the general consensus among the analysts the author interviewed in Damascus.

37. Washington tends to focus only on the political tools it has available, notably, exerting U.S. diplomatic and political power to help Syria regain the Golan Heights from Israel and win international acceptance of Syria's special role in Lebanon.

38. Leverett, *Inheriting Syria*, 84–85.

39. See http://www.delsyr.cec.eu.int/en/eu_and_syria/projects/10.htm.

40. Western governments have practiced some of the antiliberal measures suggested here when confronted by secessionists in the past, such as when the United Kingdom and Spain limited certain freedoms in the face of Irish and Basque separatist movements. Since 9/11, many more Western countries have limited some of their cherished freedoms in the face of the threat of domestic terrorism.

Chapter 8

1. U.S. aid has actually declined since 2002 from what was already a very modest level. See David H. Shinn, "Somaliland, the Horn of Africa, and U.S. Policy" (remarks made at the Somaliland Convention, Crystal City, VA, September 8, 2006).

2. See Andrew Cawthorne, "U.S. Says al Qaeda behind Somali Islamists," Reuters, December 14, 2006.

3. See http://www.cfr.org/publication/10781/somalias_terrorist_infestation.html.

4. Virginia Luling, "Come Back Somalia? Questioning a Collapsed State," *Third World Quarterly* 18(2) (June 1997): 292. The following description of the clan system of governance borrows from this article.

5. Ken Menkhaus, "Somalia: Political Order in a Stateless Society," *Current History* 97(619) (May 1998): 220.

6. Roland Marchal and Ken Menkhaus, *Somalia Human Development Report 1998* (Nairobi, Kenya: United Nations Development Programme, October 1998), 12.

7. There is no census data for either Somaliland or Somalia. The United Nations estimated Somalia's population at 8,228,000 in 2005. Somaliland's population is generally estimated at between 2.5 and 3.5 million. See International Crisis Group (ICG), *Somaliland: Time for African Union Leadership*, Africa Report No. 110 (Brussels, Belgium: ICG, May 23, 2006), 4.

8. Asteris Huliaras, "The Viability of Somaliland: Internal Constraints and Regional Geopolitics," *Journal of Contemporary African Studies* 20(2) (July 2002): 158.

9. Ian Spears, "Reflections on Somaliland and Africa's Territorial Order," *Review of African Political Economy* 30(95) (March 2003): 94.

10. This last point was mentioned repeatedly in interviews conducted by the author in Hargeysa (Somaliland) in September 2006. See also Matt Bryden, "The Banana Test: Is Somaliland Ready for Recognition?" (unpublished manuscript), 6; and Mark Bradbury, Adan Yusuf Abokor, and Haroon Ahmed Yusuf, "Somaliland: Choosing Politics Over Violence," *Review of African Political Economy* 30(97) (September 2003): 462.

11. Academy for Peace and Development (APD), "A Self-Portrait of Somaliland: Rebuilding from the Ruins" (draft manuscript, APD, Hargeysa, Somaliland, 2000).

12. Carolyn Logan, *Overcoming the State-Society Disconnect in the Former Somalia: Putting Somali Political and Economic Resources at the Root of Reconstruction*, United States Agency for International Development, Regional Economic Development Services Office for East and Southern Africa (September 2000), 20.

13. Huliaras, "The Viability of Somaliland," 162.

14. Bradbury, Abokor, and Yusuf, "Somaliland: Choosing Politics over Violence," 475.

15. Ibid., 455 and 458.

16. Shinn, "Somaliland."

17. Initiative and Referendum Institute (IRI) Election Monitoring Team, *Somaliland National Referendum: May 31, 2001* (Washington, DC: Citizen Lawmaker Press, July 27, 2001).

18. See http://www.state.gov/p/af/rls/fs/2007/96359.htm.

19. Interview with Somaliland's foreign minister, Abdillahi M. Duale, Hargeysa, Somaliland, September 17, 2006.

20. Bradbury, Abokor, and Yusuf, "Somaliland: Choosing Politics Over Violence," 458.

21. This discussion borrows from ICG, "Somaliland: Time for African Union Leadership," 19–21.

22. African Union Commission, *Resume: AU Fact-Finding Mission to Somaliland (30 April to 4 May 2005)* (Addis Ababa, Ethiopia: African Union, 2005).

23. Ann Scott Tyson, "U.S. Debating Shift of Support in Somali Conflict," *Washington Post*, December 4, 2007, A17.

24. ICG, "Somaliland: Time for African Union Leadership," 21.

25. Dan Simpson, "The Ghost of Somalia: Somaliland Should Be Allowed to Depart a Chaotic Country in Transition," *Pittsburgh Post-Gazette*, August 11, 2006.

26. See, for example, David H. Shinn, "Somaliland: The Little Country That Could," *Addis Tribune* November 29, 2002.

27. Logan, *Overcoming the State-Society Disconnect*, 3.

28. Ibid., 28.

29. Ian Spears, "Reflections on Somaliland and Africa's Territorial Order," *Review of African Political Economy* 30(95) (March 2003): 94.

Chapter 9

1. "The Latinobarómetro Poll: Democracy's Ten-Year Rut," *Economist*, October 29, 2005, 39–40. The poll, carried out annually since 1995 by Latinobarómetro, a Chilean organization, was taken by "local opinion-research companies in eighteen countries, and involved 20,209 interviews in August and September 2005."

2. As quoted in William Ratliff, "The Democracy Problem," *Hoover Digest* 2005(3) (Fall 2005): 78.

3. "The Latinobarómetro Poll: Democracy's Ten-Year Rut," *Economist*.

4. As quoted in Juan Forero, "In Latin America, a Leftist Vision Is Taking Hold," *New York Times*, December 9, 2005.

5. Instituto Nacional de Estadística and United Nations Development Programme, *Atlas Estadístico de Municipios de Bolivia 2005* (La Paz: INE/UNDP).

6. See http://www.cne.org.bo/ for complete election results.

7. U.S. Agency for International Development, *Bolivia Country Strategic Plan, 2005–2009* (February 22, 2005), 1.

8. George Gray-Molina, "Exclusion, Participation and Democratic State-building," in *Towards Democratic Viability: The Bolivian Experience*, ed. John Crabtree and Laurence Whitehead (New York: Palgrave, 2001), 66.

9. The World Bank figure averages six governance indicators ranging from −2.5 to 2.5. These measure voice and accountability; political stability; government effectiveness; regulatory quality; rule of law; and control of corruption. See http://www.worldbank.org/wbi/governance/govdata/.

10. See http://www.transparency.org/.

11. World Bank, *Doing Business in 2005: Removing Obstacles to Growth* (Washington, DC: World Bank, International Finance Corporation, and Oxford University Press, 2005).

12. See INE and UNDP, *Atlas Estadístico de Municipios de Bolivia 2005*, and Instituto Nacional de Estadística, *Anuario Estadístico 2004* (La Paz: INE).

13. USAID, *Bolivia Country Strategic Plan, 2005–2009*, 5.

14. As quoted in Paulo Sotero, "Democracy in Latin America: Alive but Not Well," included in the special advertising supplement "Latin America: The Coming Changes," *Foreign Policy* (January–February 2005): 26.

15. Gray-Molina, "Exclusion, Participation and Democratic State-building," 66.

16. Aymara is the largest indigenous group in Bolivia. Allyus are self-governing, land-based, extended kinship groups that have roots in the pre-Columbian agricultural conditions and social structure.

17. See Donna Le Van Cott, "Constitutional Reform in the Andes: Redefining Indigenous-State Relations," in *Multiculturalism in Latin America: Indigenous Rights, Diversity, and Democracy*, ed. Rachel Sieder (New York: Palgrave Macmillan, 2002), 55–58.

18. USAID, *Bolivia Country Strategic Plan, 2005–2009*, 64. Numbers compare 2003 and 1998. Since 2003, investment has fallen even further, and while income levels have steadied, the country continues to grow more slowly than its neighbors—despite significant increases in royalties from its natural resources.

19. International Crisis Group (ICG), "Bolivia's Reforms: The Danger of New Conflicts," *Latin America Briefing*, no. 13 (Bogotá, Colombia: ICG, January 8, 2007), 1.

20. "Bolivia's Breaking Point?" *Economist Intelligence Unit (EIU) ViewsWire*, December 14, 2007.

21. Donna Lee Van Cott, "Latin America's Indigenous Peoples," *Journal of Democracy* 18(4) (October 2007): 139.

22. Antonio Aranibar Arze, interview with the author, November 2005 (senior member of UNDP Bolivia).

23. "Bolivia's Blues," *Economist Intelligence Unit (EIU) ViewsWire*, August 10, 2007.

24. United Nations Conference on Trade and Development, http://www.unctad.org/Templates/Page.asp?intItemID=3198&lang=1.

25. According to the IMF. See "Highly Flammable," *Economist*, September 11, 2003.

26. ICG, "Bolivia's New Constitution: Avoiding Violent Confrontation," *Latin America Report*, no. 23 (Bogotá, Colombia: ICG, August 31, 2007), 1.

27. "A Year of Evo Morales," *EIU ViewsWire*, February 2, 2007.

28. There have been numerous articles promoting the concept of distributing natural resource revenue directly to citizens as a way to bypass state corruption and profligacy, especially in the aftermath of the Iraq War. See, for example, Nancy Birdsall and Arvind Subramanian, "Saving Iraq from Its Oil," *Foreign Affairs* (July–August 2004): 77–89. The idea originated in Xavier Sala-i-Martin and Arvind Subramanian, *Addressing the Natural Resource Curse: An Illustration from Nigeria* (Cambridge, MA: National Bureau of Economic Research, June 2003).

29. See United Nations Development Programme, *La Economía más allá del Gas, Segunda Edición* (La Paz: UNDP, 2005).

30. "Friends, Not Clones," *Economist*, June 9, 2007, 41.

31. Jules Lampell, interview with the author, December 2005. Lampell is director of the La Paz-based Bolivia Competitiva en Comercio Negocios, a USAID-funded project promoting exports.

32. USAID, *Bolivia Country Strategic Plan, 2005–2009*, 20.

33. Indeed, as USAID has observed, "the 'community justice' system functions effectively and efficiently throughout much of Bolivia, thereby relieving the formal court system of what would otherwise be an overwhelming caseload." See USAID, *Bolivia Country Strategic Plan, 2005–2009*, 47.

34. Ibid., 14.

35. See http://www.deliberative-democracy.net/.

36. Ibid.

37. Van Cott, "Latin America's Indigenous Peoples," 135.

38. "Enter the Man in the Stripy Jumper," *Economist*, January 21, 2006, 38–40.

39. Monte Reel, "For Bolivian Majority, a New Promise," *Washington Post*, January 23, 2006, A1.

40. He has, however, rejected the idea of a free trade agreement modeled on agreements signed by Colombia and Peru.

41. USAID, *Bolivia Country Strategic Plan, 2005–2009*, 3.

42. "Bolivia's Industry, *EIU ViewsWire*, February 19, 2007.

43. "Brazil Cuts Investments in Bolivia Due to New Oil Law," http://www.brazzilmag.com, May 20, 2005. Originally from Mercopress.

44. See http://education.yahoo.com/reference/factbook/bl/econom.html.

45. As quoted in Bill Faries, "After Win, Morales Faces Tough Task," *Christian Science Monitor*, December 20, 2005.

46. "Bush Calls for Dialogue with Bolivian Leader," Reuters, February 1, 2006.

Chapter 10

1. The White House and State Department have used many varieties of this expression since 9/11 to describe both Pakistan and General Musharraf. See, for example, http://nation.com.pk/daily/feb-2007/9/index10.php.

2. U.S. Undersecretary for Political Affairs, R. Nicholas Burns, called Pakistan "arguably the most important partner of United States" in its struggle against global terrorist groups, while warning that "what happens in that country (Pakistan) has a profound and direct impact on our country" in the same meeting in October 2007. See http://www.cfr.org/publication/14709/us_officials_mull_pakistan_position.html?breadcrumb=%2Fbios%2F13611%2Fjayshree_bajoria.

3. See http://www.cia.gov/cia/publications/factbook/geos/pk.html#People.

4. Stephen Philip Cohen, *The Idea of Pakistan* (Washington, DC: Brookings Institution Press, 2005), 2.

5. Ibid. The quotation comes from "a senior Indian diplomat."

6. "Unfortunately, the United States has only a few true Pakistan experts and knows remarkably little about this country. Much of what has been written is palpably wrong, or at best superficial." Cohen, *The Idea of Pakistan*, 1.

7. Christopher Jaffrelot, "Islamic Identity and Ethnic Tensions," in *A History of Pakistan and Its Origins*, ed. Christopher Jaffrelot (London, UK: Anthem Press, 2002), 20.

8. No Afghanistan government has ever recognized the Durand Line, as the border between the two countries is known, because it was decided unilaterally by the British in 1893 and cuts right through the Pashtun inhabited area.

9. Cohen, *The Idea of Pakistan*, 224.

10. International Crisis Group (ICG), *The State of Sectarianism in Pakistan*, Asia Report No. 95 (Islamabad, Pakistan, and Brussels, Belgium: ICG, April 18, 2005), 6.

11. Mahabub ul-Haq, chief economist of the Planning Commission, estimated in 1968 that twenty-two families controlled about two-thirds of Pakistan's industrial assets, 80 percent of its banking sector, and 79 percent of its insurance business. Gilbert Étienne, "Economic Development," in *A History of Pakistan and Its Origins*, ed. Christopher Jaffrelot (London, UK: Anthem Press, 2002), 309n1. In 1996, the country's establishment consisted of "a small culturally and socially intertwined elite" numbering perhaps only five hundred people. See Cohen, *The Idea of Pakistan*, 69. The children of the elite who attend private, English-language schools "live in different worlds" from the poor masses who study in Urdu at the madrassa." Tariq Rahman, "Tolerance and Militancy among Schoolchildren," *Dawn* (Karachi), February 23, 2003.

12. S. Akbar Zaidi, "State, Military, and Social Transition: Improbable Future of Democracy in Pakistan," *Economic and Political Weekly* 40(49) (December 3, 2005): 5174.

13. Ibid., 5173–5181. Some of this analysis borrows from Zaidi's writings.

14. Three elected governments were dissolved—in 1990, 1993, and in 1996—at the behest of the army.

15. The parliament elected in February 2008 has indicated that it will reverse at least some of these changes; even so, the fundamental nature of the military-gavernment relationship will change only very gradually.

16. Zaidi, "State, Military and Social Transition," 5177.

17. Ayesha Siddiqa, "Pakistan's Permanent Crisis." Ehsan Masood, "Pakistan: The Army as the State," *OpenDemocracy*, April 12, 2007. See http://www. opendemocracy.net/node/4519.

18. From an interview with Musharraf on BBC, "Musharraf Defends Power to Sack Government," reported in *The News* (Karachi, Lahore, and Rawalpindi/Islamabad), June 23, 2002.

19. Cohen, *The Idea of Pakistan*, 207.

20. Pakistan Institute of Legislative Development and Transparency (PILDAT), *Dynamics of Federalism in Pakistan: Current Challenges and Future Directions*, Briefing Paper No. 31 (Islamabad: PILDAT, December 2006), 16.

21. "Baluchistan: Turning a Fight into a War," *Economist*, June 29, 2006.

22. See "A Survey of Pakistan," *Economist*, July 8, 2006, 8; and Husain Haqqani, "Weeding Out the Heretics: Sectarianism in Pakistan," *Current Trends in Islamist Ideology*, vol. 4 (Washington, DC: Hudson Institute, November 2006).

23. Jane Perlez, "Ex-Pakistani Official Says Policy on Taliban Is Failing," *New York Times*, January 27, 2008, A10.

24. ICG, *The State of Sectarianism in Pakistan*, 5.

25. Perlez, "Ex-Pakistani Official Says Policy on Taliban Is Failing," A10.

26. Cohen, *The Idea of Pakistan*, 241.

27. Ibid., 72.

28. S. Akbar Zaidi, *Issues in Pakistan's Economy* (Oxford, UK: Oxford University Press, 1999), 7.

29. Ibid., 241.

30. Ibid., 8 and 482.

31. Ibid., 9 and 482.

32. See "Pakistan's Tribal Areas: A Safe Haven for Terrorists," *Economist*, April 14, 2007, 13.

33. "Pakistan's Militant Drift: Taliban All Over," *Economist*, April 14, 2007, 43–46.

34. "Too Much for One Man: A Survey of Pakistan," *Economist*, July 8, 2006, 4–5.

35. "The Trouble with Pakistan," *Economist*, July 6, 2006.

36. The National Commission on Terrorist Attacks upon the United States, set up in the aftermath of 9/11 by the U.S. government, argued that this "ought to be central to U.S. engagement in Pakistan." Craig Cohen and Derek Chollet, "When $10 Billion Is Not Enough: Rethinking U.S. Strategy toward Pakistan," *Washington Quarterly* 30(2) (Spring 2007): 12.

37. Glenn Kessler, "Democracy Gets Small Portion of U.S. Aid," *Washington Post*, January 6, 2008, A17.

38. Ibid., 7–19.
39. Interview with Akbar Zaidi in Karachi, January 3, 2007.
40. See http://www.wto.org/english/res_e/statis_e/statis_e.htm.
41. Mohammed bin Yusoff, Suhaila Abdul Jalil, and Fauziah Abu Hasan, "Globalization, Economic Policy, and Equity: The Case of Malaysia." Background Paper for the OECD Workshop, "Poverty and Income Inequality in Developing Countries: A Policy Dialogue on the Effects of Globalisation," Paris, France, November 30 to December 1, 2000.

Chapter 11

1. "Instability in the South Caucasus is a threat to European Union (EU) security. Geographic proximity, energy resources, pipelines and the challenges of international crime and trafficking make stability in the region a clear EU interest." International Crisis Group (ICG), *Conflict Resolution in the South Caucasus: The EU's Role* (Brussels, Belgium: ICG, March 2006), i.
2. See http://www.eia.doe.gov/emeu/cabs/azerbjan.html.
3. Yigal Schleifer, "Azerbaijan Oil: A Mixed Blessing," *Christian Science Monitor*, December 30, 2005. The post-2005 escalation in oil prices would yield an even higher figure.
4. He made this declaration during the visit of President Aliyev to Washington, DC. Aida Sultanova, "Bush, Azerbaijan Leader Discuss Oil, Iran," *Associated Press*, April 28, 2006.
5. U.S. strategists were no doubt pleased to see Kazakhstan sign an agreement with Azerbaijan on June 16, 2006, to send Kazakh oil through the BTC pipeline.
6. Jim Nichol, *Armenia, Azerbaijan, and Georgia: Political Developments and Implications for U.S. Interests*, CRS Issue Brief for Congress (Washington, DC: Congressional Research Service, updated May 9, 2006), 12.
7. Yaakov Katz, "Azerbaijan an Ally in Iran Nuke Crisis," *Jerusalem Post*, February 11, 2006.
8. The contradictions in U.S. policy in Central Asia have been commented upon by a number of regional specialists. See, for example, Fiona Hill, "Une stratégie incertaine: la politique des Etats-Unis dans le Caucase et en Asie centrale depuis 1991," *Politique étrangère* (Paris), no. 1 (2001); and Eugene Rumer, "The U.S. Interests and Role in Central Asia after K2," *Washington Quarterly* (Summer 2006): 141–154.
9. See http://usinfo.state.gov/eur/Archive/2005/Nov/07=749512.html. Other Western countries and international organizations such as the Organization for Security and Cooperation in Europe (OSCE) made similar comments.
10. See http://www.jamestown.org/terrorism/news/article.php?articleid=2373767.
11. Some two-thirds of Azeris still live in Iran today.
12. Thomas de Waal, *Black Garden: Armenia and Azerbaijan through Peace and War* (New York: New York University Press, 2003), 29.
13. See http://ww1.transparency.org/cpi/2004/cpi2004.en.html#cpi2004.
14. See http://www.heritage.org/research/features/index/countries.cfm.
15. Svetlana Tsalik, *Caspian Oil Windfalls: Who Will Benefit?* Caspian Revenue Watch, Central Eurasia Project (New York: Open Society Institute [OSI], 2003), 90.
16. Despite accounting for 30 percent of GDP in 2000, the oil sector constituted only 1 percent of total employment. Ibid., 96.

17. Ibid., 97.

18. Ibid., 97.

19. Anar Ahmadov, Leila Alieva, and Dr. Nasib Nassibli all mentioned this in interviews with the author in April and May 2006. Also see ICG, *Azerbaijan: Turning Over a New Leaf?* (Brussels, Belgium: ICG, May 13, 2004), 24. Ahmadov, in an interview on May 3, 2006, estimated that the number of observant Muslims had risen tenfold since independence.

20. See http://www.jamestown.org/terrorism/news/article.php?articleid=2373767.

21. Leila Alieva, "Azerbaijan's Frustrating Elections," *Journal of Democracy* (April 2006): 148.

22. See http://www.freedomhouse.org/template.cfm?page=22&country=6689&year=2005&view=mof.

23. Jose-Manuel Barroso "highlighted extenuating factors, praising Azerbaijan's relative successes. 'Let's not forget that Azerbaijan never had a democratic state as we consider it in the European Union,' he said. 'So Azerbaijan is making efforts [toward] economic and political reform.'" Ahto Lobjakas, "Azerbajan: EU Taking Note of Baku's Strength," Radio Free Europe/Radio Liberty, November 7, 2006, http://www.rferl.org/featuresarticle/2006/11/0f418e0f-3f21=4ae3=8f3e-bceeb1c4be40.html.

24. See http://www.freedomhouse.hu/nit.html.

25. See http://www.osce.org/item/16887.html.

26. Jim Nichol, *Azerbaijan's 2005 Legislative Election: Outcome and Implications for U.S. Interests*, CRS Report for Congress (Washington, DC: Congressional Research Service, November 30, 2006), 5.

27. Jackson Diehl, "Retreat from the Freedom Agenda," *Washington Post*, April 24, 2006, A17.

28. See, among others, Philip Stephens, "Next Guest Says More about Bush," *Financial Times*, April 20, 2006.

29. Michael McFaul, "Ukraine Imports Democracy: External Influences on the Orange Revolution," *International Security* 32(2) (Fall 2007): 70.

30. C. J. Chivers, "Azerbaijan Leader, Under Fire, Hopes U.S. Visit Improves Image," *New York Times*, April 23, 2006, 10.

31. Ahto Lobjakas, "Azerbaijan: EU Doubtful of Baku's Commitment to Democracy," Radio Free Europe/Radio Liberty, October 27, 2005.

32. "EU: Armenia, Azerbaijan, and Georgia Sign Accords," Radio Free Europe/Radio Liberty, November 14, 2006.

33. Many cited the growth of such sentiments during my April and May 2006 interviews.

34. This is documented in a number of places. See, for example, the most authoritative work on the war, de Waal, *Black Garden*, 130. On the other hand, the area is on the Azeri side of the watershed and was economically closely integrated with Azerbaijan.

35. State consolidation would be enhanced, for example, if the two sides agreed to a peace deal that guaranteed transit rights between Azerbaijan's two parts (currently separated by Armenian territory) or even that involved an exchange of land so that the two parts could become contiguous. A peace deal that guaranteed a special political and administrative relationship between Azerbaijan and those parts of Nagorno-Karabakh, such as Shusha, that were predominantly Azeri before the war would both encourage Azeri refugees to return to their homes in Nagorno-Karabakh and ensure that there was less friction between

those towns and the Karabakh government, which will most likely be dominated by the Armenian majority.

36. de Waal, *Black Garden*, 286. Many in Azerbaijan argue that the proportion is higher.

37. ICG, *Conflict Resolution in the South Caucasus*, 2.

38. Ibid.

39. ICG, *Nagorno-Karabakh: Viewing the Conflict from the Ground* (Brussels, Belgium: ICG, September 2005), 28.

40. ICG, *Nagorno-Karabakh: Risking War* (Brussels, Belgium: ICG, November 14, 2007), i.

41. "The EU has mostly avoided the Nagorno-Karabakh issue in its relations with both countries.... Compared with other ENP [European Neighborhood Policy] action plans, such as those of Georgia and Moldova, Armenia's and Azerbaijan's are vague and do not link progress in the peace process to further EU aid." The EU special representative (EUSR) for the South Caucasus is barely active in the political process at all. Ibid., 7.

42. Nichol, *Armenia, Azerbaijan, and Georgia*, 4.

43. ICG, *Nagorno-Karabakh: A Plan for Peace* (Brussels, Belgium: ICG, October 2005), 8.

44. This reason has been mentioned by many analysts. See, for example, Laurence Broers, ed., "The Limits of Leadership: Elites and Societies in the Nagorny Karabakh Peace Process," in *Accord* (London, UK: Conciliation Resources, 2005). See http://www.c-r.org/our-work/accord/nagorny-karabakh/contents.php.

45. Also high on the U.S. agenda should be the implementation of part or all of Transparency International's anticorruption prescriptions, which constitute a comprehensive, systemic approach encompassing laws, regulations, and practices. See http://ww1.transparency.org/. For further suggestions along these lines, see Tsalik, *Caspian Oil Windfalls*.

46. Some of these ideas come from Sufyan Alissa, *The Challenge of Economic Reform in the Arab World: Toward More Productive Economies* (Washington, DC: Carnegie Endowment for International Peace, 2007), 9.

47. See http://ec.europa.eu/world/enp/policy_en.htm.

48. Azerbaijan planned to align its military closely with NATO standards by the end of 2007. Rovshan Ismayilov, "Azerbaijan's Military Build Up," *EurasiaNET*, July 3, 2007.

Index

About the Author

SETH D. KAPLAN is a business consultant who has run multinational firms and founded successful local corporations in Asia, Africa, and the Middle East. His articles on fragile states and development have appeared in the *Washington Quarterly, Orbis*, the *Wall Street Journal*, and the *New York Times*.

CPSIA information can be obtained at www.ICGtesting.com
Printed in the USA
BVOW06*0357090816

457984BV00009B/38/P

9 780275 998288